MARTHA WHITE'S

# Southern Sampler

# MARTHA WHITE'S

## Southern Sampler

*Ninety years of baking tradition*

RUTLEDGE HILL PRESS

NASHVILLE, TENNESSEE

Published in Nashville, Tennessee, by Rutledge Hill Press, Inc., 513 Third Avenue South, Nashville, Tennessee 37210.

All color photographs of food by Tad Ware & Company/Studio 3, Minneapolis, MN.

Photographs on pages 14, 71, 126, 130, 131, 174, and 199 courtesy of Tennessee Photographic Services.

Photograph on page 20 courtesy of the Country Music Foundation, Inc. and used by permission.

Photograph on page 23 by Donnie Beauchamp and used by permission of Opryland USA, Inc.

Photograph on page 44 by Jeff Frazier; poster courtesy of Larry Singleton, Cracker Barrel Old Country Stores.

Photographs on pages 28, 48, 69, 84, 96, 109, and 189 courtesy of the Grand Ole Opry.

Painting on page 51 by Donny Finley and used by permission of Gray Stone Press.

Photograph on page 53 by Steve Ramsey and used by permission.

Photographs on pages 55, 65, 115, 134, and 172 by Robin Hood and used by permission.

Photograph on page 128 by Jim McGuire and used by permission.

Photographs on page 146 and 171 copyright © 1984 by Paul Weigle and used by permission.

Photograph on page 157 by Guider Photography and used by permission.

Photograph on page 158 of Cool Springs Farm courtesy of Southeast Venture Companies.

Photograph on page 191 copyright © 1987 by J. D. Stigall and used by permission.

Photograph on page 193 by Don Putnam and used by permission.

Text design by Harriette Bateman
Typography by Bailey Typography, Nashville, Tennessee
Printed in the United States of America by R. R. Donnelley.

**Library of Congress Cataloging-in-Publication Data**

Martha White's southern sampler.
    p.    cm.
    Recipes from Martha White Foods.
    ISBN 1-55853-035-5
    1. Baking. 2. Cookery, American—Southern style. I. Martha White Foods. II. Title: Southern sampler.
TX765.M3518  1989           89-39568
641.7'1—dc20              CIP

3 4 5 6 7 8 9 - 95 94 93 92 91 90

# CONTENTS

# INTRODUCTION

## Welcome to
## Martha White's Southern Sampler

When you go to a family reunion, homecoming or potluck dinner, the polite thing to do is to sample a little bit of everything.

And that's precisely what Martha White's Southern Sampler is—a little bit of everything.

Since 1899, Martha White Foods has provided home bakers with quality baking ingredients, mixes and a wealth of baking tips and recipe information. We're celebrating Martha White's 90th anniversary as a Southern baking institution.

During its 90-year history, Martha White has tried to do its part to improve the quality of family life.

To that end, the company developed baking mixes to ease the toil of folks working in the kitchen, assisted 4-H Clubs and home economics classes with millions of recipes and sponsored unknown country musicians who have since risen to stardom on the Grand Ole Opry stage.

It's a humble beginning, but we're proud of it. And because we managed to do a few things right along the way, 90 years later Martha White continues to bring old-fashioned country homemade goodness to tables throughout the South and the rest of the country.

Collected in the following pages are the results of Martha White's rich tradition—90 years of the best recipes from the good folks at the Martha White Test Kitchen.

Each recipe has been formulated, tested and improved over the years by a trained staff of home economists. In addition to fine recipes, you'll find home baking tips, photos and remembrances throughout for added flavor.

Blended together, these assorted ingredients provide a warm, rich taste of Southern family tradition as expressed through the simple, unadorned act of baking at home.

But it's just a sample.

Because in the South, folks have their own way of doing things, their own family recipes reverently passed down along with the family Bible, their very own story to tell and their very own way of telling that story.

This is Martha White's story—a celebration of 90 years of homemade goodness.

# Martha White Test Kitchen's Ten All-Time Favorite Recipes

\* \* \* \* \* \* \* \* \* \*

How do the home economists at the Martha White Test Kitchen know when they've got a crowd-pleasing recipe on their hands?

They cook it up, set it out on the cooling rack and watch the crowd gather. Even though everyone around the Martha White headquarters sees a lot of good cooking, there are a few special recipes that folks watch for and come running when they're prepared.

According to the Martha White home economists, these 10 recipes cause a considerable amount of commotion among their co-workers. You might want to give them a try and see what kind of crowd they draw at your house.

Each of these recipes has a star like this * before it so you can't miss it.

* Mom's Apple Cobbler—page 140
* Butter Bite Hoecakes—page 32
* Chocolate Chip Cookies—page 191
* Buttermilk Pie—page 135
* Biscuits . . . any shape, any kind—Chapter 1
* Sausage Cheese Grits Casserole—page 100
* Lemon Meringue Pie—page 137
* Aunt Lois' Banana Nut Bread—page 62
* Cream Cheese Pound Cake—page 166
* Cinnamon Rolls—page 77

# Martha White's

## Southern Sampler

# BISCUITS

In the South, there is a special waking moment just at the edge of early morning light known as "Biscuit Time."

It takes place in those precious few seconds before the rooster's crow, Mama's call and the day's chores begin, when children stretch and struggle from beneath the weight of the feather tick. Slowly, these small dreamers are lulled into consciousness by the powerful aroma of hot buttermilk biscuits baking in the stove and the scratchy sound of an old familiar country tune on the radio:

"How many biscuits can you eat this morning?

How many biscuits can you eat this evening?

How many biscuits can you eat?

Forty-nine and a ham of meat,

This morning. This evening. Right now . . . ."*

"Biscuit Time" plays forever in the South. In fact, a taste of Southern culture naturally begins with a biscuit. For the humble biscuit is more than a regional specialty, it is the daily bread of Southern life.

Quickly in and out of the oven, the biscuit sped farmers to their fields in the morning and hastened wives from hot kitchen climes in the days before air conditioning. And even though it began each morning, the biscuit allowed for variety. By subtly altering the measure of ingredients, introducing new ingredients or baking them just a little bit differently, a thousand thick or thin versions of the basic biscuit are possible.

So diverse are the possible variations of shape, size, texture and taste, that biscuits serve as a kind of family tree as faithful as the one tucked in the front of the big black family Bible. Many are the displaced Southerners who live in search of the perfect biscuit, also known as "just like my Mama used to make."

Today, the search for the perfect biscuit has spread from the South to the rest of the country. And to feed this growing national biscuit hunger, fast-food purveyors have added this traditional Southern staple to their menus.

While fast-food biscuits certainly have their place in the faster-paced New South, their recipes lack one special ingredient that has always been the secret of the Southern biscuit's mouth-watering flavor:

Home.

---

*How Many Biscuits Can I Eat? by Gwen Foster.

Martha White's Old-Fashioned Buttermilk Biscuits (page 12)

## Martha White's Old-Fashioned Buttermilk Biscuits

*Buttermilk gives these traditional Southern biscuits a moist texture and rich flavor.*

**2 cups sifted Martha White Self-Rising Flour**

**¼ cup shortening**
**⅞ cup buttermilk (1 cup less 2 tablespoons)**

Preheat oven to 450°F. Lightly grease baking sheet. Cut shortening into flour with pastry blender or two knives until mixture resembles coarse crumbs. Add buttermilk and stir with a fork only until dough leaves sides of bowl. Turn

# A Short History of Southern Home Cooking

The gathering of fine food and family has long been the centerpiece of the agriculturally rich South. At the root of celebrated Southern hospitality is food and its distinctive preparation.

The rich bounty that has traditionally ladened the tables of Southern settlers, plantation owners, farmers, coastal fishermen and the simple folk of the hills and hollows is a menu more than 300 years in the making. Over the centuries, those who have come to call the South home have contributed their best recipes to the grand and gracious spread that is revered throughout the world today as Southern-style cooking.

The Native Americans favored the settlers with the enduring gift of corn and its kin—grits and hominy. Europeans journeying to the South crossed the ocean with their sturdy companion, the pig. From Africa came okra, collard greens and watermelon. From South America came chocolate, peanuts and tomatoes. And from the native Southern soil itself rose harvests of pecans, persimmons, black walnuts and blackberries, as well as an abundance of wild game and fish, including deer, rabbit, squirrel, possum, pigeon, quail, catfish, crab and shrimp.

These foods flourished in the abundance of the antebellum age and were nourished through the hardships of the Civil War, Reconstruction, the Great Depression and two world wars. These foods were the fruits of hardy men and women laboring from dawn till dusk on the land and in the kitchen. They sustained a way of life.

Today, mass communications blur the charm of regional accents and mass transportation has all but erased the boundaries once imposed by geography. But the Southern way of life is still preserved through the distinctive flavor of its food.

dough out onto lightly floured board or pastry cloth; knead gently just until smooth. Roll out to ½-inch thickness. Cut into rounds with floured 2-inch cutter. Place on prepared baking sheet. Bake for 10 to 12 minutes or until golden brown. Makes 12 to 14 biscuits.

**Note:** If using Martha White All-Purpose Flour, sift 1 tablespoon baking powder and ¾ teaspoon salt with flour.

## Martha White's Basic Biscuits

*The basic biscuit—try all the delicious variations.*

>     2 cups sifted Martha White
>        Self-Rising Flour
>  ¼ cup shortening
>  ¾ cup milk

Preheat oven to 450°F. Lightly grease a baking sheet. Cut shortening into flour with pastry blender or two knives until mixture resembles coarse crumbs. Add milk and stir with a fork only until dough leaves sides of bowl. Turn dough out onto lightly floured board or pastry cloth; knead gently just until smooth. Roll out to ½-inch thickness. Cut into rounds with floured 2-inch cutter. Place on prepared baking sheet. Bake for 10 to 12 minutes or until golden brown. Makes 12 to 14 biscuits.

**Note:** If using Martha White All-Purpose Flour, sift 1 tablespoon baking powder and ¾ teaspoon salt with flour.

**Drop Biscuits**

*Often called bachelor biscuits because they're so easy to make.*

Prepare Basic Biscuits as directed; except—increase milk to 1 cup. Drop dough by spoonfuls onto prepared baking sheet. Bake as directed.

## Cinnamon Raisin Biscuits

*All the goodness of a cinnamon roll, but easier to prepare.*

>  1 recipe Martha White's Basic
>     Biscuits
>  1 teaspoon cinnamon
>  1 cup raisins
>     Confectioners' Icing, below

Prepare Basic Biscuits as directed; except—stir cinnamon into flour. Stir in raisins after cutting in shortening and before adding milk. Bake as directed. Dip tops of warm biscuits in Confectioners' Icing. Makes 12 to 14 biscuits.

**Confectioners' Icing**

>  1 cup sifted confectioners' sugar
>  1 tablespoon milk
>  ½ teaspoon vanilla

Combine ingredients in order listed; stir until smooth.

## Easy Cinnamon Rolls

*A classic made easy with biscuit dough.*

    1 recipe Martha White's Basic
      Biscuits (page 13)
 ¼ cup (½ stick) butter or margarine,
      melted
 ½ cup sugar
   2 teaspoons cinnamon
      Confectioners' Icing, following

Preheat oven to 425°F. Grease a 9-inch round baking pan. Prepare Basic Biscuits as directed; except—roll dough into a 14x10-inch rectangle, about ⅛-inch thick. Brush dough with melted butter. Combine sugar and cinnamon; sprinkle evenly over dough. Roll up jelly-roll style, beginning with a long side. Slice into ¾-inch rounds. Place rounds in prepared pan. Bake for 18 to 20 minutes or until golden brown. Cool rolls for about 2 minutes; drizzle with Confectioners' Icing. Makes 16 to 18 rolls.

**Note:** Easy Cinnamon Rolls may be baked in greased muffin cups for 12 to 15 minutes or until golden brown.

### Confectioners' Icing

    1 cup sifted confectioners' sugar
    1 tablespoon milk
 ½ teaspoon vanilla

Combine ingredients in order listed; stir until smooth.

## Cinnamon Twists

*These figure-8 twists are easy to make with a doughnut cutter.*

    1 recipe Martha White's Basic
      Biscuits (page 13)
 ½ cup (1 stick) butter or margarine,
      melted
    1 cup sugar
    2 teaspoons cinnamon

Prepare Basic Biscuits as directed; except—roll dough out to ¼-inch thickness. Cut into rounds with floured doughnut cutter. Dip biscuit into melted butter, then in mixture of sugar and cinnamon. Twist once and place about 1 inch apart on prepared baking sheet. Bake as directed. Makes 12 to 14 twists.

Clockwise from top: Whole Wheat Biscuits (page 18), Thimble Biscuits (page 15), Cinnamon Twists (page 14), Easy Cinnamon Rolls (page 14)

## Thimble Biscuits

*Kids love these biscuits filled with their favorite jam.*

**1 recipe Martha White's Basic
    Biscuits (page 13)**
**¼ cup jam or jelly**

Prepare Basic Biscuits as directed; except—roll dough out to ¼-inch thickness. Cut into rounds with floured 2-inch cutter. Place half of rounds on prepared baking sheet. Cut a small hole in center of remaining rounds with a thimble or other small cutter. Stack rounds with holes on top of those already on baking sheet. Fill each hole with about ¼ teaspoon jam or jelly. Bake as directed. Makes 12 to 14 biscuits.

## Sausage Show-Offs

*Savory sausage & biscuit swirls.*

**1 recipe Martha White's Basic
    Biscuits (page 13)**
**1 pound sausage, at room
    temperature**

Preheat oven to 350°F. Prepare Basic Biscuits as directed; except—roll dough into a 14x10-inch rectangle, about ⅛-inch thick. Spread sausage almost to edges of dough. Roll up jelly-roll style, beginning with a long side. Slice into ½-inch thick rounds. Place rounds about 1 inch apart on prepared baking sheet. Bake for 30 to 35 minutes or until golden brown. Makes 25 to 30 rounds.

## Cheese Biscuits

*A cheesy version of the basic biscuit.*

**1 recipe Martha White's Basic
   Biscuits (page 13)**
**1 cup (4 ounces) grated sharp
   Cheddar cheese**
**½ teaspoon dry mustard**
**⅛ teaspoon cayenne pepper**

Prepare Basic Biscuits as directed; except—stir in cheese, mustard and pepper after cutting in shortening. Bake as directed. Makes 12 to 14 biscuits.

---

### BEYOND BASIC BISCUITS

**O**nce you've mastered the technique of creating tender, mouth-watering biscuits, your options in biscuit baking are endless. Here are a few ideas on getting better mileage out of simple biscuit dough:

♦ Dip dough in melted butter and roll in brown sugar and cinnamon for a succulent sweet roll.
♦ Roll dough and wrap it around a sausage link for a spicy sausage roll-up.
♦ Add ½ cup shredded sharp Cheddar cheese to flour for moist cheese biscuits.
♦ Add Italian seasoning to flour, roll dough and cut into thin strips for breadsticks.

---

## Bacon Biscuits

*Great for breakfast, or toast and serve with creamy tomato soup.*

**1 recipe Martha White's Basic
   Biscuits (page 13)**
**8 strips bacon, cooked and
   crumbled**

Prepare Basic Biscuits as directed; except—stir in bacon after cutting in shortening. Bake as directed. Makes 12 to 14 biscuits.

## Basic Biscuit Mix

*The easy way to make just a few biscuits at a time.*

**8 cups (2 pounds) sifted Martha
   White Self-Rising Flour**
**1 cup shortening**

Cut shortening into flour with pastry blender or two knives until mixture resembles coarse crumbs. Store in a tightly covered container at room temperature. Mix will keep up to 4 months. To prepare biscuits, preheat oven to 450°F. Lightly grease a baking sheet. Add ⅓ cup milk to 1 cup Basic Biscuit Mix for 5 to 6 biscuits (double for more biscuits). Stir with a fork only until dough leaves sides of bowl. Turn dough out onto lightly floured board or pastry cloth; knead gently just until smooth. Roll out to ½-inch thickness. Cut into rounds with floured 2-inch cutter. Place on prepared baking sheet. Bake for 10 to 12 minutes or until golden brown. Makes 5 to 6 biscuits per 1 cup mix.

**Note:** If using Martha White All-Purpose Flour, sift ¼ cup baking powder and 1 tablespoon salt with flour.

## Rich Sesame Biscuits

*Sour cream gives these biscuits a rich texture while sesame seeds add extra crunch.*

> 1½ **cups sifted Martha White**
> **Self-Rising Flour**
> ½ **cup Martha White Self-Rising**
> **Corn Meal Mix**
> 1 **tablespoon sugar**
> ¼ **teaspoon baking soda**
> ¼ **cup shortening**
> 1 **egg, lightly beaten**
> ¾ **cup dairy sour cream**
> 2 **tablespoons butter or margarine,**
> **melted**
> 1 **tablespoon sesame seeds**

Preheat oven to 450°F. Stir together flour, corn meal, sugar and soda in mixing bowl. Cut shortening into flour mixture with pastry blender or two knives until mixture resembles coarse crumbs. Add egg and sour cream; stir with a fork only until dough leaves sides of bowl. Turn dough out onto lightly floured board or pastry cloth; knead gently just until smooth. Roll out to ¼-inch thickness. Cut into rounds with floured 2½-inch cutter. Make an off-center crease in each round. Fold over so large half overlaps small half. Moisten

edges lightly to seal. Brush with melted butter and sprinkle with sesame seeds. Place biscuits on ungreased baking sheet. Bake for 10 to 12 minutes or until golden brown. Makes 14 to 16 biscuits.

**Note:** If using Martha White All-Purpose Flour and Plain Corn Meal, stir 1 tablespoon baking powder and ¾ teaspoon salt into dry ingredients.

---

### MEASURING

**A**ll measurements in this book are level. You will be most successful if ingredients are measured accurately.

- *Flour:* When recipe calls for sifted flour, sift before measuring. Spoon flour lightly into correct size measuring cup—do not tap cup or pack down. Fill to overflowing and level off with spatula.
- *Sugar:* Do not sift; otherwise, use same method as for flour.
- *Brown sugar:* Pack into correct size dry measuring cup just firmly enough for sugar to keep the shape of the cup when turned out.
- *Shortening:* Pack into correct size dry measuring cup and level off.
- *Liquids:* Place standard liquid measuring cup on level surface. Pour liquid into cup to correct measurement.
- *Baking powder, salt, spices:* Use standard measuring spoons. Heap ingredient in spoon. Level off with spatula.

## Whole Wheat Biscuits

*Wholesome biscuits with great texture and flavor.*

> 1 cup sifted Martha White
>   All-Purpose Flour
> 1 cup Martha White Whole Wheat
>   Flour
> 3 tablespoons sugar
> 1 tablespoon baking powder
> ¾ teaspoon salt
> ¾ cup milk
> ¼ cup vegetable oil

Preheat oven to 450°F. Lightly grease a baking sheet. Combine flours, sugar, baking powder and salt in medium bowl. Make a well in dry ingredients. Add milk, then oil to well. Stir with a fork only until dough leaves sides of bowl. Turn dough out onto lightly floured board or pastry cloth; knead gently just until smooth. Roll out to ½-inch thickness. Cut into rounds with floured 2½-inch cutter. Place on prepared baking sheet. Bake for 12 to 15 minutes or until golden brown. Makes 10 to 12 biscuits.

## Sour Cream Biscuits

*Great for little party biscuits.*

> 1 package (5½ ounces) Martha
>   White BixMix
> ½ teaspoon sugar
> 1 cup (8 ounces) dairy sour cream*

Preheat oven to 450°F. Lightly grease a baking sheet. Combine BixMix and

Bunny Biscuits

sugar in medium bowl. Add sour cream and stir with a fork only until dough leaves sides of bowl. Turn dough out onto lightly floured board or pastry cloth; knead gently just until smooth. Roll out to ½-inch thickness. Cut into rounds with floured 2-inch cutter. Place on prepared baking sheet. Bake for 10 to 12 minutes or until golden brown. Makes 10 to 12 biscuits.

*The consistency of dairy sour cream varies slightly, so begin with about 2 tablespoons less than one cup. If dough is stiff, add remaining dairy sour cream.

# Easy Mix Biscuits

*Vegetable oil makes mixing quick and easy.*

**2 cups sifted Martha White
  Self-Rising Flour**
**½ cup milk**
**⅓ cup vegetable oil**

Preheat oven to 450°F. Lightly grease a baking sheet. Place flour in medium bowl; make a well in flour. Add milk, then oil to well. Stir with a fork only until dough leaves sides of bowl. Turn dough out onto lightly floured board or pastry cloth; knead gently just until smooth. Roll out to ½-inch thickness. Cut into rounds with floured 2-inch cutter. Place on prepared baking sheet. Bake for 12 to 15 minutes or until golden brown. Makes 12 to 14 biscuits.

**Note:** If using Martha White All-Purpose Flour, sift 1 tablespoon baking powder and ¾ teaspoon salt with flour.

Preheat oven to 450°F. Lightly grease a large baking sheet. Stir together flour and sugar in mixing bowl. Cut butter into flour with pastry blender or two knives until mixture resembles coarse crumbs. Beat egg in measuring cup; add enough milk to make ⅔ cup. Add liquid mixture to flour and stir with fork only until dough leaves sides of bowl. Turn dough out onto lightly floured board or pastry cloth; knead gently just until smooth. Roll out to ½-inch thickness. For each bunny, cut one large circle (2 inches) for body, three circles (1 inch each) for ears and head and one small circle (½ inch) for tail. Assemble bunnies on prepared baking sheet as sketched below, rolling circles for ears between hands to lengthen. Bake for 10 to 12 minutes or until golden brown. Makes about 8 bunny biscuits.

**Note:** If using Martha White All-Purpose Flour, sift 1 tablespoon baking powder and ¾ teaspoon salt with flour.

# Bunny Biscuits

*A special occasion treat for kids of all ages.*

**2 cups sifted Martha White Self-
  Rising Flour**
**3 tablespoons sugar**
**⅓ cup (5⅓ tablespoons) butter or
  margarine, softened**
**1 egg**
  **About ½ cup milk**

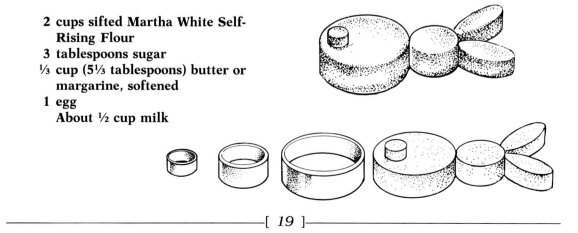

# A Request at Carnegie Hall

Regarded as the master of banjo picking, Earl Scruggs enjoyed a storied relationship with Martha White Foods. Along with his partner Lester Flatt, Scruggs and the Foggy Mountain Boys toured the country promoting Martha White from 1953 until 1969, when the bluegrass duo disbanded. They popularized the Martha White theme while scaling heights on their own in the record industry with such hits as "Foggy Mountain Breakdown" and "The Ballad of Jed Clampett," theme of "The Beverly Hillbillies" show. Lester Flatt died in May 1979. Scruggs lives in Nashville with his wife Louise. Earl Scruggs remembers when the legendary bluegrass duo played Carnegie Hall in 1962.

"The Flatt and Scruggs Carnegie Hall concert was a landmark appearance. First, we were playing this very prestigious hall. Second, the concert would become a live album.

"Anyone who has the album can hear somebody in the audience yelling for Martha White throughout the show. He was wanting to hear the theme. You wonder where he could've heard it before. We had learned to expect those kind of requests playing pie suppers in East Tennessee, but this was New York.

"The first thought that hit me during the show was that Cohen Williams [former Martha White chairman of the board] had planted somebody out in the audience.

"Finally I told Lester, 'Let's do the thing and get them to shut up so they won't destroy the whole album.' Well, we went ahead and did the thing. They loved it. The tune was catching on.

"Later, we found out the guy making the commotion was an attorney and caught our show in New York. I don't remember his name or where he was from, but I'll never forget his voice hollering 'Play the Martha White song!'

"And you know what, the same thing happened again at another big show several years later. But this time in Japan. They called it the 'Martha White theme' or they'd just holler Martha White. The Carnegie Hall album had been released in Japan and the people there picked up on it."

Earl Scruggs demonstrates his famous banjo-picking style at Carnegie Hall.

## Earl Scruggs' Famous Buttermilk Biscuits

2 cups sifted Martha White
    Self-Rising Flour
1 teaspoon sugar
⅓ cup shortening
⅞ cup buttermilk (1 cup less 2
    tablespoons)
    Melted butter or margarine

Preheat oven to 450°F. Sift together flour and sugar. Cut shortening into flour with pastry blender or two knives until mixture resembles coarse crumbs. Add buttermilk and stir with a fork only until dough leaves sides of bowl. Turn dough out onto lightly floured board or pastry cloth; knead gently just until smooth. Roll out to ½-inch thickness. Cut into rounds with floured 2½-inch cutter. Place on ungreased baking sheet. Bake for 12 to 14 minutes or until golden brown. Brush hot biscuits with melted butter. Makes 10 to 12 biscuits.

**Note:** If using Martha White All-Purpose Flour, sift 1 tablespoon baking powder and ¾ teaspoon salt with flour.

## Scones with Devon Cream

*Originally a Scottish bread often served with tea. Perfect for brunch—just a hint of refreshing orange flavor.*

2 cups sifted Martha White
    Self-Rising Flour

2 tablespoons sugar
1 teaspoon grated orange peel
¼ teaspoon baking soda
¼ cup (½ stick) butter or margarine,
    melted
1 egg, lightly beaten
½ cup buttermilk
    Devon Cream, below
    Strawberry preserves (optional)

Preheat oven to 400°F. Lightly grease a baking sheet. Stir together flour, sugar, orange peel and soda in mixing bowl. Add butter, egg, and buttermilk; stir with a fork only until dough leaves sides of bowl. Turn dough out onto lightly floured board or pastry cloth; knead gently just until smooth. Divide dough in half. Pat or roll each half into a ½-inch thick round. Cut each round into 8 wedges using a floured sharp knife or pizza cutter. Place wedges about 1 inch apart on prepared baking sheet. Bake for 15 to 18 minutes or until golden brown. Serve hot with Devon Cream and strawberry preserves, if desired. Makes 16 scones.

**Note:** If using Martha White All-Purpose Flour, sift 1 tablespoon baking powder and ¾ teaspoon salt with flour.

### Devon Cream

1 package (8 ounces) cream cheese,
    softened
⅓ cup dairy sour cream
1 tablespoon sugar

Beat all ingredients together until smooth and light.

## Fast Food Biscuits

*Rich jumbo biscuits, ideal for breakfast sandwiches.*

¾ cup shortening
4 cups sifted Martha White
    Self-Rising Flour
1⅔ cups buttermilk
    Melted butter or margarine

Preheat oven to 475°F. Grease a large baking sheet with low sides. Blend shortening into flour by hand, leaving large pea-sized pieces of shortening. Add buttermilk and stir with a fork only until dough leaves sides of bowl. Turn dough out onto lightly floured board or pastry cloth; knead gently just until smooth. Roll out to ½-inch thickness. Cut into rounds with floured 2¾-inch cutter. Place on prepared baking pan. Bake for 12 to 15 minutes or until golden brown. Brush hot biscuits generously with melted butter. Makes 18 to 20 biscuits.

**Note:** If using Martha White All-Purpose Flour, sift 2 tablespoons baking powder and 1½ teaspoons salt with flour.

---

### SELF-RISING FLOUR EQUIVALENTS

**O**ne cup Self-Rising Flour equals 1 cup All-Purpose Flour plus 1½ teaspoons baking powder and a scant ½ teaspoon salt.

---

## Cheesy Corn Meal Biscuits

*The crunch of corn meal and the tang of Cheddar cheese come together to add variety to the basic biscuit.*

1½ cups sifted Martha White
    Self-Rising Flour
½ cup Martha White Self-Rising
    Corn Meal Mix
¼ cup shortening
1 cup (4 ounces) grated sharp
    Cheddar cheese
¾ cup milk

Preheat oven to 450°F. Lightly grease a baking sheet. Stir together flour and corn meal in mixing bowl. Cut shortening into flour mixture with pastry blender or two knives until mixture resembles coarse crumbs. Stir in cheese. Add milk and stir with a fork only until dough leaves sides of bowl. Turn dough out onto lightly floured board or pastry cloth; knead gently just until smooth. Roll out to ½-inch thickness. Cut into rounds with floured 2-inch cutter. Place on prepared baking sheet. Bake for 10 to 12 minutes or until golden brown. Makes 12 to 14 biscuits.

**Note:** If using Martha White All-Purpose Flour and Plain Corn Meal, stir 1 tablespoon baking powder and ¾ teaspoon salt into dry ingredients.

# Biscuits From Lake Wobegon

I grew up in Minnesota, home of Gold Medal® and Pillsbury's Best®, which sponsored plenty of radio shows between them, but none as memorable to me as the Martha White segment of the Opry that I heard one hot summer night in 1973.

I'd driven from Minneapolis to Nashville in 20 hours to catch the Saturday night show, not thinking that it might be sold out, which of course it was, so I had to watch from the parking lot next to the Ryman Auditorium. This was not a bad deal, considering. The Ryman wasn't air-conditioned and the windows were open wide—wide enough so that when we crouched down we could see all of the short performers like Stonewall Jackson and Dolly Parton and most of the tall ones.

It was sociable out in the lot. Beer was passed around, and we discussed the people on stage pretty freely ("Don't you think she's gained weight?"), and then Lester Flatt & Earl Scruggs and the Foggy Mountain Boys came on for Martha White and cranked up that theme song, and it was like the lights went out and the rockets went up.

The Martha White theme is sort of the Aristotle-Contemplating-the-Bust-of-Homer of bluegrass jingles, a real dazzling masterpiece, and it stuck with me. The next year when I started up "A Prairie Home Companion," I invented Powdermilk Biscuits as a sponsor, in homage to Martha White, and wrote a theme to the tune of "Roli In My Sweet Baby's Arms":

> Has your family tried 'em,
>    Powdermilk?
> Oh, has your family tried
>    'em, Powdermilk?
> Well, if your family's tried 'em,
> You know you've satisfied 'em.
> They're the real hot item,
>    Powdermilk

It doesn't come up to the lyric grandeur of Martha White's, but the Powdermilk Biscuits themselves are exemplary. As we say on the show, "They're made from whole wheat raised in the rich bottomlands of the Lake Wobegon River valley by Norwegian bachelor farmers. So you know they're not only good for you, they're also pure, mostly. Heavens, they're tasty! And expeditious. They give shy persons the strength to get up and do what needs to be done." This outrageous claim, made repeatedly over the years, has done more good for shyness than all the books on the subject, I believe, which goes to show the power of advertising, especially when the product is fictional.

—Garrison Keillor

## Honey Pecan Biscuits

*A caramel layer laced with crunchy pecans adorns the top of these upside-down treats.*

3 tablespoons brown sugar
2 tablespoons butter or margarine, melted

1 tablespoon honey
½ cup pecan halves
2 cups sifted Martha White Self-Rising Flour
½ cup granulated sugar
2 teaspoons cinnamon
¾ cup milk
⅓ cup vegetable oil

# Biscuit Basics

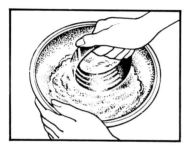

(1) Cut shortening into flour until mixture resembles coarse crumbs.

(2) Add liquid and stir only until dough leaves sides of bowl.

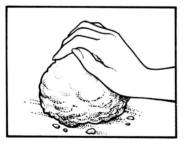

(3) Turn dough out onto lightly floured surface; knead gently just until smooth.

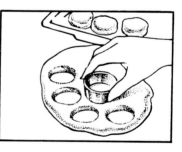

(4) Roll out to ½-inch thickness, or as directed (biscuits will double in height while baking). Cut with floured cutter.

Preheat oven to 450°F. Grease muffin cups. Combine brown sugar, butter and honey in small bowl. Spoon 1 teaspoon brown sugar mixture into each prepared muffin cup. Arrange pecan halves evenly among cups. Stir together flour, sugar and cinnamon in mixing bowl. Add milk and oil; stir just until blended. (Batter will be slightly stiff.) Spoon batter into prepared muffin cups, filling each ⅔ full. Bake for 15 to 17 minutes or until golden brown. Remove from pans and serve pecan-side up. Makes 10 to 12 biscuits.

**Note:** If using Martha White All-Purpose Flour, sift 1 tablespoon baking powder and ¾ teaspoon salt with flour.

## Basic Rich Biscuits

*Spoon sweetened fruit between layers and over the top. Serve with whipped cream for a tempting shortcake.*

> 2 cups sifted Martha White
>   Self-Rising Flour
> 3 tablespoons sugar
> ⅓ cup (5⅓ tablespoons) butter or
>   margarine, softened
> 1 egg, lightly beaten
>   About ½ cup milk

Preheat oven to 450°F. Lightly grease a baking sheet. Stir together flour and sugar in mixing bowl. Cut butter into flour mixture with pastry blender or two knives until mixture resembles coarse crumbs. Beat egg in measuring cup; add enough milk to make ⅔ cup. Add milk mixture to flour mixture and stir with a fork only until dough leaves sides of bowl. Turn dough out onto lightly floured board or pastry cloth; knead gently just until smooth. Roll out to ½-inch thickness. Cut into rounds with floured 3-inch cutter. Place on prepared baking sheet. Bake for 10 to 12 minutes or until golden brown. Makes 6 to 9 biscuits.

**Note:** If using Martha White All-Purpose Flour, sift 1 tablespoon baking powder and ¾ teaspoon salt with flour.

## Whipping Cream Biscuits

*So good and so simple—just two ingredients in these mouth-watering biscuits.*

> 2 cups sifted Martha White
>   Self-Rising Flour
> 1 cup (8 ounces) whipping cream

Preheat oven to 450°F. Lightly grease a baking sheet. Combine flour and whipping cream in mixing bowl; stir with a fork only until dough leaves sides of bowl. (Dough will be stiff.) Turn dough out onto lightly floured board or pastry cloth; knead gently just until smooth. Roll out to ½-inch thickness. Cut into rounds with 2-inch cutter. Place on prepared baking sheet. Bake for 10 to 12 minutes or until golden brown. Makes 12 to 14 biscuits.

**Note:** If using Martha White All-Purpose Flour, sift 1 tablespoon baking powder and ¾ teaspoon salt with flour.

# CORNBREAD

There is a certain amount of Southern history that can't be written in a book, restored in an antebellum mansion, commemorated on a battlefield or honored with a limestone monument on the courthouse lawn.

It is the real-life record of the region and its people. It is the rich family history entrusted only to its best oral traditions—Grandpa's stories and Grandma's cornbread.

Southern history travels best when it is personally handed down from generation to generation . . . on a plate and still hot from the oven.

The history of cornbread *is* a history of the South. And like all early American history, cornbread begins with the Native Americans.

When the first Europeans settled in America during the 17th century, Native Americans greeted them with corn and the secret of making it into bread. It turned out to be the secret of life. Corn and cornbread sustained the early settlers struggling to survive those first winters of famine in the new land. It would later sustain the ravaged South through Reconstruction and the Great Depression.

Called ash cakes, the simple recipe involved taking pones of corn meal and water and tossing them into a fire to bake in the hot ashes. When done, the pone was removed from the fire, dusted off and eaten.

Already exhibiting a keen sense of refinement, Southerners quickly adapted this recipe to their own tastes. The story goes that, instead of throwing the pones directly into the ashes, they placed them on a flat hoe and held it over the fire to bake.

Once free of ashes, the resulting bread was also out of a name. It became hoecakes.

As all good stories are improved upon with constant retelling, cornbread has improved with time. From its humble beginning as basic Native American bread, cornbread is often disguised today as a sophisticated soufflé or sweet cake. The once simple mixture of meal, salt, water and grease is now regularly joined by a whole pantry of ingredients, including eggs, milk, buttermilk, baking powder, baking soda, and even sugar and flour. The result is a smorgasbord of cornbreads. Corn dodgers, cornpone, johnnycake, cracklin' cornbread, lacy cornbread, hush puppies, corn light bread and spoonbread are all tasteful, unique variations on a single theme.

Martha White's Southern Cornbread (page 28)

## Martha White's Southern Cornbread

*A hot cast-iron skillet gives Southern cornbread its distinctive crisp brown crust.*

> 1 egg
> 1⅓ cups milk or 1¾ cups buttermilk
> ¼ cup vegetable oil or melted shortening
> 2 cups Martha White Self-Rising Corn Meal Mix

Preheat oven to 450°F. Grease a 9-inch cast-iron skillet or baking pan and place in oven to heat. Beat egg in mixing bowl. Add remaining ingredients; stir until smooth. (Batter should be creamy and pourable. If batter seems too thick, add a little more liquid.) Pour batter into prepared pan. Bake for 20 to 25 minutes or until golden brown. Makes 6 to 8 servings.

## ★ Grant Turner ★

The dean of Opry announcers, Grant Turner, came to Nashville's WSM radio in 1944. Turner was anxious to "make my mark on a big 50,000-watt station." He had gone on the radio at 16 in his hometown of Abilene, Texas. After a few minor successes at Longview and Sherman, Texas, and Knoxville, Tennessee, a great opportunity beckoned . . . working on Nashville's Grand Ole Opry.

### GRANT'S RANCHO DELIGHT CORNBREAD

1 egg
¾ cup milk
1 package (6½ ounces) Martha White Mexican Cornbread Mix
2 sausage patties, cooked and chopped
⅔ cup crushed corn chips

Preheat oven to 425°F. Grease an 8-inch cast-iron skillet or baking pan. Beat egg in mixing bowl; add milk and cornbread mix and stir until smooth. Stir in sausage and corn chips. Pour batter into prepared skillet. Bake for 15 to 18 minutes or until golden brown. Makes 4 to 6 servings.

**Hint:** Roll corn chips between paper towels with a rolling pin to cut down on cleanup.

MUFFINS OR CORN STICKS: Preheat oven to 450°F. Grease muffin cups or corn stick molds and place in oven to heat. Prepare batter for Southern Cornbread; pour into prepared pans. Bake for 15 to 20 minutes or until golden brown. Makes about 12 medium muffins or 16 corn sticks.

## Country-Style Cornbread

*An old-fashioned stick-to-your ribs cornbread.*

> 2 cups Martha White Self-Rising
>    Corn Meal Mix
> 1¾ cups buttermilk
> ¼ cup vegetable oil or melted
>    shortening

Preheat oven to 450°F. Grease a 9-inch cast-iron skillet or baking pan and place in oven to heat. Combine ingredients in mixing bowl; stir until smooth. (Batter should be creamy and pourable. If batter seems too thick, add a little more liquid.) Pour batter into prepared pan. Bake for 20 to 25 minutes or until golden brown. Makes 6 to 8 servings.

MUFFINS OR CORN STICKS: Preheat oven to 450°F. Grease muffin cups or corn stick molds and place in oven to heat. Prepare batter as directed above; pour into prepared pans. Bake for 15 to 20 minutes or until golden brown. Makes about 12 medium muffins or 16 corn sticks.

## THE DIFFERENCE A LITTLE BUTTERMILK MAKES

Ever wonder why some folks' biscuits and cornbread turn out moist every time and have a great distinctive taste? Southern bakers may not want to give away their secret, but it's probably buttermilk.

Good cooks have recognized the benefits of baking with buttermilk. Nothing else provides the special flavor buttermilk gives to biscuits, cornbread and fluffy pancakes.

While adding flavor and moisture to cooking, buttermilk is low in fat and calories because the fat goes into the butter when it separates from the milk.

To catch up on a few facts about cooking with buttermilk, read the following tips:

♦ Buttermilk will keep for as long as two weeks after purchase. Its acidity retards the growth of bacteria. The date stamped on the carton is when the buttermilk should be withdrawn from retail sale but does allow additional storage time in your home.

♦ Although the finished product may not be as flavorful, when there's no buttermilk on hand and a recipe calls for it, the following substitution can be made: In place of 1 cup of buttermilk, add enough regular milk to 1 tablespoon vinegar or lemon juice to make 1 cup. Let stand 5 minutes.

Corn sticks and muffins prepared from Martha White's Southern Cornbread recipe (page 28)

## Sausage Cornbake

*Serve with a fresh vegetable summer lunch.*

    1 **egg**
 1½ **cups milk**
   ¼ **cup vegetable oil or melted**
      **shortening**
    2 **cups Martha White Self-Rising**
      **Corn Meal Mix**
    1 **teaspoon sugar**
   ½ **pound (8 ounces) sausage,**
      **browned and drained**

Preheat oven to 450°F. Grease a 10-inch cast-iron skillet and place in oven to heat. Beat egg in mixing bowl. Add milk, oil, corn meal and sugar; stir until smooth. Add sausage; blend well. Pour batter into prepared pan. Bake for 20 to 25 minutes. This cornbread should be baked thin and quite brown. Makes 6 to 8 servings.

MUFFINS OR CORN STICKS: Preheat oven to 450°F. Grease muffin cups or corn stick molds and place in oven to heat. Prepare batter as directed above; pour into prepared pans. Bake for 15 to 20 minutes or until golden brown. Makes 14 muffins or 18 corn sticks.

## Golden Cornbread

*A lighter textured, slightly sweet cornbread often made with yellow corn meal.*

    2 **eggs**
    1 **cup milk**
   ¼ **cup vegetable oil or melted**
      **shortening**

1½ cups **Martha White Self-Rising Corn Meal Mix**
1 cup **Martha White All-Purpose Flour**
¼ cup **sugar**

Preheat oven to 450°F. Grease an 8- or 9-inch square baking pan. Beat eggs in mixing bowl. Add remaining ingredients; stir until smooth. (Batter should be creamy and pourable. If batter seems too thick, add a little more liquid.) Pour batter into prepared pan. Bake for 20 to 25 minutes or until golden brown. Makes 6 to 9 servings.

**Note:** Martha White Yellow Self-Rising Corn Meal Mix may be used in this recipe.

CORN MUFFINS: Preheat oven to 450°F. Grease 12 medium muffin cups. Prepare batter as directed above; pour into prepared muffin cups. Bake for 15 to 20 minutes or until golden brown. Makes about 12 medium muffins.

**Note:** More sugar may be added for sweeter muffins, if desired.

## Corn Dodgers

*Reminiscent of the simple corn pones introduced by Native Americans to early settlers.*

3 cups **Martha White Self-Rising Corn Meal Mix**
2¼ cups **boiling water**
3 tablespoons **vegetable oil or melted shortening, divided**

Preheat oven to 450°F. Grease a 10-inch cast-iron skillet. Gradually stir boiling water into corn meal. Add two tablespoons oil and blend thoroughly. Dip hands into cool water. Shape 2-inch balls of corn meal mixture into oblong pones, about 3x2-inches. (Dip hands in cool water before shaping each pone.) Place pones in skillet with sides lightly touching. Brush tops with remaining oil. Bake for 40 to 45 minutes or until lightly browned. Makes about 10 dodgers.

## Cracklin' Corn Dodgers

*Pork cracklings have been a favorite addition to cornbread since colonial days.*

3⅔ cups **water**
1½ cups **small pork cracklings pieces**
3 cups **Martha White Self-Rising Corn Meal Mix**
1 tablespoon **vegetable oil**

Preheat oven to 450°F. Grease a 10-inch cast-iron skillet. Bring water and cracklings to a boil in medium saucepan. Cover, reduce heat and simmer for 10 minutes or until cracklings are tender. Gradually stir crackling mixture into corn meal; blend thoroughly. Dip hands into cool water. Shape 2-inch balls of corn meal mixture into oblong pones, about 3x2-inches. (Dip hands into cool water before shaping each pone.) Place pones in skillet with sides lightly touching. Brush tops with oil. Bake for 45 to 50 minutes or until lightly browned. Makes about 15 dodgers.

## *Butter Bite Hoecakes

*Crisp little corn cakes that get their characteristic flavor and texture from scalding the corn meal before frying.*

     Vegetable oil or shortening for
     frying
   1 cup Martha White Self-Rising
     Corn Meal Mix
   1¾ cups boiling water
     Butter or margarine (optional)

In large skillet, heat ¼-inch deep oil over medium-low heat until a drop of water sizzles when dropped in skillet. Place corn meal in large mixing bowl. Gradually stir boiling water into corn meal. Continue to add boiling water in small amounts as batter thickens. Batter should be thick enough to hold its shape, but not stiff. Drop batter by large spoonfuls into hot skillet. Fry on one side until golden brown; turn and fry on other side until golden brown. Serve hot with butter, if desired. Makes about 10 hoecakes.

## Sweet Milk Corn Cakes

*The term "sweet" is used to distinguish regular milk from buttermilk, the traditional Southern baker's favorite.*

   1 egg
   ¾ cup milk
   1 tablespoon vegetable oil or melted
     shortening
   1 cup Martha White Self-Rising
     Corn Meal Mix
   ½ teaspoon sugar

Preheat a lightly greased skillet or griddle on medium heat (350°F). Beat egg in mixing bowl. Add remaining ingredients; stir until smooth. Pour batter onto hot skillet or griddle; ¼ cup batter makes a nice size corn cake. Brown on one side; turn and brown on other side. For thinner corn cakes, add a little more milk. Makes 6 corn cakes.

**Note:** These corn cakes are good topped with barbecue or may be buttered and served with any meal.

## Lacy Cornbread

*A lacy-edged corn cake, popular in South Georgia.*

   1 cup Martha White Self-Rising
     Corn Meal Mix
     About ¾ cup water

Preheat a lightly greased skillet or griddle on medium-high heat (400°F). Combine corn meal and water in small mixing bowl. Batter should be thin and watery. Pour ⅛ cup (2 tablespoons) batter onto heated surface. Patties should be about 4 inches in diameter with a solid center and lacy edges. If batter seems too thick, add up to ¼ cup more water. Brown on one side; carefully turn and brown on other side. Drain on absorbent paper. Best served hot. Makes about 12 patties.

**Note:** A nonstick electric skillet works well.

*One of Martha White Test Kitchen's ten all-time favorite recipes.

## Scalded Corn Cakes

*Serve hot from the skillet with plenty of butter.*

Vegetable oil or shortening for frying
1 cup Martha White Self-Rising Corn Meal Mix
¼ teaspoon sugar
1 cup boiling water
¼ cup buttermilk
Butter or margarine (optional)

In large skillet, heat ¼-inch deep oil over medium-low heat until a drop of water sizzles when dropped in skillet. Combine corn meal and sugar in large mixing bowl. Gradually stir boiling water into corn meal. Stir in buttermilk. Drop batter by small spoonfuls into hot skillet. Fry on one side until golden brown; turn and fry on other side until golden brown. Serve hot with butter, if desired. Makes about 20 small corn cakes.

## Old Virginia Spoonbread

*Light and airy, like a corn meal soufflé.*

1 cup Martha White Self-Rising Corn Meal Mix
1½ cups boiling water
3 eggs, separated
1 tablespoon butter or margarine, melted
1 cup buttermilk
1 teaspoon sugar
Butter or margarine (optional)

Preheat oven to 375°F. Grease a deep 2-quart casserole dish. Place corn meal in large mixing bowl. Pour boiling water over corn meal; stir until slightly cooled. Beat egg yolks in separate bowl with electric mixer until lemon-colored. Stir egg yolks and butter into corn meal; blend well. Stir in buttermilk and sugar. Beat egg whites in small mixing bowl with electric mixer until soft peaks form. Gently fold egg whites into corn meal mixture until blended. Pour batter into prepared dish. Bake for 45 to 50 minutes or until golden brown. Serve hot with butter, if desired. Makes 6 to 8 servings.

## Sour Cream Cornbread

*Sour cream dresses up basic cornbread.*

1 egg
1 cup (8 ounces) dairy sour cream
½ cup milk
2 tablespoons vegetable oil or melted shortening
1⅓ cups Martha White Self-Rising Corn Meal Mix
⅓ cup Martha White Self-Rising Flour
1 tablespoon sugar
¼ teaspoon baking soda

Preheat oven to 400°F. Grease a 9-inch square baking pan. Beat egg in mixing bowl. Add remaining ingredients; stir until smooth. Pour batter into prepared pan. Bake for 20 to 25 minutes or until golden brown and toothpick inserted in center comes out clean. Makes 6 to 8 servings.

## Pea-Picker's Cornbread

*Just a little flour gives this cornbread a light texture.*

 1 egg
 ⅔ cup buttermilk
 1 tablespoon water
 1 tablespoon vegetable oil or melted
  shortening
 1 cup Martha White Self-Rising
  Corn Meal Mix
 3 tablespoons Martha White
  Self-Rising Flour

Preheat oven to 450°F. Grease an 8-inch cast-iron skillet or baking pan and place in oven to heat. Beat egg in mixing bowl. Add remaining ingredients; stir until smooth. Pour batter into prepared pan. Bake for 20 to 25 minutes or until golden brown. Makes 4 to 6 servings.

## Corn Meal Waffles

*Crisp and flavorful—a suppertime favorite topped with chili.*

 1½ cups Martha White Self-Rising
  Corn Meal Mix
 1½ cups milk
 ¼ cup vegetable oil or melted
  shortening
  No-stick cooking spray

Preheat waffle iron according to manufacturer's directions. Combine corn meal, milk and oil in mixing bowl; stir until smooth. Spray top and bottom cooking surfaces of iron with no-stick cooking spray. Pour batter into heated waffle iron. Bake until steaming stops and waffles are dark golden brown, about 10 minutes. Makes twelve 4-inch waffles.

Tex-Mex Cornbread

## Tex-Mex Cornbread

*Livens up a bowl of bean soup.*

1 egg
1 cup Martha White Self-Rising
   Corn Meal Mix
1 can (8½ ounces) cream-style corn
½ cup milk
2 tablespoons vegetable oil or
   melted shortening
1 teaspoon sugar
1 cup (4 ounces) grated sharp
   Cheddar cheese
2 tablespoons chopped jalapeño
   peppers or chopped green chilies

Preheat oven to 450°F. Grease an 8-inch square baking pan. Beat egg in large mixing bowl. Add remaining ingredients; blend well. Pour batter into prepared pan. Bake for 25 to 30 minutes or until golden brown. Cool in pan 10 minutes before serving; cornbread will be very moist. Makes 6 to 9 servings.

**Note:** Martha White Yellow Self-Rising Corn Meal Mix may be used in this recipe.

## Garden Cornbread

*Fresh garden vegetables make this casserole bread perfect with grilled pork chops.*

2 eggs
1½ cups milk
2 cups Martha White Self-Rising
   Corn Meal Mix
2 cups (8 ounces) grated sharp
   Cheddar cheese

1½ cups peeled, chopped tomatoes
1 cup chopped green pepper
¼ cup chopped onion

Preheat oven to 400°F. Grease a 9-inch square baking pan. Beat eggs in mixing bowl. Add remaining ingredients; blend well. Pour batter into prepared pan. Bake for 35 to 40 minutes or until toothpick inserted in center comes out clean. Cool in pan for 10 minutes before serving. Best served warm. Makes 6 to 8 servings.

## Tennessee Cornbread

*The perfect size for smaller families—scalded corn meal makes it moist.*

2 cups Martha White Self-Rising
   Corn Meal Mix
⅓ cup boiling water
1¼ cups milk
¼ cup vegetable oil or melted
   shortening
1 egg, lightly beaten
1 teaspoon sugar

Preheat oven to 450°F. Grease a 9-inch cast-iron skillet or baking pan and place in oven to heat. Remove 2 tablespoons corn meal from 2 cups and combine with boiling water in a small bowl; stir to blend and set aside. Pour remaining corn meal into mixing bowl. Add remaining ingredients in order listed; stir until smooth. Add scalded corn meal and blend well. Pour batter into prepared pan. Bake for 18 to 22 minutes or until golden brown. Makes 6 to 8 servings.

# The Joy of Cast-Iron Cooking

For generations Southern cooks have known the joy of cooking with cast iron. Tradition is reason enough.

Cooking with cast iron is healthful. Foods cooked in iron cookware actually show an increase in iron content, a necessary mineral for our daily diet. Foods that are high in acidity and water content—apples, for example—tend to absorb more iron than others.

A better reason for cooking with iron, perhaps, is the flavor it imparts to great Southern recipes. An iron skillet greased with bacon drippings and preheated in a hot oven almost fries the cornbread batter when it is first poured into the pan, making a crisp and crunchy crust on the bottom.

You can expect your skillet cornbread to have a dark crust on the bottom since a dark utensil absorbs more heat than conventional cookware does. And do turn your cornbread out onto a plate bottom-side-up to preserve the crispness of the crust; otherwise moisture condensation will make it soggy.

Above all, treat your iron pot or pan right and it will treat you to years of pleasurable cooking. Never leave it to soak or air-dry—you'll have a rusty pan. Instead, wash and dry your iron utensil right away. Then oil it after each use.

## How to Season Your Cast-Iron Cookware

- Wash a new pot or pan with mild dishwashing soap and a stiff brush. Never use abrasives or steel wool.
- Grease the inside of the utensil with vegetable oil or shortening. (Do not use a salted fat, such as margarine or salted butter.) Also lightly grease the outside of the cookware, wiping away any excess. Do the same for cast-iron lids.
- Place the greased cast-iron cookware in a 300° to 350°F. oven and let it "season" for 30 to 40 minutes. Turn the oven off. Leave the utensil in the oven overnight or until cooled to room temperature.
- Some cooks repeatedly oil the pot or pan, then fill it with potato peels before slow-cooking to temper the iron taste.
- Be sure to oil the utensil before putting it away and oil after each cleaning.

## Rich Honey Cornbread

*Sweet, moist and light in texture—almost like cake.*

2 eggs
1 cup (8 ounces) whipping cream
¼ cup vegetable oil or melted shortening
¼ cup honey
¼ cup sugar
1 cup Martha White Self-Rising Corn Meal Mix
1 cup Martha White Self-Rising Flour

Preheat oven to 400°F. Grease a 9-inch square baking pan. Beat eggs in mixing bowl. Add remaining ingredients; stir until smooth. Pour batter into prepared pan. Bake for 20 to 25 minutes or until golden brown and toothpick inserted in center comes out clean. Makes 6 to 8 servings.

## Corn Light Bread

*Sweet cornbread baked in a loaf. A Tennessee favorite served with barbecue.*

1½ cups Martha White Self-Rising Corn Meal Mix
½ cup Martha White All-Purpose Flour
½ cup sugar
1½ cups buttermilk
½ cup (1 stick) butter or margarine, melted

Preheat oven to 350°F. Grease bottom of an 8½x4½x2½-inch loaf pan. Combine ingredients in mixing bowl; stir until smooth. Set aside for 20 minutes; stir lightly. Pour batter into prepared pan. Bake for one hour or until toothpick inserted in center comes out clean. Cool in pan 10 minutes; turn out onto wire rack until ready to serve. Makes 8 to 10 servings.

## Easy Cheesy Muffins

*Adds a homemade touch to a simple soup and salad.*

1 cup sifted Martha White Self-Rising Flour
1 cup Martha White Self-Rising Corn Meal Mix
1 cup (4 ounces) grated sharp Cheddar cheese
1 teaspoon dry mustard
1 egg
1 cup milk
¼ cup vegetable oil or melted shortening

Preheat oven to 450°F. Grease muffin cups. Combine flour, corn meal, cheese and dry mustard in medium bowl. Beat egg in separate bowl; stir in milk and oil. Add liquid mixture to dry ingredients; blend thoroughly. Spoon batter into prepared muffin cups, filling each ⅔ full. Bake for 18 to 20 minutes or until golden brown. Makes about 12 medium muffins.

## Bacon and Corn Meal Muffins

*The aroma of smoky bacon escapes when you break one open—serve with a salad.*

1 cup Martha White Self-Rising Corn Meal Mix
1 cup sifted Martha White Self-Rising Flour
3 tablespoons sugar
1 egg
1 cup buttermilk
¼ cup vegetable oil or melted shortening
8 strips bacon, cooked and crumbled

Preheat oven to 425°F. Grease muffin cups. Stir together corn meal, flour and sugar in mixing bowl. Beat egg in separate bowl; stir in buttermilk and oil. Add liquid mixture to dry ingredients, stirring just until blended. Stir in crumbled bacon. Spoon batter into prepared muffin cups, filling each ⅔ full. Bake for 15 to 18 minutes or until golden brown. Makes about 12 medium muffins.

---

### CORNBREAD WITH A CRISP BROWN CRUST

Traditional Southern cornbread has a crisp brown crust and is tender on the inside. To make it this way, grease and heat a black cast-iron pan. It may be heated in the oven or on top of the stove. When the pan is hot and just begins to smoke, pour in the batter—it should sizzle. Then put in the oven to bake. When done, turn out of pan immediately so moisture does not form on the bottom.

For a thicker crust, melt a tablespoon of shortening in the pan and sprinkle a little dry corn meal evenly over the bottom. When corn meal browns, pour in batter and bake.

---

## Hush Puppies

*A necessity with fried catfish.*

2 cups Martha White Self-Rising Corn Meal Mix
3 tablespoons Martha White Self-Rising Flour
1 tablespoon finely chopped onion
1¼ cups buttermilk
1 egg, lightly beaten

Combine corn meal, flour and onion in large mixing bowl. Gradually beat in buttermilk and egg. Set aside for 5 minutes; do not stir. Drop small spoonfuls of batter into hot fat where fish was fried. Fry until golden brown, turning occasionally; drain on paper towels. Serve hot. Makes about 20 hush puppies.

**Note:** For more flavor, add 1 additional tablespoon finely chopped onion and 1 teaspoon onion powder.

## Corn Meal Muffins

*Cooked grits make a moist muffin with a crisp crust—reminiscent of old-fashioned stone-ground corn meal muffins.*

    1 egg
    ¾ cup milk
    ¼ cup vegetable oil or melted
       shortening
    1 teaspoon sugar
    1 cup cooked Jim Dandy Quick
       Grits
    1½ cups Martha White Self-Rising
       Corn Meal Mix

Hush Puppies

Preheat oven to 450°F. Grease muffin cups. Beat egg in mixing bowl. Add remaining ingredients; stir until smooth. Spoon batter into prepared muffin cups, filling each ¾ full. Bake for 18 to 20 minutes or until golden brown. Makes about 12 medium muffins.

## Firecracker Corn Sticks

*Not the ordinary corn stick recipe—lots of crushed red pepper adds quite a kick.*

    1 egg
    1¼ cups milk
    ¼ cup vegetable oil or melted
       shortening
    2 cups Martha White Self-Rising
       Corn Meal Mix
    2 teaspoons sugar
    2 teaspoons crushed red pepper

Preheat oven to 450°F. Grease corn stick molds and place in oven to heat. Beat egg in mixing bowl. Add remaining ingredients; stir until smooth. Pour batter into prepared molds. Bake for 15 to 18 minutes or until golden brown. Makes about 15 corn sticks.

## Texas Cornbread

*Moist and dense with the addition of cream-style corn.*

    1 egg
    ½ cup milk
    2 tablespoons vegetable oil or
       melted shortening
    1 teaspoon sugar
    1 can (8½ ounces) cream-style corn
    1 cup Martha White Self-Rising
       Corn Meal Mix

Preheat oven to 450°F. Grease an 8-inch square baking pan. Beat egg in mixing bowl. Add remaining ingredients; stir until smooth. Pour batter into prepared pan. Bake for 25 to 30 minutes or until golden brown. Makes 6 to 8 servings.

## TIPS FOR COOL SUMMER BAKING

**E**nergy conservation in the kitchen helps keep the cook cool and pays dividends when the gas or electric bill comes. Alternatives to heating up the oven will keep the kitchen cooler and save energy. However, there are times when the oven will have to be used, so take full advantage of it when it's hot.

Here are some energy-saving tips for cooler summer baking:

♦ Bake small batches in a toaster oven—make a small skillet of cornbread, muffins in a six-cup muffin pan or one recipe of biscuits.
♦ Bake waffles and serve with summer fruits like strawberries, peaches or blueberries.
♦ While the waffle iron is hot, bake an extra batch and freeze. Reheat in toaster or toaster oven as needed.
♦ Cornbread batter may also be baked in the waffle iron. Corn meal waffles are crisp and delicious served with barbecue or creamed chicken.
♦ Your favorite cornbread batter may be baked like pancakes. Use an electric skillet, griddle or a skillet on top of the range.
♦ When baking cookies, make a double batch. Freeze one batch and use as needed.

# Green Chili Cornbread

*Lots of moist, rich cornbread with a Mexican flair—perfect for a crowd.*

3 eggs
2 cups buttermilk
1 can (17 ounces) cream-style corn
½ cup mayonnaise
2 cups (8 ounces) grated sharp Cheddar cheese
1 cup chopped onion
1 can (4 ounces) chopped green chilies, drained
3 cups Martha White Self-Rising Corn Meal Mix

Preheat oven to 375°F. Grease a 13x9x2-inch baking pan. Beat eggs in large mixing bowl. Add remaining ingredients; blend well. Pour batter into prepared pan. Bake for 50 to 55 minutes or until dark golden brown and toothpick inserted in center comes out clean. Cool in pan for 15 minutes before serving. Makes 12 to 15 servings.

# Peppery Corn and Cheese Muffins

*Corn muffins with a kick. Serve with fresh green beans from the garden.*

2 eggs
1 cup buttermilk
2 tablespoons melted butter or margarine
1 cup Martha White Self-Rising Corn Meal Mix

¾ cup **Martha White Self-Rising Flour**
½ cup **grated Parmesan cheese**
1½ teaspoons **black pepper**
    **Kernels cut from 1 ear of corn**

Preheat oven to 450°F. Grease muffin cups. Beat eggs in mixing bowl. Add remaining ingredients; blend well. Spoon batter into prepared muffin cups, filling each ¾ full. Bake for 18 to 20 minutes or until golden brown. Makes about 12 medium muffins.

## Cornbread Dressing

*The highlight of a Southern holiday dinner.*

¾ cup **(1½ sticks) butter or margarine**
1 cup **chopped celery**
¼ cup **chopped onion**
1 recipe **Martha White's Basic Biscuits (page 13), crumbled (about 5 cups)**
1 recipe **Martha White's Country-Style Cornbread (page 29), crumbled (about 5 cups)**
1 teaspoon **poultry seasoning**
½ teaspoon **pepper**
2 cans **(14½ ounces each) chicken broth (about 4 cups)**

Melt butter in large skillet over medium heat. Add celery and onion; sauté until tender. Pour sautéed mixture into large bowl. Add remaining ingredients in order listed; blend well. Stuff mixture into bird; roast according to standard roasting directions. Mixture may also be baked in a greased 13x9x2-inch baking pan at 350°F for one hour or until golden brown. Makes about 12 cups stuffing or 10 to 12 servings.

## Southern-Style Sausage Stuffing

*Hearty enough to serve as a main dish casserole.*

1 pound **sausage**
1 cup **chopped celery**
¼ cup **chopped onion**
1 recipe **Martha White's Basic Biscuits (page 13), crumbled (about 5 cups)**
1 recipe **Martha White's Country-Style Cornbread (page 29), crumbled (about 5 cups)**
1 teaspoon **poultry seasoning**
½ teaspoon **pepper**
2 cans **(14½ ounces each) chicken broth (about 4 cups)**

Combine sausage, celery and onion in large skillet. Sauté mixture over medium heat until sausage is browned and vegetables are tender; drain well. Pour sausage mixture into large bowl. Add remaining ingredients in order listed; blend well. Stuff mixture into bird; roast according to standard roasting directions. Mixture may also be baked in a greased 13x9x2-inch baking pan at 350°F for one hour or until golden brown. Makes about 12 cups stuffing or 10 to 12 servings.

# BREAKFAST AND SNACK BREADS

Most folks say that life in the South passes pretty slowly and that Southerners take their own sweet time . . . and a little bit of everybody else's.

That's right. There's no need to deny it.

But when we need to be fast, we can be. One thing that gets Southerners moving is food, whether we're eating it, baking it or getting it to the table.

Speed is the essence of hot breads. And, of course, the South is the hotbed of hot breads. The hottest breads in the South are quick breads. When there is a real need for mealtime speed, Southern cooks turn to traditional quick breads such as muffins, pancakes and waffles.

What makes these breads quick?

The speed is baked right in with self-rising flour which already contains the leavening ingredients that must be added to all-purpose flour. But quick breads are more than just fast; they're good, dependable friends. And like all good friends, each is appreciated for different reasons.

Some are built around fresh and dried fruits, not to mention summer's endless supply of zucchini (threatening to overtake your prize-winning toma-toes). Yes, it's true. The best way to beat 'em *is* to join 'em. Make zucchini bread.

Other quick breads neatly cross the border between dessert and mealtime with just a touch of sugar and plenty of flavor.

Take banana bread, the frugal cook's solution to bananas past their lunchbox prime.

Second cousin to hot loaves like banana bread are muffins. A favorite with the younger set, hot muffins are a hit at the breakfast table and double throughout the day as a snack.

Hot bread is always good with a hot cup of freshly brewed coffee. And perhaps the best quick bread for any occasion is coffee cake. Usually laden with a fruit or nut filling, a good coffee cake can be breakfast in one slice.

But the quick in quick bread really sizzles when it hits a hot griddle or waffle iron. Pancakes and waffles tastefully decorated with ripe, red strawberries are a traditional Southern favorite. They're quick off the plate in most other parts of the country too.

Southerners have nothing against speed. They know when it's called for—getting to the table—and when it's not—leaving the table.

[ 43 ]

Frosty Orange Muffins (page 54)

## Buttermilk Pancakes

*Saturday morning specialty—try all the delicious variations.*

1¼ cups sifted **Martha White Self-Rising Flour**
1 tablespoon **sugar**
½ teaspoon **baking soda**
1 **egg**
1¼ cups **buttermilk**
3 tablespoons **vegetable oil**

For more than a quarter of a century, Lester Flatt traveled across the country singing the praises of Martha White products to such fine folks as the citizens of Moss, Tennessee.

Sift flour, sugar and soda together into mixing bowl. Beat egg in separate bowl; stir in buttermilk and oil. Add liquid mixture to dry ingredients, stirring just until blended. Batter will be slightly lumpy. Pour batter onto heated (340°F) lightly greased skillet or griddle, using about ¼ cup batter for each pancake. Brown on one side. Turn when tops are covered with bubbles and edges begin to look dry. Brown on other side. Makes about 10 pancakes.

**Note:** If using Martha White All-Purpose Flour, sift 1½ teaspoons baking powder and a scant ½ teaspoon salt with flour.

## Whole Wheat Buttermilk Pancakes

*Whole grain goodness—for a healthy alternative, top with fresh fruit and yogurt.*

¾ cup sifted **Martha White Self-Rising Flour**
¾ cup **Martha White Whole Wheat Flour**
2 tablespoons **sugar**
½ teaspoon **baking soda**
¼ teaspoon **salt**
1 **egg**
1 cup **buttermilk**
½ cup **vegetable oil**

Stir together flours, sugar, soda and salt in mixing bowl. Beat egg in separate bowl; stir in buttermilk and oil. Add liquid mixture to dry ingredients, stirring just until blended. Batter will be slightly lumpy. Pour batter onto heated (340°F) lightly greased skillet or griddle, using about ¼ cup batter for each pancake. Brown on one side. Turn when tops are covered with bubbles and edges begin to look dry. Brown on other side. Makes about 10 pancakes.

**Note:** If using Martha White All-Purpose Flour, sift one teaspoon baking powder and ¼ teaspoon salt with flour.

## Apple-Cinnamon Oat Pancakes

*Top with warm applesauce or warm maple syrup.*

½ **cup Martha White Whole Wheat Flour**
½ **cup quick-cooking or old-fashioned oats**
1 **tablespoon sugar**
1 **teaspoon baking powder**
½ **teaspoon cinnamon**
½ **teaspoon salt**
1 **egg**
⅔ **cup milk**
½ **cup applesauce**
2 **tablespoons vegetable oil**
½ **cup chopped walnuts**

Stir together flour, oats, sugar, baking powder, cinnamon and salt in mixing bowl. Beat egg in separate bowl; stir in milk, applesauce and oil. Add liquid mixture to dry ingredients, stirring just until blended. Fold in walnuts. Pour batter onto heated (340°F) lightly greased skillet or griddle, using about ¼ cup batter for each pancake. Brown on one side. Turn when tops are covered with bubbles and edges begin to look dry. Brown on other side. Makes about 10 pancakes.

# The Table

The clang of the dinner bell and the call to the table are more than a summons to eat. They are a call to experience family, food and conversation—an invitation to a daily family reunion.

Most of us learned and lived our family histories at the table. We were raised at the table—disciplined, rewarded, encouraged and comforted there. We learned who God was at the altar of the kitchen table by hearing our fathers repeat the blessings we would later learn and say. Family holidays were all celebrated at the table with seasonal feasts. We were honored with a seat at the head of the table and punished by being sent from the table. And in our mothers' eyes, our table manners portrayed just what manner of people we were.

The table is the center of home and family. Everywhere you go.

## Bacon Cheddar Pancakes

**1 recipe Buttermilk Pancakes
    (page 44)
4 slices bacon, cooked and
    crumbled
½ cup grated sharp Cheddar cheese**

Prepare Buttermilk Pancakes as directed; except—stir bacon and cheese into batter. Cook as directed. Makes about 10 pancakes.

## Blueberry Pancakes

**1 recipe Buttermilk Pancakes
    (page 44)
½ cup blueberries, rinsed and
    drained (fresh, frozen or canned)**

Prepare Buttermilk Pancakes as directed; except—gently fold blueberries into batter. Cook as directed. Makes about 12 pancakes.

## Cinnamon Sugar Pancakes

**1 recipe Buttermilk Pancakes
    (page 44)
2 tablespoons sugar
½ teaspoon cinnamon**

Prepare Buttermilk Pancakes as directed; except—stir sugar and cinnamon into dry ingredients. Cook as directed. Makes about 10 pancakes.

## Butter Pecan Pancakes

**1 recipe Buttermilk Pancakes
    (page 44)
⅓ cup firmly packed brown sugar
⅓ cup chopped pecans
2 tablespoons butter or margarine,
    melted**

Prepare Buttermilk Pancakes as directed; except—stir brown sugar, pecans and butter into batter. Cook as directed. Makes about 12 pancakes.

## Waffles

*All-purpose waffles are great for dessert — seasonal fresh fruit and whipped cream turn them into waffle shortcake.*

**2 eggs
1¼ cups milk
½ cup vegetable oil
1¾ cups sifted Martha White
    Self-Rising Flour**

Preheat waffle iron according to manufacturer's directions. Beat eggs in mixing bowl. Add milk and oil; blend well. Stir in flour until well blended. Pour

Waffles

batter into greased, heated waffle iron. Bake until steaming stops and waffles are light golden brown. Makes twelve 4-inch waffles.

**Note:** If using Martha White All-Purpose Flour, sift 2¾ teaspoons baking powder and 1¼ teaspoons salt with flour.

## Blackberry Roll-Ups

*A fruit muffin mix is the base for these easy pancakes rolled up with jam.*

    **1 egg**
    **1 cup milk**
    **1 package (7 ounces) Martha White Blackberry Muffin Mix**
    **½ cup blackberry jam**
    **Confectioners' sugar**

Beat egg in mixing bowl; stir in milk. Add muffin mix and stir just until blended. Batter will be thin and slightly lumpy. Pour batter onto heated (340°F) lightly greased skillet or griddle, using about ¼ cup batter for each pancake. Brown on one side. Turn when tops are covered with bubbles and edges begin to look dry. Brown on other side. For each roll-up, spoon one tablespoon jam down center of each pancake. Fold edges over to create a roll. Dust with confectioners' sugar. These are best served warm. They may also be served with maple syrup. Makes 8 roll-ups.

# Country Music Heritage

Martha White is as modern and fresh as the oat bran muffin that just came out of your oven. But this modern reputation for excellence wasn't achieved in a day. It was built over time on the company's long-standing tradition as an enduring Southern name in baking.

♦ A little girl's name—Martha White. Unlike fictitious brand symbols, Martha White was a real person. When Richard Lindsey Sr. founded the company back in 1899, he named his finest brand of flour for his 3-year-old daughter, Martha White.

♦ A secret ingredient—Hot Rize. For almost half a century Hot Rize has been emblazoned on Martha White flour and cornmeal sacks, sung about and immortalized on T-shirts for country music fans. Hot Rize is the self-rising agent blended into Martha White's self-rising flour and cornmeal.

♦ A classic theme song—the Martha White jingle. Written in the '50s and immortalized by Martha White spokesmen Earl Scruggs and Lester Flatt, the Martha White jingle is a bluegrass standard.

♦ An entertaining means of advertising—country music. In the early years of the company, Martha White used country music as a natural forum to carry its message to the biscuit-eating public. Beginning in 1948, Martha White sponsored its first Grand Ole Opry show and has been a part of the world's longest-running radio show every Saturday night since.

Today Martha White is the longest continuing sponsor of the famous Opry. Over the years, the Martha White portion of the Opry has been hosted by country music's greatest legends, from Bill Monroe to Porter Wagoner and Roy Acuff. Today a portion of the Martha White backdrop, once used onstage at the Opry, hangs on display in the Country Music Hall of Fame in Nashville.

## Classic Muffins

*The master recipe, ready for your creative additions.*

> 2 cups sifted Martha White
>   Self-Rising Flour
> ¼ cup sugar
> 1 egg
> 1 cup milk
> 3 tablespoons vegetable oil

Preheat oven to 425°F. Grease muffin cups. Stir together flour and sugar in mixing bowl. Beat egg in separate bowl; stir in milk and oil. Add liquid mixture to dry ingredients, stirring just until blended. Batter will be slightly lumpy. Spoon batter into prepared muffin cups, filling each ⅔ full. Bake for 18 to 20 minutes or until golden brown. Makes about 12 medium muffins.

**Note:** If using Martha White All-Purpose Flour, sift 1 tablespoon baking powder and ¾ teaspoon salt with flour.

## Oat Bran Muffins

*A hint of cinnamon and vanilla gives these nourishing muffins unique flavor.*

> 2 cups sifted Martha White
>   Self-Rising Flour
> ½ cup oat bran or 1 cup quick-
>   cooking oats
> ½ cup sugar
> ¼ teaspoon cinnamon
> 2 eggs
> ¾ cup milk
> ½ cup vegetable oil
> 1 teaspoon vanilla

Preheat oven to 425°F. Grease muffin cups. Stir together flour, oat bran, sugar and cinnamon in mixing bowl. Beat eggs in separate bowl; stir in milk, oil and vanilla. Add liquid mixture to dry ingredients, stirring just until blended. Batter will be slightly lumpy. Spoon batter into prepared muffin cups, filling each ⅔ full. Bake for 16 to 18 minutes or until golden brown. Makes about 12 medium muffins.

**Note:** If using Martha White All-Purpose Flour, sift 1 tablespoon baking powder and ¾ teaspoon salt with flour.

## Blueberry Oat Bran Muffins

> 1 recipe Oat Bran Muffins
> 1 can (15 ounces) blueberries,
>   rinsed and drained

Prepare Oat Bran Muffins as directed; except—gently fold in blueberries after combining liquid and dry ingredients. Bake as directed. Makes about 12 medium muffins.

**Note:** One cup fresh blueberries or 1 cup frozen blueberries, thawed and drained, may be substituted for canned blueberries.

## Oat Bran Muffins Plus

1 recipe Oat Bran Muffins (page 49)
½ cup dried fruit or chopped nuts
(pecans, walnuts, raisins, chopped
dates or apricots)

Prepare Oat Bran Muffins as directed; except—fold in dried fruit or nuts after combining liquid and dry ingredients. Bake as directed. Makes about 12 medium muffins.

## English Bran Muffins

*Muffins rich in high fiber cereal—perfect for breakfast or anytime.*

1 cup All-Bran cereal
⅔ cup milk
1 egg, lightly beaten

### MUFFINS ARE EASY

Most of the muffin recipes in this book are made by this easy three-step method.
(1) Mix all the dry ingredients together in bowl.
(2) Mix all the liquid ingredients together in another bowl.
(3) Add liquid to dry and stir just until moistened.

¼ cup vegetable oil
1 cup sifted Martha White
Self-Rising Flour
¼ cup sugar

Preheat oven to 400°F. Grease muffin cups. Combine cereal and milk in mixing bowl; set aside until milk is absorbed, about 10 minutes. Stir in egg and oil; blend well. Add flour and sugar; stir just until blended. Spoon batter into prepared muffin cups, filling each ⅔ full. Bake for 20 to 25 minutes or until deep golden brown. Makes about 9 medium muffins.

**Note:** If using Martha White All-Purpose Flour, sift 1½ teaspoons baking powder and ½ teaspoon salt with flour.

## Butter Pecan Muffins

*A bowl of fresh peaches accompanied by these buttery muffins complete a summer brunch.*

1½ cups sifted Martha White
Self-Rising Flour
1 cup chopped pecans
½ cup firmly packed light brown
sugar
1 egg
¾ cup milk
¼ cup (4 tablespoons) butter or
margarine, melted and cooled
½ teaspoon vanilla

Preheat oven to 400°F. Grease muffin cups. Stir together flour, pecans and brown sugar in mixing bowl. Beat egg

The Martha White cotton flour sack, once a prominent item in many kitchens, is immortalized in this Donny Finley painting.

in separate bowl; stir in milk, butter and vanilla. Add liquid mixture to dry ingredients, stirring just until blended. Batter will be slightly lumpy. Spoon batter into prepared muffin cups, filling each ⅔ full. Bake for 15 to 18 minutes or until golden brown. Makes about 12 medium muffins.

**Note:** If using Martha White All-Purpose Flour, sift 2¼ teaspoons baking powder and ½ teaspoon salt with flour.

## Banana Nut Muffins

*Reminiscent of grandmother's banana nut bread.*

    **2 cups sifted Martha White Self-Rising Flour**
**½ cup sugar**
  **1 egg**

⅔ **cup milk**
⅓ **cup (5⅓ tablespoons) butter or margarine, melted and cooled**
½ **cup mashed banana (about 1 large)**
½ **cup chopped pecans**

Preheat oven to 425°F. Grease muffin cups. Stir together flour and sugar in mixing bowl. Beat egg in separate bowl; stir in milk, butter and banana. Add liquid mixture to dry ingredients, stirring just until blended. Batter will be slightly lumpy. Fold in pecans. Spoon batter into prepared muffin cups, filling each ⅔ full. Bake for 15 to 18 minutes or until golden brown. Makes about 12 medium muffins.

**Note:** If using Martha White All-Purpose Flour, sift 1 tablespoon baking powder and ¾ teaspoon salt with flour.

## Corn 'N' Wheat Muffins

*Serve hot with butter and strawberry preserves—good enough for dessert.*

- 1½ cups Martha White Self-Rising Corn Meal Mix
- ½ cup Martha White Whole Wheat Flour
- ⅓ cup firmly packed light brown sugar
- 2 eggs
- 1 cup milk
- ¼ cup vegetable oil or melted shortening

Preheat oven to 400°F. Grease muffin cups. Stir together corn meal, flour and brown sugar in mixing bowl. Beat eggs in separate bowl; stir in milk and oil. Add liquid mixture to dry ingredients, stirring just until blended. Spoon batter into prepared muffin cups, filling each ⅔ full. Bake for 20 to 25 minutes or until golden brown. Makes about 12 medium muffins.

## Homemade Blueberry Muffins

*This classic recipe may be made year 'round using fresh, frozen, or canned berries.*

- 2 cups sifted Martha White Self-Rising Flour
- ½ cup sugar
- 1 egg
- ⅔ cup milk
- ⅓ cup (5⅓ tablespoons) butter or margarine, melted and cooled

- 1 cup canned blueberries, rinsed and drained*

Preheat oven to 425°F. Grease muffin cups. Stir together flour and sugar in mixing bowl. Beat egg in separate bowl; stir in milk and butter. Add liquid mixture to dry ingredients, stirring just until blended. Batter will be slightly lumpy. Gently fold in blueberries. Spoon batter into prepared muffin cups, filling each ⅔ full. Bake for 15 to 18 minutes or until golden brown. Makes about 12 medium muffins.

*One cup fresh blueberries or 1 cup frozen blueberries, thawed and drained, may be substituted for canned blueberries.

**Note:** If using Martha White All-Purpose Flour, sift 1 tablespoon baking powder and ¾ teaspoon salt with flour.

## Apple Streusel Muffins

*Awaken overnight guests with the spicy aroma of these wholesome muffins.*

- 1 cup sifted Martha White All-Purpose Flour
- 1 cup Martha White Whole Wheat Flour
- 1 cup chopped apple (about 1 medium)
- ⅓ cup firmly packed brown sugar
- 1 tablespoon baking powder
- 1 teaspoon salt
- 1 egg
- 1 cup milk
- ¼ cup vegetable oil
  Streusel Topping, following

Preheat oven to 400°F. Grease muffin cups. Stir together flours, apple, sugar, baking powder and salt in mixing bowl. Beat egg in separate bowl; stir in milk and oil. Add liquid mixture to dry ingredients, stirring just until blended. Spoon batter into prepared muffin cups, filling each ⅔ full. Sprinkle evenly with Streusel Topping. Bake for 15 to 18 minutes or until golden brown. Makes about 12 medium muffins.

**Streusel Topping**

- ½ cup firmly packed brown sugar
- 1 tablespoon butter or margarine, softened
- ½ teaspoon cinnamon
- ¼ cup chopped pecans

Combine sugar, butter and cinnamon in small mixing bowl using fingers or pastry blender. Add pecans and mix well.

## ★ Pete Wernick of Hot Rize ★

In the late 1970s, the leader of a new Colorado bluegrass band took a deep breath and wrote to Martha White to ask if he could use one of the company's most identifiable trademarks, "Hot Rize," as the name for the band. To Pete Wernick's complete delight, the company agreed and thus set in motion a relationship that endures to this day.

### WHOLE WHEAT MUFFINS

*Add your favorite dried fruit or nuts for variety and extra nutrients.*

- 1 cup sifted Martha White All-Purpose Flour
- 1 cup Martha White Whole Wheat Flour
- ⅓ cup granulated sugar or firmly packed brown sugar
- 1 tablespoon baking powder
- 1 teaspoon salt
- 1 egg
- 1 cup milk
- ¼ cup vegetable oil

Preheat oven to 400°F. Grease muffin cups. Stir together flours, sugar, baking powder and salt in mixing bowl. Beat egg in separate bowl; stir in milk and oil. Add liquid mixture to dry ingredients, stirring just until blended. Spoon batter into prepared muffin cups, filling each ⅔ full. Bake for 15 to 18 minutes or until golden brown. Makes about 12 medium muffins.

## Savory Cheese Muffins

*Dry mustard is the secret ingredient that enhances the cheese flavor.*

> 2 cups sifted Martha White
>   Self-Rising Flour
> 1 cup (4 ounces) grated sharp
>   Cheddar cheese
> 1 teaspoon dry mustard
> ½ teaspoon chili powder
> 1 egg
> 1 cup milk
> ¼ cup vegetable oil

Preheat oven to 425°F. Grease muffin cups. Stir together flour, cheese, mustard and chili powder in mixing bowl. Beat egg in separate bowl; stir in milk and oil. Add liquid mixture to dry ingredients, stirring just until blended. Batter will be slightly lumpy. Spoon batter into prepared muffin cups, filling each ⅔ full. Bake for 18 to 20 minutes or until golden brown. Makes about 12 medium muffins.

**Note:** If using Martha White All-Purpose Flour, sift 1 tablespoon baking powder and ¾ teaspoon salt with flour.

## Applesauce Muffins

*A welcome afternoon snack with a glass of milk.*

> 2 cups sifted Martha White
>   Self-Rising Flour
> ⅓ cup sugar
> ½ teaspoon cinnamon

> ¼ teaspoon nutmeg
> 1 egg
> 1 cup applesauce
> ½ cup milk
> 3 tablespoons vegetable oil

Preheat oven to 425°F. Grease muffin cups. Stir together flour, sugar, cinnamon and nutmeg in mixing bowl. Beat egg in separate bowl; stir in applesauce, milk and oil. Add liquid mixture to dry ingredients, stirring just until blended. Batter will be slightly lumpy. Spoon batter into prepared muffin cups, filling each ⅔ full. Bake for 18 to 20 minutes or until golden brown. Makes about 12 medium muffins.

**Note:** If using Martha White All-Purpose Flour, sift 1 tablespoon baking powder and ¾ teaspoon salt with flour.

## Frosty Orange Muffins

*The zest of orange and rich cream cheese icing make these refreshing muffins good enough for dessert.*

> 2 cups sifted Martha White
>   Self-Rising Flour
> ⅓ cup sugar
> 1 tablespoon grated orange peel
> 1 egg
> ¾ cup orange juice
> ¼ cup vegetable oil
>   Orange Icing, following

Preheat oven to 400°F. Grease muffin cups. Stir together flour, sugar and orange peel in mixing bowl. Beat egg in separate bowl; stir in orange juice and oil. Add liquid mixture to dry ingredients, stirring just until blended. Batter will be slightly lumpy. Spoon batter into prepared muffin cups, filling each ⅔ full. Bake for 18 to 20 minutes or until golden brown. Remove muffins from pan and cool for 5 minutes. Spread with Orance Icing. Makes about 12 medium muffins.

**Note:** If using Martha White All-Purpose Flour, sift 1 tablespoon baking powder and ¾ teaspoon salt with flour.

### Orange Icing

> 1 **package (3 ounces) cream cheese, softened**
> 2 **tablespoons sugar**
> 1 **teaspoon grated orange peel**
> 2 **teaspoons orange juice**

Combine cream cheese, sugar and orange peel in small bowl; blend well. Add orange juice and stir until smooth.

## French Cinnamon Muffins

*Rich buttery muffins that melt in your mouth—crowned with a cinnamon-sugar topping.*

> 2 **cups sifted Martha White Self-Rising Flour**
> ½ **cup sugar**
> ¼ **teaspoon cinnamon**
> 1 **egg**
> ⅔ **cup milk**
> ⅓ **cup (5⅓ tablespoons) butter or margarine, melted and cooled**

> ¼ **cup sugar**
> 1 **teaspoon cinnamon**
> ¼ **cup (4 tablespoons) butter or margarine, melted**

Preheat oven to 425°F. Grease muffin cups. Stir together flour, ½ cup sugar and ¼ teaspoon cinnamon in mixing bowl. Beat egg in separate bowl; stir in milk and ⅓ cup butter. Add liquid mixture to dry ingredients, stirring just until blended. Batter will be slightly lumpy. Spoon batter into prepared muffin cups, filling each ⅔ full. Bake for 15 to 18 minutes or until golden brown. Stir together ¼ cup sugar and 1 teaspoon cinnamon in small bowl. Remove muffins from pans. Dip tops of warm muffins in ¼ cup butter and then in cinnamon-sugar mixture. Makes about 12 medium muffins.

**Note:** If using Martha White All-Purpose Flour, sift 1 tablespoon baking powder and ¾ teaspoon salt with flour.

## MUFFIN TIPS

**M**uffins brown best when baked in shiny aluminum pans. Dark pans tend to brown muffins more quickly on the bottom. If you have dark pans, simply reduce temperature 25°F. and bake for the length of time recommended in the recipe.

The muffin recipes in this book were tested in pans with cups that are 2½ inches in diameter and 1 inch deep, but any size may be used. Just remember to fill the cups only ⅔ full for a nice round-topped muffin.

If you prefer large mushroom-shaped muffins, fill the cup almost to the top with batter. It may be necessary to bake a minute or two longer than the recipe specifies.

## Deluxe Fruit Muffins

*Sour cream gives these muffins their deluxe flavor.*

>   2 packages (7 ounces each) Martha White Fruit Muffin Mix (Blueberry, Strawberry, Blackberry or Raspberry)
>   1 cup (8 ounces) dairy sour cream
>   ⅔ cup milk

Preheat oven to 425°F. Grease muffin cups. Pour dry muffin mix into mixing bowl. In separate bowl, gradually stir milk into sour cream until blended. Add sour cream mixture to muffin mix, stirring just until blended. Batter will be slightly lumpy. Spoon batter into prepared muffin cups, filling each ⅔ full. Bake for 15 to 18 minutes or until golden brown. Makes about 12 medium muffins.

## Sugar Plum Muffins

*Chock full of high-fiber goodness.*

>   1¼ cups sifted **Martha White Self-Rising Flour**
>   ¾ cup **oat bran**
>   ⅓ cup **sugar**
>   1 **egg**
>   ¾ cup **milk**
>   3 tablespoons **vegetable oil**
>   ½ cup **pitted cooked prunes, chopped**

Preheat oven to 425°F. Grease muffin cups. Stir together flour, oat bran and sugar in mixing bowl. Beat egg in separate bowl; stir in milk and oil. Add liquid mixture to dry ingredients, stirring just until blended. Stir in prunes. Spoon batter into prepared muffin cups, filling each ⅔ full. Bake for 15 to 18 minutes or until golden brown. Makes about 12 medium muffins.

**Note:** If using Martha White All-Purpose Flour, sift 1¾ teaspoons baking powder and ½ teaspoon salt with flour.

## Treasure Bran Muffins

*A luscious cheesecake-like topping forms as the muffin bakes.*

    1 package (8 ounces) cream cheese, softened
   ¼ cup sugar
    1 egg, lightly beaten
    2 packages (7 ounces each) Martha White Bran Muffin Mix
   ⅔ cup milk
    2 eggs, lightly beaten

Preheat oven to 425°F. Grease muffin cups. Combine cream cheese and sugar in mixing bowl. Stir in 1 egg until well blended. Pour dry muffin mix into separate bowl. Add milk and 2 eggs, stirring just until blended. Fill each muffin cup ¼ full with batter. Spoon one teaspoon cream cheese mixture into center of batter in each cup. Fill each muffin cup to ½ full with remaining batter. Top each with one tablespoon of remaining cream cheese mixture. Bake for 12 to 15 minutes or until golden brown. Makes about 12 medium muffins.

## Date Nut Muffins

*Dates and pecans baked in a light, buttery muffin.*

    2 cups sifted Martha White Self-Rising Flour
   ½ cup sugar
    1 egg
   ¾ cup milk
   ½ cup (1 stick) butter or margarine, melted
    1 cup chopped dates
   ½ cup chopped pecans

Preheat oven to 425°F. Grease muffin cups. Stir together flour and sugar in mixing bowl. Beat egg in separate bowl; stir in milk and butter. Add liquid mixture to dry ingredients, stirring just until blended. Batter will be slightly lumpy. Stir in dates and pecans. Spoon batter into prepared muffin cups, filling each ¾ full. Bake for 15 to 18 minutes or until golden brown. Makes about 15 medium muffins.

**Note:** If using Martha White All-Purpose Flour, sift 1 tablespoon baking powder and ¾ teaspoon salt with flour.

---

### SIFTING THROUGH THE FLOUR FACTS

**W**hen baking with flour, here are a few facts to remember:

♦ Most flour today is pre-sifted before being packaged.
♦ It is not necessary to sift again for standard, everyday baking.
♦ Sifting adds air and tends to make a lighter product.
♦ When making delicate foods, such as cakes, you may want to sift the flour before measuring for accuracy.

## Easy Date Muffins

*Dates complement quick and easy Apple Cinnamon Muffin Mix.*

**1 package (7 ounces) Martha White Apple Cinnamon Muffin Mix**
**½ cup chopped dates**
**⅓ cup milk**

Preheat oven to 400°F. Grease muffin cups. Stir together muffin mix and dates in mixing bowl. Add milk and stir just until blended. Batter will be slightly lumpy. Spoon batter into prepared muffin cups, filling each ⅔ full. Bake for 15 to 18 minutes or until golden brown. Makes about 6 medium muffins.

## Quick Cheese Bread

*Warm slices complement soup, salads and chili.*

**2 packages (5½ ounces each) Martha White BixMix**
**¾ cup water**
**2 eggs, lightly beaten**
**2 teaspoons dry mustard**
**1½ cups (6 ounces) grated sharp Cheddar cheese, divided**
**2 tablespoons butter or margarine**

Preheat oven to 350°F. Grease bottom of an 8½x4½x2½-inch loaf pan. Combine biscuit mix and water in mixing bowl; stir until smooth. Add eggs, mustard and one cup cheese; blend well. Pour batter into prepared pan. Sprinkle with remaining ½ cup cheese and dot with butter. Bake for 40 to 45 minutes or until toothpick inserted in center comes out clean. Cool in pan for 10 minutes. Remove from pan and cool on wire rack before slicing. Makes 8 to 10 servings.

**Note:** To serve as a snack or with salads, cut slices of Quick Cheese Bread into strips. Brush with melted butter and toast under broiler or in toaster oven.

## Little Date Nut Loaves

*Let the kids help prepare these miniature loaves as a gift for the teacher.*

**2 eggs**
**⅔ cup milk**
**2 packages (7 ounces each) Martha White Bran Muffin Mix**
**1 cup chopped dates**
**1 cup chopped pecans**

Preheat oven to 350°F. Grease bottoms of six 4½x2½x1½-inch miniature loaf pans. Beat eggs in mixing bowl. Add remaining ingredients, stirring just until blended. Divide batter evenly among prepared pans. Bake for 25 to 30 minutes or until toothpick inserted in center comes out clean. Cool in pans for 5 minutes. Remove from pans and cool on wire racks. Makes six miniature loaves.

# Who is Martha White?

If you grew up in the South on home-made cornbread and cobbler, you might have thought Martha White was some unseen cousin who helped your mama in the kitchen with the baking.

And the truth is, unlike fictitious brand symbols, Martha White was a real person. In fact, the founding father of the company was also the father of the little girl who gave the company its name.

Martha White Lindsey was the daughter of Richard Lindsey Sr. and Katherine Jordan Lindsey. Richard Lindsey Sr. founded Nashville's Royal Flour Mill back in 1899 and named his finest flour brand for his then 3-year-old daughter. When the Williams family acquired the Royal Flour Mill in 1941,

An oil portrait of little Miss Martha in her famous pose.

the first thing they did was change the company's name to match that of its best-selling flour—Martha White.

Today that little girl's name graces Martha White products. And, until 1988, little Martha's smiling face accompanied her name as the company's logo.

Martha was first featured in the "barrel head" logo. The trademark's distinctive red ring was reminiscent of the red ring painted on the head of the Martha White flour barrel. In the years since, the Martha White logo has been refined and even animated for television commercials. In 1988, Martha underwent her latest facelift when the little girl finally came of age and was transformed into a woman. The new logo features the stylized silhouette of a woman holding a fresh-baked pie.

Off the package, the real-life Martha grew up in Nashville and attended Warner Elementary School and Hume Fogg High School. In 1923, Martha was married to Dr. George M. Russell, an orthodontist. The couple had three children and lived in Nashville until 1931, at which time they moved to Memphis where they lived until Martha White Lindsey Russell died in 1949.

But little Martha lives on.

Several years ago a child mailed a letter with the lone address: Martha, Nashville, Tennessee. Sure enough, the letter found its way to the right place, Martha White Foods, all on the strength of a little girl's name.

## Lemon Tea Bread

*For the perfect tea-time sandwiches, spread thin slices with Ginger Cream Spread.*

>     2 cups sifted Martha White
>        Self-Rising Flour
>    ¾ cup sugar
>     1 tablespoon grated lemon peel
>     2 eggs, lightly beaten
>    ½ cup buttermilk
>    ⅓ cup vegetable oil
>    ½ cup chopped walnuts
>     2 tablespoons sugar
>     1 tablespoon lemon juice
>        Ginger Cream Spread, below

Preheat oven to 350°F. Grease bottom of an 8½x4½x2½-inch loaf pan. Stir together flour, ¾ cup sugar and lemon peel in mixing bowl. Add eggs, buttermilk and oil; stir to blend. Stir in walnuts. Pour batter into prepared pan. Bake for 55 to 60 minutes or until toothpick inserted in center comes out clean. Stir together 2 tablespoons sugar and lemon juice. Pour mixture over hot bread immediately after removing from oven. Cool in pan for 10 minutes. Remove from pan and cool on wire rack. For easier slicing, wrap loaf and store overnight in a cool place. Slice and serve with Ginger Cream Spread, if desired. Makes 8 to 10 servings.

**Note:** If using Martha White All-Purpose Flour, sift 1 tablespoon baking powder and ¾ teaspoon salt with flour.

### Ginger Cream Spread

>     1 package (3 ounces) cream cheese,
>        softened

>     1 teaspoon milk
>     2 tablespoons finely chopped
>        crystallized ginger
>     2 tablespoons finely chopped
>        blanched almonds

Combine cream cheese and milk in small bowl; stir to blend. Add ginger and almonds; blend well.

## Strawberry Bread

*This moist bread, made with strawberry jam, is wonderful spread with cream cheese.*

>    ½ cup (1 stick) butter or margarine,
>        softened
>    ½ cup sugar
>     2 eggs
>     1 teaspoon vanilla
>     2 cups sifted Martha White
>        All-Purpose Flour
>    ½ teaspoon salt
>    ¼ teaspoon baking soda
>     1 cup strawberry preserves
>    ½ cup buttermilk
>    ½ cup chopped pecans

Preheat oven to 325°F. Grease bottom of an 8½x4½x2½-inch loaf pan. Cream butter and sugar together in mixing bowl until light and fluffy. Add eggs one at a time, beating well after each addition. Blend in vanilla. Stir together flour, salt and soda in small bowl. Combine preserves and buttermilk in separate bowl. Add flour to creamed mixture alternately with preserves, beginning and ending with flour. Stir in pecans. Pour batter into prepared pan.

Bake for 1 hour and 20 minutes or until toothpick inserted in center comes out clean. Cool in pan for 15 minutes. Remove from pan and cool on wire rack. For easier slicing, wrap loaf and store overnight in a cool place. Makes 8 to 10 servings.

## Zucchini Nut Bread

*A creative use for this summer vegetable.*

> 2 cups sifted Martha White
>   All-Purpose Flour
> 1 cup sugar
> 1 tablespoon cinnamon
> 2 teaspoons baking powder
> 1 teaspoon salt
> 3 eggs
> 2 cups unpeeled grated zucchini
>   (about 1 large)
> ¾ cup vegetable oil
> 1 tablespoon vanilla
> 1 cup chopped walnuts

Preheat oven to 325°F. Grease and flour a 9x5x3-inch loaf pan. Stir together flour, sugar, cinnamon, baking powder and salt in large mixing bowl. Beat eggs in separate bowl; stir in zucchini, oil and vanilla. Add zucchini mixture to dry ingredients, stirring just until blended. Fold in walnuts. Pour batter into prepared pan. Bake for 1 hour and 5 minutes or until toothpick inserted in center comes out clean. Cool in pan for 10 minutes. Remove from pan and cool on wire rack. For easier slicing, wrap loaf and store overnight in a cool place. Makes 10 to 12 servings.

### BAKE BREAD AHEAD AND FREEZE

Do you ever wish you had a fresh, hot muffin or biscuit for breakfast but were pressed for time and settled for just a cup of coffee instead?

Try baking breads ahead and freezing for convenience. If frozen properly, breads will still taste oven fresh for about three months.

The key to fresh-tasting frozen breads is proper storage:

♦ Freeze only the amount you will use at any one time.
♦ Wrap the bread tightly with foil as soon as it cools.
♦ Press excess air from package and place in freezer as soon as possible.

When you are ready to serve the bread, follow these simple steps:

♦ Thaw bread at room temperature in original package for 1 to 3 hours or in refrigerator overnight.
♦ Reheat bread in foil; to make a crisper crust remove foil during the last 5 minutes of heating.
♦ An alternative is to remove thawed bread from foil, wrap in paper towel, and reheat on HIGH in the microwave for 15 to 20 seconds.
♦ Frozen bread may be reheated in the microwave by thawing on DEFROST for 1 to 2 minutes and then heating on HIGH for about 15 seconds.

## *Aunt Lois' Banana Nut Bread

*A Tennessee family's favorite handed down for generations. Just about the best you'll ever taste.*

   1½ **cups sifted Martha White All-Purpose Flour**
   ¾ **teaspoon baking soda**
   ¼ **teaspoon salt**
   1 **cup sugar**
   2 **eggs, lightly beaten**
   ¾ **cup vegetable oil**
   3 **tablespoons buttermilk**
   1 **cup mashed bananas (about 2 large)**
   ½ **cup chopped pecans**

Preheat oven to 325°F. Grease and flour an 8½x4½x2½-inch loaf pan. Stir together flour, soda and salt in mixing bowl. Add sugar, eggs, oil and buttermilk; stir to blend. Stir in bananas and pecans. Pour batter into prepared pan. Bake for 1 hour and 10 minutes or until toothpick inserted in center comes out clean. Cool in pan for 15 minutes. Remove from pan and cool on wire rack. For easier slicing, wrap loaf and store overnight in a cool place. Makes 8 to 10 servings.

**Note:** For an extra moist, rich bread, wrap warm loaf tightly after removing from pan. Store overnight for best flavor and easier slicing.

Cranberry Banana Nut Bread

## Apple Butter Spice Bread

*A comforting snack bread with spicy homespun flavor.*

   2 **cups sifted Martha White All-Purpose Flour**
   1 **cup sugar**
   1 **teaspoon cinnamon**
   1 **teaspoon nutmeg**
   1 **teaspoon baking powder**
   ¾ **teaspoon salt**
   ¼ **teaspoon baking soda**
   3 **eggs**
   ¾ **cup apple butter**
   ¾ **cup vegetable oil**
   1 **cup raisins, boiled and drained (optional)**
   ½ **cup chopped pecans**

*One of Martha White Test Kitchen's ten all-time favorite recipes.

Preheat oven to 325°F. Grease bottoms of two 8½x4½x2½-inch loaf pans. Stir together flour, sugar, cinnamon, nutmeg, baking powder, salt and soda in mixing bowl. Beat eggs in separate bowl; stir in apple butter and oil. Add liquid mixture to dry ingredients, stirring just until blended. Fold in raisins and pecans. Pour batter into prepared pans. Bake for 55 to 60 minutes or until toothpick inserted in center comes out clean. Cool in pans for 10 minutes. Remove from pans and cool on wire rack. For easier slicing, wrap loaves and store overnight in a cool place. Makes 8 to 10 servings each.

## Bran and Raisin Bread

*Slice and serve with a cup of hot coffee to get the day off to a good start.*

>    1 cup Bran Buds cereal
>    1 cup raisins
>    1 cup milk
>    ¾ cup sugar
>    1 cup sifted Martha White
>       All-Purpose Flour
>    1 teaspoon baking powder

Combine cereal, raisins, milk and sugar in medium bowl; blend well. Cover and refrigerate several hours or overnight. Preheat oven to 375°F. Grease bottom of an 8½x4½x2½-inch loaf pan. Add flour and baking powder to refrigerated cereal mixture; blend well. Pour batter into prepared pan. Bake for 50 to 55 minutes or until toothpick inserted in center comes out clean. Cool in pan for 10 minutes. Remove from pan and cool on wire rack. For easier slicing, wrap

loaf and store overnight in a cool place. This is a very dense, compact loaf. Makes 8 to 10 servings.

## Cranberry Banana Nut Bread

*Whole cranberry sauce adds holiday flair to a classic favorite.*

>    ⅔ cup shortening
>    1⅓ cups sugar
>    3 eggs
>    2 cups mashed bananas (about 4
>       large)
>    3½ cups sifted Martha White
>       Self-Rising Flour
>    ¼ teaspoon baking soda
>    1 cup chopped walnuts
>    1 can (16 ounces) whole berry
>       cranberry sauce (1¾ cups)

Preheat oven to 350°F. Grease bottoms of two 8½x4½x2½-inch loaf pans. Cream shortening and sugar together in mixing bowl until light and fluffy. Add eggs one at a time, beating well after each addition. Add bananas, flour, soda, walnuts and cranberry sauce; stir gently to blend. Pour batter into prepared pans. Bake for 1 hour or until toothpick inserted in center comes out clean. Cool in pans for 10 minutes. Remove from pans and cool on wire rack. For easier slicing, wrap loaves and store overnight in a cool place. Makes 8 to 10 servings each.

**Note:** If using Martha White All-Purpose Flour, sift 5¼ teaspoons baking powder and 1½ teaspoons salt with flour.

# Whole Wheat Health Bread

*A hearty, honey-sweetened bread chock full of good things like whole wheat flour, raisins and nuts.*

1 cup sifted Martha White Self-Rising Flour
1 cup Martha White Whole Wheat Flour
¼ cup sugar
½ teaspoon salt
¼ teaspoon baking soda
1 egg
1½ cups buttermilk
¼ cup (½ stick) butter or margarine, melted
¼ cup honey
½ cup raisins
½ cup chopped walnuts

Preheat oven to 375°F. Grease bottom of an 8½x4½x2½-inch loaf pan. Stir together flours, sugar, salt and soda in mixing bowl. Beat egg in separate bowl; stir in buttermilk, butter and honey. Add liquid mixture to dry ingredients, stirring just until blended. Fold in raisins and walnuts. Pour batter into prepared pan. Bake for 45 to 50 minutes or until toothpick inserted in center comes out clean. Cool in pan for 10 minutes. Remove from pan and cool on wire rack. This loaf will be more compact and will not rise as high as some quick bread loaves. For easier slicing, wrap loaf and store overnight in a cool place. Makes 8 to 10 servings.

**Note:** If using Martha White All-Purpose Flour, sift 1½ teaspoons baking powder and a scant ½ teaspoon salt with flour.

# Whole Wheat Cardamom Bread

*Cardamom lends an exotic touch to this wholesome bread.*

2 cups Martha White Whole Wheat Flour
1 teaspoon baking powder
½ teaspoon baking soda
½ teaspoon cardamom
¼ teaspoon salt
1 egg
1¼ cups buttermilk
½ cup honey
⅓ cup (5⅓ tablespoons) butter or margarine, melted
½ cup raisins
½ cup chopped walnuts

Preheat oven to 350°F. Grease bottom of an 8½x4½x2½-inch loaf pan. Stir together flour, baking powder, soda, cardamom and salt in mixing bowl. Beat egg in separate bowl. Stir in buttermilk, honey and butter. Add liquid mixture to dry ingredients, stirring just until blended. Fold in raisins and walnuts. Pour batter into prepared pan. Bake for 55 to 60 minutes or until toothpick inserted in center comes out clean. Cool in pan for 10 minutes. Remove from pan and cool on wire rack. For easier slicing, wrap loaf and store overnight in a cool place. Makes 8 to 10 servings.

## Lemon Streusel Coffee Cake

*The added zest of grated lemon peel is a flavor bonus.*

⅓ cup (5⅓ tablespoons) butter or
    margarine, softened
¾ cup sugar
1 egg
1½ cups sifted Martha White
    Self-Rising Flour
¼ teaspoon cinnamon
¼ teaspoon nutmeg
¼ teaspoon baking soda
½ cup buttermilk
½ cup raisins
¼ cup chopped walnuts
1 teaspoon grated lemon peel
    Streusel Topping, following

Preheat oven to 350°F. Grease a 9-inch square baking pan. Cream butter and sugar together in mixing bowl until light and fluffy. Add egg; beat well. Sift flour, cinnamon, nutmeg and soda together; add to creamed mixture alternately with buttermilk, beginning and ending with dry ingredients. Mix well after each addition. Stir in raisins, walnuts and lemon peel. Pour batter into prepared pan. Sprinkle Streusel Topping evenly over batter. Bake for 30 to 35 minutes or until golden brown. Cool in pan for 15 minutes before serving. Makes 6 to 9 servings.

**Note:** If using Martha White All-Purpose Flour, sift 2¼ teaspoons baking powder and ½ teaspoon salt with flour.

### Streusel Topping

⅓ cup firmly packed brown sugar
2 tablespoons Martha White
    Self-Rising Flour
2 tablespoons butter or margarine,
    softened
1 teaspoon grated lemon peel
¼ teaspoon cinnamon
¼ teaspoon nutmeg
¼ cup chopped walnuts

Combine all ingredients in mixing bowl; blend well using fingertips or pastry blender.

Carolina Coffee Cake

## Sour Cream Streusel Coffee Cake

*Sour cream and streusel topping transform fruit muffin mix into a quick-to-fix coffeecake.*

> 1  egg
> 1  cup (8 ounces) dairy sour cream
> ½  cup milk
> 2  packages (7 ounces each) Martha White Blueberry Muffin Mix
>    Streusel Topping, following

Preheat oven to 350°F. Grease a 9-inch square baking pan. Beat egg in mixing bowl. Add sour cream, milk and muffin mix; stir just until blended. Pour batter into prepared pan and sprinkle evenly with Streusel Topping. Bake for 35 to 40 minutes or until cake begins to pull away from sides of pan. Makes 6 to 9 servings.

### Streusel Topping

> ½  cup firmly packed brown sugar
> 2  tablespoons Martha White Self-Rising or All-Purpose Flour
> 1  teaspoon cinnamon
> 2  tablespoons butter or margarine, softened

Combine ingredients in mixing bowl using fingertips or pastry blender.

## Carolina Coffee Cake

*Pools of brown sugar topping form as this fine-textured cake bakes.*

> ⅓  cup shortening
> ¾  cup sugar
> 2  eggs
> ¾  cup milk
> 1¾  cups sifted Martha White Self-Rising Flour
> ⅓  cup chopped pecans

Crumble Topping, below
Confectioners' Icing, below

Preheat oven to 375°F. Grease a 10-inch cast-iron skillet or 9-inch square baking pan. Cream shortening and sugar together in mixing bowl until light and fluffy. Add eggs one at a time, beating well after each addition. Blend in milk. Stir in flour and pecans; blend well. Pour batter into prepared pan. Sprinkle evenly with Crumble Topping. Bake for 30 to 35 minutes or until cake begins to pull away from sides of pan. Cool in pan for 15 minutes and drizzle with Confectioners' Icing. Makes 12 to 15 servings.

**Note:** If using Martha White All-Purpose Flour, sift 2½ teaspoons baking powder and ¾ teaspoon salt with flour.

### Crumble Topping

    ½ cup firmly packed brown sugar
    2 tablespoons Martha White
      Self-Rising or All-Purpose Flour
    1 teaspoon cinnamon
    2 tablespoons butter or margarine,
      softened

Combine ingredients in mixing bowl using fingertips or pastry blender.

### Confectioners' Icing

    1½ cups sifted confectioners' sugar
     2 tablespoons hot milk
     ½ teaspoon vanilla

Combine all ingredients in mixing bowl. Stir until smooth.

## Whole Wheat Coffee Cake

*Just stir up this easy cake for a satisfying snack. The pecan glaze makes it moist.*

    1¼ cups boiling water
     1 package (8 ounces) chopped dates
     2 cups Martha White Whole Wheat
       Flour
     1 cup firmly packed light brown
       sugar
    2¼ teaspoons baking powder
     ½ teaspoon salt
     ½ cup (1 stick) butter or margarine,
       melted
     2 eggs, lightly beaten
    1½ teaspoons vanilla
       Pecan Glaze, below

Pour boiling water over dates in large bowl; stir. Set aside to cool. Preheat oven to 375°F. Grease a 13x9x2-inch baking pan. Stir together flour, sugar, baking powder and salt in mixing bowl. Add date mixture, butter, eggs and vanilla, stirring just until blended. Pour batter into prepared pan. Bake for 25 to 30 minutes or until cake begins to pull away from sides of pan. Pour Pecan Glaze over hot cake. Cool in pan for 15 minutes. Makes 12 to 15 servings.

### Pecan Glaze

    2 cups sifted confectioners' sugar
    ¼ cup milk
    1 teaspoon vanilla
    ½ teaspoon almond extract
    ½ cup chopped pecans

Combine sugar, milk, vanilla and almond extract in mixing bowl; stir until smooth. Add pecans and blend well.

## Danish Coffee Cake

*Raspberry jam in almond-studded pastry makes an impressive brunch dessert.*

 1 package (5½ ounces) Martha
  White BixMix
 2 tablespoons sugar
 1 package (3 ounces) cream cheese,
  softened
 2 tablespoons butter or margarine,
  softened
 ½ cup chopped blanched almonds
 ¼ cup milk
 ½ cup red raspberry preserves
  Confectioners' Glaze, following

Stir together biscuit mix and sugar in mixing bowl. Cut in cream cheese and butter using pastry blender or two knives until mixture is crumbly. Stir in almonds. Add milk and stir just until blended. Turn dough out onto lightly floured board or pastry cloth and knead 8 to 10 times. Roll dough out on waxed paper into a 12x8-inch rectangle. Carefully invert rectangle onto large greased baking sheet. Remove waxed paper. Spread preserves lengthwise down the center third of the dough. At one inch intervals cut strips along sides of dough, cutting from filling outward toward edges. Beginning at one end, fold strips inward at an angle across preserves, alternating from side to side. Chill for 30 minutes. Preheat oven to 400°F. Bake for 20 to 25 minutes or until golden brown. Cool on baking sheet for 10 minutes and drizzle with Confectioners' Glaze. Makes 6 to 8 servings.

### Confectioners' Glaze

 1 cup sifted confectioners' sugar
 1½ tablespoons milk

Combine sugar and milk; stir until smooth.

## Sour Cream Coffee Loaf

*Cut off the first slice to reveal a ribbon of streusel in the center as well as on top.*

 ½ cup (1 stick) butter or margarine,
  softened
 1¼ cups granulated sugar
 3 eggs
 1 cup (8 ounces) dairy sour cream
 1 teaspoon grated lemon peel
 2 cups sifted Martha White
  Self-Rising Flour
 ½ cup chopped pecans
 3 tablespoons brown sugar
 1 teaspoon cinnamon

Preheat oven to 325°F. Grease bottom of a 9x5x3-inch loaf pan. Cream butter and sugar together in mixing bowl until light and fluffy. Add eggs one at a time, beating well after each addition. Fold in sour cream and lemon peel. Gradually fold flour into creamed mixture (do not beat). Spoon half of batter into prepared pan. Combine pecans, brown sugar and cinnamon in small bowl; sprinkle half of topping over batter. Spoon remaining half of batter into pan; sprinkle with remaining half of topping. Gently pat down. Bake for 60 to 70 minutes or until toothpick inserted in center comes out clean. Cool in pan for 15 minutes. Remove from pan and cool on wire rack. For easier slicing, wrap loaf and store overnight in a cool place. Makes 10 to 12 servings.

**Note:** If using Martha White All-Purpose Flour, sift 1 tablespoon baking powder and ¾ teaspoon salt with flour.

# ★ Tom T. Hall ★

Just say "The Storyteller," and two generations of country music fans will know instantly that you're talking about Tom T. Hall. Part poet and part folklorist, Hall has written and sung some of the most moving and acute lyrics in modern music, including "Old Dogs, Children and Watermelon Wine," "The Year Clayton Delaney Died," "Homecoming" and "Ballad Of Forty Dollars."

## STORYTELLER'S COFFEE CAKE

2 cups sifted Martha White Self-Rising Flour
½ cup sugar
2 eggs
½ cup milk
¼ cup (½ stick) butter or margarine, melted
½ teaspoon vanilla
Brown Sugar Topping, following

Preheat oven to 375°F. Grease a 9-inch square baking pan. Stir together flour and sugar in mixing bowl. Beat eggs in separate bowl; stir in milk, butter and vanilla. Add liquid mixture to dry ingredients, stirring just until blended. Pour batter into prepared pan. Sprinkle evenly with Brown Sugar Topping. Bake for 25 to 30 minutes or until cake begins to pull away from sides of pan. Makes 6 to 9 servings.

**Note:** If using Martha White All-Purpose Flour, sift 1 tablespoon baking powder and ¾ teaspoon salt with flour.

Brown Sugar Topping

½ cup firmly packed brown sugar
2 tablespoons Martha White Self-Rising or All-Purpose Flour
1 teaspoon cinnamon
2 tablespoons butter or margarine, softened

Combine ingredients in mixing bowl using fingertips or pastry blender.

## Upside Down Coffee Cake

*Quick and easy to make with convenient biscuit mix.*

⅓ cup (5⅓ tablespoons) butter or
   margarine
½ cup firmly packed brown sugar
½ teaspoon cinnamon
¼ cup chopped pecans
1 package (5½ ounces) Martha
   White BixMix
½ cup milk

Preheat oven to 425°F. Melt butter in an 8-inch round or square baking pan. Stir in brown sugar, cinnamon and pecans. Combine biscuit mix and milk in mixing bowl, stirring just until blended. Drop biscuit dough by spoonfuls on top of butter mixture in pan. Bake for 20 to 25 minutes or until golden brown. Immediately turn upside down on serving plate. Makes 6 to 8 servings.

## Quick Doughnuts

*These quick doughnuts made from rich biscuit dough will be a hit with the neighborhood kids.*

Vegetable oil or shortening for
   deep frying
2 cups sifted Martha White
   Self-Rising Flour
3 tablespoons sugar

⅓ cup (5⅓ tablespoons) butter or
   margarine, softened
1 egg
About ½ cup milk
Confectioners' Glaze, below

In heavy saucepan or electric fryer, heat 2 to 3 inches of oil over medium-high heat to 375°F. Stir together flour and sugar in mixing bowl. Cut butter into flour with pastry blender or two knives until mixture resembles fine crumbs. Beat egg in measuring cup; add enough milk to make ⅔ cup. Add liquid to flour mixture and stir with a fork only until dough leaves sides of bowl. Turn dough out onto lightly floured board or pastry cloth; knead gently just until smooth. Roll out to ¼-inch thickness. Cut into rounds with floured doughnut cutter. Fry three or four doughnuts at a time in hot oil for two minutes or until golden brown. Drain on paper towels. Dip warm doughnuts in Confectioners' Glaze. These are best when served warm. Makes about 15 doughnuts.

**Note:** If using Martha White All-Purpose Flour, sift 1 tablespoon baking powder and ¾ teaspoon salt with flour.

### Confectioners' Glaze

2 cups sifted confectioners' sugar
6 tablespoons milk
½ teaspoon vanilla

Combine all ingredients in mixing bowl; stir until smooth.

# Cranberry Coffee Cake

*A moist sour cream coffee cake, topped with pools of cranberry sauce. Bake ahead and freeze for a special holiday breakfast.*

> 1 cup (2 sticks) butter or margarine, softened
> 1 cup sugar
> 2 eggs
> ½ teaspoon almond extract
> 2 cups sifted Martha White Self-Rising Flour
> 1 cup (8 ounces) dairy sour cream
> 1 cup whole berry cranberry sauce
> ½ cup chopped blanched almonds
> Confectioners' Glaze, following

Preheat oven to 350°F. Grease a 13x9x2-inch baking pan. Cream butter and sugar together in mixing bowl until light and fluffy. Add eggs and extract; beat well. Add flour alternately with sour cream to creamed mixture, beginning and ending with flour. Mix well after each addition. Pour batter into prepared pan. Spoon cranberry sauce evenly over batter; spread lightly but do not try to cover batter. Sprinkle evenly with almonds. Bake for 35 to 40 minutes or until cake begins to pull away from sides of pan. Cool in pan on wire rack for 5 minutes. Drizzle with Confectioners' Glaze before serving. Makes 12 to 15 servings.

**Note:** If using Martha White All-Purpose Flour, sift 1 tablespoon baking powder and ¾ teaspoon salt with flour.

## Confectioners' Glaze

> 1 cup sifted confectioners' sugar
> 2 tablespoons milk
> ½ teaspoon vanilla

Combine all ingredients; stir until smooth.

# From Our Kitchen to Yours

The Martha White Test Kitchen—sounds like a pretty high-tech operation, doesn't it?

It would probably be full of baking "technicians" wearing white lab coats with plastic name tags and working with all kinds of electronic kitchen gadgetry—like computerized measuring cups and solar-powered mixers. Right?

Wrong.

Take a look at your kitchen—a four-burner stove, stainless steel sink, a color-coordinated refrigerator with fruit magnets and a coffee pot sitting in the corner of the countertop—and you've got a pretty good picture of our kitchen.

It wouldn't make much sense for Martha White to test its baking products and formulate its recipes in a kitchen that was different than the one the folks at home were using. Like you, we want every recipe that we give to our friends to turn out just right.

Since 1952 the Martha White Test Kitchen has tested every Martha White product and its ingredients, developed new recipes and provided consumer assistance and education.

Like you, we share our favorite recipes with our friends. We mail more than one million recipe leaflets annually to folks all over the country who have requested them.

Like you, we like to visit folks. And so our home economists travel to conduct cooking demonstrations and to attend food festivals and shows.

And like you, we want our kitchen to be handy to the folks we care about. That's why our test kitchen is located right in the middle of our corporate offices. Stop by and you're liable to smell the sweet scent of hot cinnamon rolls and have one of our folks in the kitchen pass you a cup of coffee like you're family.

Martha White Test Kitchen yesterday . . .    and today.

## Doughnut Puffs

*Biscuit mix simplifies the preparation of these drop doughnuts accented with a cinnamon-sugar coating.*

Vegetable oil or shortening for deep frying
1 package (5½ ounces) Martha White BixMix
2 tablespoons sugar
1 egg, lightly beaten
¼ cup water
Cinnamon-Sugar Coating, below

In a heavy saucepan or electric fryer, heat 2 to 3 inches of oil over medium-high heat to 375°F. Stir together biscuit mix and sugar in mixing bowl. Add egg and water; stir with a fork only until dough leaves sides of bowl. Drop dough by rounded spoonfuls into hot oil. Fry about two minutes or until golden brown, turning often. Drain on paper towels. Coat warm puffs with Cinnamon-Sugar Coating by shaking a few at a time in plastic bags with coating. These are best when served warm. Makes about 20 puffs.

**Cinnamon-Sugar Coating**

¾ cup sugar
2 tablespoons cinnamon

Combine sugar and cinnamon in plastic bag.

## Favorite Funnel Cakes

*These fun spiral-shaped cakes are formed as the batter runs through an ordinary funnel.*

2 eggs
1¼ cups milk
1 tablespoon sugar
½ teaspoon vanilla
2 packages (5½ ounces each) Martha White FlapStax
Vegetable oil or shortening for frying
Confectioners' sugar

Beat eggs in mixing bowl. Add milk, sugar, vanilla and pancake mix; stir until smooth. In large skillet, heat one inch of oil over medium-high heat to 375°F. Cover bottom opening of wide-mouth funnel with finger; pour ¼ cup batter into funnel. When ready to fry, release finger and run batter into hot oil using a slow, wide circular motion; maintain as steady a stream as possible. Fry, turning once, until golden brown, 1 to 1½ minutes on each side. Drain on paper towels. Repeat procedure until all batter is used. Cool funnel cakes 5 minutes before dusting with confectioners' sugar. These are best when served warm. Makes about 10 funnel cakes.

# YEAST BREADS

There was a time in this great country of ours when folks grew up kneading . . . yeast bread for their family.

But for the most part those days have passed. Nowadays the act of snatching our daily bread in the rush between office and home is part of a savage shopping-cart demolition derby generally viewed as one of life's little drudgeries. The modern means of putting bread on the table doesn't offer the same sense of well-being and good taste that comes from secretly cutting a fresh, hot slice off a homemade loaf.

In getting back to the basics that made this country strong, America is in need once more of the rich, relaxing and, yes, therapeutic countertop aerobics known as kneading. And while it hasn't been proven that kneading bread dough is a cure for ulcers, headaches, juvenile delinquency and job burnout, . . . it just might be.

More than a few psychologists have actually prescribed the restful act of kneading and baking yeast breads as a way of reducing the effects of stress. There's something about the rhythmic and repetitive act of kneading that soothes our savage nature.

But this modern, scientific bread-baking breakthrough is something that those who have baked have always known. We didn't need highly educated behavioral scientists to tell us what our grandmother had already taught us.

In a corner of her kitchen, there hung a child-sized apron of our own, perhaps with our name embroidered on it, waiting for the day each week when we would bake the family's bread. Scooting the kitchen stool to the counter, she raised us gently up to join her as a respected equal in the act of providing something good for our people. And while our exuberant pounding and pressing of the dough were far less efficient than her easy rocking motion, it wasn't wasted energy. Kneading was her sly grandmotherly way of capturing and containing our youthful spirit, of entertaining us and tiring us.

We left that childhood experience feeling needed. In another sense, we were kneaded along with the bread. For during the physical act of preparing the bread for baking, grandma kneaded into our minds and memories volumes of family history, appreciation for hard work and a sense of purpose and usefulness as breadmakers.

And, of course, kneading relieved us of a lifetime of stress in a way that science would take more than 40 years to discover.

Swedish Tea Ring (page 78)

## Sweet Yeast Dough

*Master this sweet rich dough, then create an endless variety of sweet breads and coffee cakes.*

> 2 packages active dry yeast
> ½ cup warm water (105°F to 115°F)
> ½ cup milk, scalded
> ½ cup sugar
> 2 teaspoons salt
> ½ cup shortening
> 2 eggs, lightly beaten
> 4½ to 5 cups Martha White
>    All-Purpose Flour

Dissolve yeast in measuring cup with warm water; set aside. Combine hot milk, sugar, salt and shortening in large mixing bowl. Cool to lukewarm. Add eggs; blend well. Blend in 2 cups flour. Stir in dissolved yeast. Add enough of remaining flour to make a soft dough. Turn dough out onto lightly floured board or pastry cloth. Cover with bowl and let rest for 10 minutes. Knead dough until smooth and elastic, 8 to 10 minutes. Place dough in large greased bowl; turn once to grease top. Cover and let rise in warm draft-free area until doubled in bulk, about 1 hour and 30 minutes. Punch dough down; let rest for 10 minutes. Shape and bake as directed for Cinnamon Rolls, Cinnamon Raisin Bread, Swedish Tea Ring, Bake Shop Doughnuts or Coconut Coffee Cake.

## Cinnamon Raisin Bread

*Each slice reveals a spiral of cinnamon. Try a warm slice buttered and toasted.*

> 1 recipe Sweet Yeast Dough
> ½ cup raisins
> ¼ cup (½ stick) butter or margarine, melted
> 1 cup sugar
> 2 tablespoons cinnamon
>    Butter or margarine, melted
>    Confectioners' Icing, below

Lightly knead raisins into dough. Divide dough in half. On lightly floured board or pastry cloth, roll out one half into a 9x7-inch rectangle. Brush with 2 tablespoons butter to within one inch of edges. Combine sugar and cinnamon in small bowl; sprinkle half of mixture over dough. Roll up jelly-roll style, beginning with a long side; press to seal edges. Press each end with side of hand and fold under. Place seam-side down in greased 8½x4½x2½-inch loaf pan. Brush with melted butter. Repeat procedure with remaining dough. Cover and let rise in warm draft-free area until doubled in bulk, about 45 minutes. Preheat oven to 350°F. Bake for 40 to 45 minutes or until golden brown. Remove from pans; place on wire racks. Drizzle with Confectioners' Icing while warm. Makes 2 loaves (8 to 10 servings each).

### Confectioners' Icing

> 3 cups sifted confectioners' sugar
> ¼ cup hot milk
> 1 teaspoon vanilla

Combine all ingredients; beat until smooth.

# *Cinnamon Rolls

*Nothing is more welcoming than the aroma of homemade cinnamon rolls.*

> 1 recipe Sweet Yeast Dough
> (page 76)
> ¼ cup (½ stick) butter or margarine, melted
> 1 cup sugar
> 1 tablespoon cinnamon
> Confectioners' Icing, below

Divide dough into 4 equal pieces. On floured board or pastry cloth, roll out one piece into a 12x6-inch rectangle. Brush with about 1 tablespoon butter to within one inch of edges. Combine sugar and cinnamon in small bowl; sprinkle ¼ of mixture over dough. Roll up jelly-roll style, beginning with a long side; press to seal edges. Cut into 1-inch slices. Place slices cut-side down in greased 8-inch round baking pan or in greased muffin cups. Repeat procedure with remaining pieces of dough. Cover and let rise in warm draft-free area until doubled in bulk, about 45 minutes. Preheat oven to 350°F. Bake for 20 to 25 minutes, or until golden brown. Remove from pans; place on wire racks. Drizzle with Confectioners' Icing while warm. Makes about 4 dozen rolls.

## Confectioners' Icing

> 3 cups sifted confectioners' sugar
> ¼ cup hot milk
> 1 teaspoon vanilla

Combine all ingredients; beat until smooth.

## THE ETERNAL PURSUIT OF THE HOT ROLL

Grandmas never seem to sit down at family meals.

What keeps these spry little ladies hopping from the table to the stove and back? It's their pursuit of the elusive state of keeping a hot roll on everyone's plate.

Why, some grandmothers have been known to yank a tepid roll from between a set of anxious teeth just to replace it with a steaming hot one from the oven.

You must understand that the quality of these yeasty delights doesn't depend upon their temperature. In fact, some swear the rolls are best in the middle of the afternoon long after the stove has cooled, the table is cleared and the dishes are washed.

Like grandmothers themselves, these rolls come in a variety of soft shapes. With loving hands, grandma spends the extra time it takes to make pocket rolls that have little flaps under which every pat of butter in the kitchen wants to melt. Other shapes include cloverleafs, circles, squares and triangles.

Why does grandma go to all that trouble to get you a roll while it's still hot? It's because that little bit of warmth baked into every bite is love.

*One of Martha White Test Kitchen's ten all-time favorite recipes.

## Bake Shop Doughnuts

*Surprise the kids with homemade doughnuts and hot chocolate.*

**1 recipe Sweet Yeast Dough (page 76)**
**Vegetable oil or shortening for deep frying**
**Confectioners' Icing, following**

Divide dough in half. On floured board or pastry cloth, roll out one half about ⅓-inch thick. Cut with floured doughnut cutter. Place doughnuts on oiled baking sheet. Repeat procedure with remaining dough. Let rise, uncovered, in a warm draft-free area until doubled in bulk, about 45 minutes. In heavy saucepan or electric fryer, heat 2 to 3 inches of oil over medium-high heat to 375°F. Gently drop 3 or 4 doughnuts at a time into hot oil. Fry for 2 to 3 minutes, turning frequently until golden brown. Drain on paper towels. Dip warm doughnuts in Confectioners' Icing. Place on wire racks to cool. Makes about 2 dozen doughnuts and holes.

### Confectioners' Icing

**3 cups sifted confectioners' sugar**
**½ cup hot milk**
**1 teaspoon vanilla**

Combine all ingredients; beat until smooth.

## Swedish Tea Ring

*This festive circle of cinnamon rolls will delight holiday guests.*

**1 recipe Sweet Yeast Dough (page 76)**
**¼ cup (½ stick) butter or margarine, melted**
**1 cup sugar**
**1 tablespoon cinnamon**
**Confectioners' Glaze, following**

Divide dough in half. On lightly floured board or pastry cloth, roll out one half into a 20x7-inch rectangle. Brush with 2 tablespoons butter to within one inch of edges. Combine sugar and cinnamon in small bowl; sprinkle half of mixture

The packages may have changed over the years, but the quality of Martha White's mixes remains the same.

over dough. Roll up jelly-roll style, beginning with a long side; press to seal edges. Place roll seam-side down on greased baking sheet. Shape into a ring and pinch ends together to seal. Use scissors or sharp knife to cut dough at 1-inch intervals around ring, cutting two-thirds through with each cut. Gently turn each cut piece on its side, slightly overlapping slices. Repeat procedure with remaining dough. Cover and let rise in warm draft-free area until doubled in bulk, about 45 minutes. Preheat oven to 375°F. Bake for 18 to 20 minutes or until golden brown. Remove from baking sheets; place on wire racks. Drizzle Confectioners' Glaze over warm rings. Makes 2 rings (6 to 8 servings each).

### Confectioners' Glaze

> 1 cup sifted confectioners' sugar
> 1½ to 2 tablespoons milk

Combine ingredients in small bowl; beat until smooth.

## Coconut Coffee Cake

*An elegant coffee cake that boasts a rich honey-coconut filling.*

> 1 recipe Sweet Yeast Dough
>    (page 76)
> 3 cups flaked coconut, divided
> ½ cup sugar
> ½ cup (1 stick) butter or margarine
> ¼ cup honey
> 2 tablespoons milk

> ¼ teaspoon almond extract
> Confectioners' Icing, below

While dough is rising, prepare filling. Measure ½ cup coconut and set aside. Combine remaining coconut, sugar, butter, honey and milk in a large saucepan. Bring to a boil over medium heat, stirring constantly. Remove from heat; set aside until cool. Stir in almond extract. When dough has doubled, punch down and let rest for 10 minutes. Divide dough in half. On lightly floured board or pastry cloth, roll out one half into a 14x8-inch rectangle. Spread half the coconut lengthwise down the center of the dough, about 3 inches wide. On each long side of dough make 6 cuts at 2-inch intervals from filling outward to edges. Beginning at one end, fold strips diagonally across filling, alternating from side to side and overlapping ends. Tuck end strips underneath. Place on greased baking sheet. Repeat procedure with remaining dough. Cover and let rise in warm draft-free area until doubled in bulk, about 35 minutes. Preheat oven to 350°F. Bake for 25 to 30 minutes or until golden brown. Remove from baking sheets; place on wire racks. Drizzle with Confectioners' Icing while warm. Sprinkle each coffee cake with ¼ cup reserved coconut. Makes 2 coffee cakes (8 to 10 servings each).

### Confectioners' Icing

> 3 cups sifted confectioner's sugar
> ¼ cup hot milk
> 1 teaspoon vanilla

Combine all ingredients; beat until smooth.

## Cream Cheese Coffee Cake

*A rich cheesecake-like filling makes this coffee cake an elegant addition to brunch.*

½ cup milk
½ cup water
¼ cup vegetable oil
3 to 3¼ cups Martha White All-Purpose Flour
1 package active dry yeast
¼ cup sugar
1 teaspoon salt
2 eggs
Cream Cheese Filling, following

Heat milk, water and oil in saucepan until very warm (120°F to 130°F). Stir together 1 cup flour, yeast, sugar and salt in large mixing bowl. Add heated mixture and eggs; beat with electric mixer on high speed for 2 minutes or 300 strokes by hand. Add 1 cup flour and beat 1 minute on medium speed or 150 strokes by hand. Stir in enough remaining flour to make a thick batter. Cover and let rise in warm draft-free area until doubled in bulk, about 1 hour. Stir batter down. Spead batter into two greased 9-inch round baking pans. Cover and let rise in warm draft-free area until doubled in bulk, about 30 minutes. Preheat oven to 350°F. Lightly spread Cream Cheese Filling over batter, using half on each coffee cake. Bake for 20 to 25 minutes or until filling is set and lightly browned. Serve warm. Makes 2 coffee cakes (6 to 9 servings each).

### Cream Cheese Filling

1 package (8 ounces) cream cheese, softened
¼ cup sugar
1 egg, lightly beaten
2 tablespoons Martha White All-Purpose Flour
¼ teaspoon almond extract (optional)

Combine cream cheese and sugar in mixing bowl. Stir in egg, flour and almond extract, if desired. Beat until smooth.

## Sesame Bread

*The easy mix batter bakes into a feathery light-textured bread with a buttery sesame seed crust.*

1 package active dry yeast
1¼ cups warm water (105°F to 115°F)
¼ cup sugar
1 teaspoon salt
2 eggs, lightly beaten
½ cup (1 stick) butter or margarine, melted and cooled
3½ cups Martha White All-Purpose Flour
½ cup (1 stick) butter or margarine, melted and cooled
⅓ cup sesame seeds

Dissolve yeast in large mixing bowl with warm water. Stir in sugar, salt, eggs, ½ cup butter and flour; blend thoroughly. Cover and let rise in warm draft-free area until doubled in bulk, about 1 hour. Stir dough down and pour into greased 13x9x2-inch baking pan. Pour remaining ½ cup butter evenly over top of batter and sprinkle with sesame seeds. Cover and refrigerate overnight. Remove from refrigerator 25 minutes before baking. Preheat oven to 400°F. Bake for 20 to 25 minutes or until golden brown. Cut into 3-inch squares and serve hot. Makes 12 squares.

**Note:** If not refrigerating, allow dough to rise in pan about 45 minutes or until doubled in bulk. Bake as directed.

# Yeast Bread Basics

**MIXING:** Vigorously mix in enough flour to make dough stiff enough to knead. This may be done with a mixer or by hand.

**KNEADING:** Fold dough toward you. Push away with heels of hands. Turn dough one quarter turn and repeat. Continue until dough is smooth and elastic.

**RISING:** Place dough in greased bowl; turn once to grease top; cover and place in a warm place (80°F. to 85°F.) to rise.

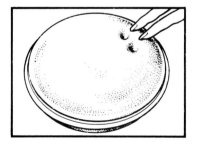

**TESTING FOR DOUBLE IN BULK:** Press two fingers lightly and quickly ½-inch into dough. If dent stays, it is doubled.

**PUNCHING DOUGH:** Push fist into center of dough. Fold dough over and form into a ball.

**SHAPING:** Follow directions for shapes. For loaves, roll dough into a rectangle. Beginning with a short side, roll up and seal seam. Press ends down; fold under.

## French Bread

*Diagonal slashes add authentic flair to these chewy loaves.*

     4 to 4½ cups Martha White
          All-Purpose Flour
     1½ teaspoons salt
      1 package active dry yeast
     1½ cups very warm water
          (120°F to 130°F)
      1 tablespoon Martha White Plain
          Corn Meal or Self-Rising Corn
          Meal Mix
      1 egg
      ½ teaspoon salt

Stir together 2 cups flour, 1½ teaspoons salt and yeast in large mixing bowl. Add water; stir until moistened, then beat well. Add enough of remaining flour to make a stiff dough. Turn dough out onto floured board or pastry cloth. Knead dough until smooth and elastic, 8 to 10 minutes. Place dough in large greased bowl; turn once to grease top. Cover and let rise in warm draft-free area until doubled in bulk, about 1 hour. Punch dough down; divide in half. Roll out one half into a 15x8-inch rectangle. Roll up jelly-roll style, beginning with a long side; press to seal edges. Pinch ends to seal. Repeat procedure with remaining dough. Grease two baking sheets and sprinkle with corn meal. Place loaves seam-side down on prepared baking sheets. Use a very sharp knife to make diagonal slashes 2 inches apart across tops of loaves. Cover and let rise in warm draft-free area until doubled in bulk, about 45 minutes. Preheat oven to 400°F. Combine egg yolk and ½ teaspoon salt in small bowl; beat lightly. Brush tops of loaves with egg wash. Bake for 35 to 40 minutes or until golden brown and loaves sound hollow when tapped. Remove from baking sheets and cool on wire racks. Makes 2 loaves (8 to 10 servings each).

## Homemade White Bread

*Nothing compares with a slice of buttered homemade bread hot out of the oven.*

      1 package active dry yeast
      ¼ cup warm water (105°F to 115°F)
      2 cups milk, scalded
      3 tablespoons sugar
      1 tablespoon salt
      3 tablespoons shortening
      5 to 5½ cups Martha White
          All-Purpose Flour
          Melted butter or margarine

Dissolve yeast in measuring cup with warm water; set aside. Combine hot milk, sugar, salt and shortening in large mixing bowl. Cool to lukewarm. Blend in 2 cups flour. Stir in dissolved yeast. Add enough of remaining flour to make a stiff dough. Turn dough out onto lightly floured board or pastry cloth. Cover with bowl and let rest for 10 minutes. Knead dough until smooth and elastic, 6 to 8 minutes. Place dough in large greased bowl; turn once to grease top. Cover and let rise in warm draft-free area until doubled in bulk, about 1 hour and 30 minutes. Punch dough down; let rest for 10 minutes. Divide dough in half. Shape each half into a loaf. Place in two greased 9x5x3-inch or 8½x4½x2½-inch loaf pans. Cover and

Sesame Bread (page 80)

let rise in warm draft-free area until doubled in bulk, about 1 hour. Preheat oven to 400°F. Bake for 15 minutes. Reduce temperature to 300°F and bake for 20 to 25 minutes or until loaves are golden brown and sound hollow when tapped. Remove from pans; place on wire racks. Brush with melted butter. Makes 2 loaves (8 to 10 servings each).

## County Fair Bread

*This beautiful braided loaf would be an unforgettable addition to a casual buffet.*

> 1½ cups milk
> ¼ cup (½ stick) butter or margarine, cut in pieces
> 5½ to 6 cups Martha White All-Purpose Flour, divided
> 1 package active dry yeast
> ¼ cup sugar
> 2 teaspoons salt
> 2 eggs

1 egg white
1 tablespoon water
Sesame seeds

Heat milk and butter in saucepan until very warm (120°F to 130°F). Butter does not need to melt. Stir together 1 cup flour, yeast, sugar and salt in large mixing bowl. Add heated mixture and eggs; beat until well blended. Add 2 cups of flour and beat vigorously. Add enough remaining flour to make a stiff dough. Turn out onto floured board or pastry cloth. Knead dough until smooth and elastic, about 5 minutes. Place dough in large greased bowl; turn once to grease top. Cover and let rise in warm draft-free area until doubled in bulk, about 1 hour and 30 minutes. Punch dough down. Pinch off about one-third of the dough, return to bowl, cover and set aside. Divide remaining two-thirds dough into 3 equal pieces. Roll each piece into a rope about 18 inches long; braid ropes and pinch ends to seal. Place on greased baking sheet. Divide reserved one-third dough into 3 equal pieces. Roll each piece into a rope about 12 inches long; braid ropes and pinch ends to seal. Place smaller braid on top of large braid. Cover and let rise in warm draft-free area until doubled in bulk, about 1 hour. Preheat oven to 375°F. Beat egg white and water together in small bowl. Brush braid with egg mixture. Sprinkle with sesame seeds. Bake for 40 to 45 minutes or until golden brown and loaf sounds hollow when tapped. If bread begins to brown too rapidly, cover with loose tent of aluminum foil or brown paper. Remove from baking sheet; place on wire rack. Makes 1 loaf (12 to 15 servings).

## Onion Bread

*Onions sprinkled on top turn a rich golden brown during baking.*

    1 package active dry yeast
    1 cup warm water (105°F to 115°F)
 3¼ to 3¾ cups Martha White
       All-Purpose Flour
    2 teaspoons sugar
    1 teaspoon salt
    2 tablespoons butter or margarine,
       melted
 ⅔ cup chopped onions
       Salt
       Paprika

Dissolve yeast in large mixing bowl with warm water. Add 2 cups flour, sugar and 1 teaspoon salt; blend thoroughly. Add enough of the remaining flour to make a soft dough. Turn out onto floured board or pastry cloth. Knead dough until smooth and elastic, 8 to 10 minutes. Place dough in large greased bowl; turn once to grease top. Cover and let rise in warm draft-free area until doubled in bulk, about 1 hour. Punch dough down. Divide dough in half. Press each half into a greased 9-inch round baking pan. Brush each loaf with 1 tablespoon butter and sprinkle with half the onions. Press onions gently into dough. Cover and let rise in warm draft-free area until doubled in bulk, about 40 minutes. Preheat oven to 450°F. Sprinkle each loaf lightly with salt and paprika. Bake for 20 to 25 minutes or until deep golden brown. Remove from pans; place on wire racks. Makes 2 loaves (6 to 8 servings each).

## Rye Bread

*Baked in round loaves, this robust bread adds flair to a casual buffet of cheeses and cold sliced meats.*

    2 packages active dry yeast
 ½ cup warm water (105°F to 115°F)
 1½ cups water, divided
 ¼ cup firmly packed brown sugar
    2 teaspoons salt
    2 teaspoons caraway seeds
    2 tablespoons shortening
    4 cups Martha White All-Purpose
       Flour
    1 to 1½ cups rye flour
       Melted butter or margarine

Dissolve yeast in measuring cup with warm water. Combine ½ cup water, sugar, salt, caraway seeds and shortening in saucepan. Bring to a boil, reduce heat and simmer 5 minutes. Pour into large mixing bowl; add remaining 1 cup water. Add 2 cups all-purpose flour; blend thoroughly. Stir in dissolved yeast. Add remaining all-purpose flour and enough rye flour to make a soft dough. Turn dough out onto lightly floured board or pastry cloth. Cover with bowl and let rest 10 minutes. Knead dough until smooth and elastic, 8 to 10 minutes, using more rye flour if needed. Place dough in large greased bowl; turn once to grease top. Cover and let rise in a warm draft-free area until doubled, about 1 hour and 30 minutes. Punch dough down; divide in half. Shape each half into a ball. Place on greased baking sheets. Make 3 slashes, ½-inch deep, in top of each loaf.

Brush loaves with butter. Let rise in warm draft-free area until doubled in bulk, about 45 minutes. Preheat oven to 375°F. Bake 30 to 35 minutes or until loaves sound hollow when tapped. Remove from pans; place on wire racks. Brush with melted butter. Makes 2 loaves (8 to 10 servings each).

# ★ Jim & Jesse McReynolds ★

The sweet-singing McReynolds brothers from Coeburn, Virginia, are a natural bridge between traditional bluegrass and pop music. While their songs have always featured the basics of bluegrass, Jim & Jesse adapted their music to many forms. For instance, their 1965 album *Berry Pickin' Time In The Country* is a bluegrass-flecked collection of Chuck Berry tunes.

## SOUTHERN HEARTH ROLLS

2 cups milk
¾ cup Martha White Self-Rising Corn Meal Mix
½ cup shortening
⅓ cup sugar
1½ teaspoons salt
2 eggs, lightly beaten
1 package active dry yeast, dissolved in ¼ cup warm water (105°F to 115°F)
4½ to 5 cups Martha White All Purpose Flour
Melted butter or margarine

Combine milk and corn meal in large saucepan. Cook over low heat, stirring frequently until thick, about 15 minutes. Add shortening, sugar and salt; mix well. Cool mixture to lukewarm. Stir in eggs and yeast. Gradually stir in enough flour to make a soft dough. Turn dough out onto floured board or pastry cloth and knead until smooth, about 5 minutes. Pinch off balls of dough, 1½ to 2 inches in diameter. Place on greased baking sheets. Let rise in warm draft-free area for 1 hour and 30 minutes or until doubled in bulk. Preheat oven to 375°F. Bake rolls for 15 minutes or until golden brown. Brush hot rolls with melted butter. Makes about 36 rolls.

**Whole Wheat Hearth Rolls** Prepare Southern Hearth Rolls as directed; except— substitute 2 cups Martha White Whole Wheat Flour and 2½ to 3 cups Martha White All-Purpose Flour.

## Refrigerator Whole Wheat Bread

*Busy homemakers can prepare the dough in advance and refrigerate until time to bake.*

    4 cups Martha White All-Purpose Flour, divided
    3 tablespoons sugar or honey
    4 teaspoons salt
    2 packages active dry yeast
    2 cups milk
    ¾ cup water
    ¼ cup (½ stick) butter or margarine
       About 4 cups Martha White Whole Wheat Flour
       Vegetable oil
       Melted butter or margarine

Stir together 3 cups all-purpose flour, sugar, salt and yeast in large mixing bowl. Heat milk, water and ¼ cup butter in saucepan until very warm (120°F to 130°F). Butter does not need to melt. Gradually add warm liquid mixture to dry ingredients and beat with electric mixer on medium speed for 2 minutes, scraping bowl occasionally. Add remaining cup of all-purpose flour and beat on high speed for 2 minutes. Stir in enough whole wheat flour to make a stiff dough. Sprinkle board or pastry cloth with whole wheat flour; turn dough out onto floured surface and knead until smooth and elastic, 8 to 10 minutes. Cover with plastic wrap, then a towel; let rest for 20 minutes. Divide dough in half. Shape each half into a loaf. Place in two greased 8½x4½x2½-inch loaf pans. Brush tops with oil. Cover loosely with plastic wrap. Refrig-erate for 2 to 24 hours. Remove from refrigerator, uncover and set aside for 10 minutes before baking. Puncture any gas bubbles that may have formed near surface. Preheat oven to 400°F. Bake for 40 to 45 minutes or until golden brown and loaves sound hollow when tapped. Remove from pans; place on wire racks. Brush with melted butter. Makes 2 loaves (8 to 10 servings each).

## Food Processor Bran Bread

*Bran Muffin Mix gives whole grain goodness to this loaf.*

    3 cups Martha White All-Purpose Flour
    1 package (7 ounces) Martha White Bran Muffin Mix
    2 tablespoons shortening
    1 tablespoon sugar
    ¾ teaspoon salt
    1 package quick-rising yeast
    ½ cup warm water (105°F to 115°F)
    1 egg
       About ½ cup boiling water
       Melted butter or margarine

Position knife blade in food processor bowl; add first 5 ingredients. Process on highest speed until blended, about 5 seconds. Leave mixture in bowl. Dissolve yeast in measuring cup with warm water. With processor running on highest speed, add dissolved yeast, egg and enough boiling water to make the dough form a loose ball. Stop processor

Overnight Oatmeal Bread

## Overnight Oatmeal Bread

*Serve with homemade vegetable soup and sharp Cheddar cheese for a warming winter supper.*

   1 cup boiling water
  ½ cup quick-cooking or old-fashioned oats
   1 package active dry yeast
  ⅓ cup warm water (105°F to 115°F)
  ¼ cup honey
   1 tablespoon butter or margarine
1¼ teaspoons salt
   3 to 3½ cups Martha White All-Purpose Flour
     Vegetable oil
     Melted butter or margarine

immediately so as not to overwork the dough. Turn dough out onto lightly floured board or pastry cloth; knead gently 9 or 10 times. Place dough in large greased bowl; turn once to grease top. Cover and let rise in warm draft-free area until doubled in bulk, about 1 hour. Punch dough down, divide in half. Shape each half into a loaf. Place in two small greased 7½x3¾x2½-inch loaf pans. Cover and let rise in warm draft-free area until doubled in bulk, about 40 minutes. Preheat oven to 375°F. Bake for 25 to 30 minutes or until golden brown and loaves sound hollow when tapped. Remove from pans; place on wire racks. Brush with melted butter. Makes 2 small loaves (6 to 8 servings each).

Pour boiling water over oats in mixing bowl; cool until mixture is lukewarm. Dissolve yeast in measuring cup with warm water. Stir yeast into lukewarm oatmeal mixture. Add honey, 1 tablespoon butter, salt and 2 cups flour; blend thoroughly. Add enough of the remaining flour to make a stiff dough. Turn out onto floured board or pastry cloth. Knead dough until smooth and elastic, 8 to 10 minutes. Shape into a loaf. Place in greased 8½x4½x2½-inch loaf pan. Brush top of loaf with oil. Cover loosely with plastic wrap. Refrigerate overnight or up to 24 hours. Remove from refrigerator, uncover and set aside for 10 minutes before baking. Preheat oven to 350°F. Bake for 50 to 55 minutes or until light golden brown and loaf sounds hollow when tapped. Remove from pan; place on wire rack. Brush with melted butter. Makes 1 loaf (8 to 10 servings).

# Dilly Bread

*An attractive casserole bread that pairs perfectly with a fluffy cheese omelet.*

   1 package active dry yeast
 ¼ cup warm water (105°F to 115°F)
   1 cup creamed cottage cheese
   2 tablespoons sugar
   1 tablespoon onion flakes
   1 tablespoon butter or margarine, melted
   2 teaspoons dill seed
   1 teaspoon salt
 ¼ teaspoon baking soda
   1 egg
2¼ to 2½ cups Martha White All-Purpose Flour
     Melted butter or margarine

Dissolve yeast in measuring cup with warm water; set aside. Place cottage cheese in small saucepan; heat to lukewarm. Combine cottage cheese, sugar, onion, 1 tablespoon butter, dill seed, salt, soda and egg in large mixing bowl. Stir in dissolved yeast. Add enough flour to make a stiff dough; blend thoroughly. Cover and let rise in warm draft-free area until doubled in bulk, about 1 hour. Stir dough down. Spoon into a well-greased 2-quart round baking dish. Let rise in warm draft-free area until doubled in bulk, about 30 minutes. Preheat oven to 350°F. Bake for 30 to 35 minutes or until golden brown. Remove from pan; place on wire rack. Brush with melted butter. Makes 1 round loaf (8 to 10 servings).

# German Stollen

*Traditional German Christmas bread.*

1½ cups milk, scalded
 ⅓ cup shortening
 ½ cup sugar
   2 teaspoons salt
   2 packages active dry yeast
   1 egg, lightly beaten
   5 to 5½ cups Martha White All-Purpose Flour
 ½ cup chopped blanched almonds
 ½ cup seedless raisins
 ½ cup finely chopped mixed candied fruit
 ½ teaspoon grated lemon peel
     Melted butter or margarine
     Confectioners' Icing, following

Scald milk. Pour scalded milk into large mixing bowl. Stir in shortening, sugar and salt; cool to warm (105°F to 115°F). Sprinkle yeast over milk mixture; stir to dissolve. Add egg and 2 cups flour; blend thoroughly. Add just enough of remaining flour to make a soft dough. Turn out onto floured board or pastry cloth. Knead dough until smooth and elastic, 8 to 10 minutes. Place dough in large greased bowl; turn once to grease top. Cover and let rise in warm draft-free area until doubled in bulk, about 1 hour and 30 minutes. Punch dough down. Knead almonds, raisins, fruit and lemon peel into dough. Divide into 3 equal pieces. Pat or roll each third into a 12x8-inch oval. Brush with butter. Fold in half lengthwise; press edges to seal. Place loaves on greased baking sheets; brush with butter. Cover and let rise in warm draft-free area until doubled in bulk, about

35 minutes. Preheat oven to 375°F. Bake for 25 to 30 minutes or until golden brown. Remove from pans; place on wire racks. Drizzle with Confectioners' Icing while warm. Makes 3 loaves (6 to 8 servings each).

### Confectioners' Icing

>   3 cups sifted confectioners' sugar
> ¼ cup hot milk
> 1 teaspoon vanilla

Combine all ingredients; beat until smooth.

# Cajun Biscuits

*These crunchy rolls look like drop biscuits, but the flavor resembles French bread.*

>   1 package active dry yeast
> 1¼ cups warm water (105°F to 115°F)
>   2 tablespoons vegetable oil
>   2 teaspoons sugar
> 3½ cups Martha White
>     Self-Rising Flour

Dissolve yeast in large mixing bowl with warm water. Add remaining ingredients; blend thoroughly. Cover and let rise in warm draft-free area until doubled in bulk, about 45 minutes. Stir dough down. Drop dough by rounded tablespoonfuls onto greased baking sheet. Let rise in warm draft-free area until doubled in bulk, about 45 minutes. Preheat oven to 425°F. Bake for 18 to 20 minutes or until golden brown. Remove from baking sheet; place on wire racks. Makes about 24 biscuits.

## SHAPING YEAST ROLLS

### Pan Rolls

Gently shape pieces of dough into smooth, 1½-inch balls by pulling the dough down and under with your thumb. Place, smooth-sides up, in greased muffin cups or an 8-inch round baking pan, setting rolls about ½ inch apart.

### Cloverleaf Rolls

Shape pieces of dough into smooth, ¾-inch balls. Place 3 balls in each greased muffin cup.

### Parker House Rolls

Roll out dough to ¼-inch thickness on lightly floured board or pastry cloth. Cut out with a floured 2½-inch round cutter. Use the floured handle of a knife to make a deep, off-center crease in the top of each round. Fold the larger section over the smaller section. Press edges together lightly. Place rolls about 1½ inches apart on greased baking sheet.

### Crescent Rolls

For recipe based on 5 to 6 cups of flour, divide dough into three pieces. Roll out one-third into a 12-inch circle. Spread with softened butter or margarine. Cut into 16 wedges. Roll up, beginning at rounded edge. Place on greased baking sheet with point underneath; curve slightly. Repeat with remaining dough.

## Light Dinner Rolls

*Shape the basic roll dough into cloverleaf, Parker House or pan rolls.*

       ¾ cup milk
       ¾ cup water
       ¼ cup (½ stick) butter or margarine
    4½ to 5 cups Martha White
          All-Purpose Flour
       ¼ cup sugar
        2 teaspoons salt
        1 package active dry yeast
        1 egg
          Melted butter or margarine

Heat milk, water and ¼ cup butter in saucepan until very warm (120°F to 130°F). Stir together 3 cups flour, sugar, salt and yeast in large mixing bowl. Gradually add warm liquid mixture and egg to dry ingredients and beat with electric mixer on high speed for 2 minutes, scraping bowl occasionally. Add enough remaining flour to make a soft dough. Turn out onto floured board or pastry cloth. Cover dough with bowl and let rest for 10 minutes. Knead just until smooth, about 3 minutes. Place dough in large greased bowl; turn once to grease top. Cover and let rise in warm draft-free area until doubled in bulk, about 45 minutes. Punch dough down. Shape into rolls, as desired. Place on greased baking sheets or in greased pans. Cover and let rise in warm draft-free area until doubled in bulk, about 45 minutes. Preheat oven to 350°F. Bake for 15 to 20 minutes or until golden brown. Remove from pans; place on wire racks. Brush with melted butter. Serve hot. Makes about 24 rolls.

## Quick Refrigerator Rolls

*As easy as mixing up a batch of muffins, with the flavor and aroma of yeast rolls.*

       1 package active dry yeast
       2 cups warm water (105°F to 115°F)
       ¾ cup vegetable oil
       ¼ cup sugar
       1 egg, lightly beaten
       4 cups Martha White Self-Rising
          Flour

Dissolve yeast in large mixing bowl with warm water. Add remaining ingredients; blend thoroughly. Cover and refrigerate overnight. Preheat oven to 425°F. Remove dough from refrigerator. Stir dough down. Spoon into greased muffin cups, filling each cup about ¾ full. Bake for 20 to 25 minutes or until golden brown. Remove from pans immediately and serve hot. Makes about 24 rolls.

**Note:** If not refrigerating—prepare dough as directed. Cover and set aside for 20 minutes. Stir dough down. Spoon into greased muffin cups and bake as directed.

## Tearoom Refrigerator Rolls

*A basket of these piping hot, tender rolls will be the highlight of your Sunday dinner.*

       1 cup diced raw potatoes
       2 cups water
       1 package active dry yeast
       ⅓ cup sugar

Pan Rolls, Cloverleaf Rolls and Crescent Rolls made from Light Dinner Rolls recipe.

1 tablespoon salt
½ cup shortening
2 eggs, lightly beaten
5 to 6 cups Martha White
    All-Purpose Flour
Melted butter or margarine

Cook potatoes in unsalted water until tender. Drain and reserve 1½ cups potato water; cool to warm (105°F to 115°F). Dissolve yeast in warm potato water. Mash potatoes in large mixing bowl; add sugar, salt and shortening; blend thoroughly. Stir in eggs and yeast mixture. Add enough flour to make a stiff dough. Turn out onto floured board or pastry cloth. Knead dough until smooth and elastic, 6 to 8 minutes. Place dough in large greased bowl; turn once to grease top. Cover and let rise in warm draft-free area until doubled in bulk, about 2 hours. Punch dough down; shape into smooth ball. Return to greased bowl; turn once to grease top. Cover and refrigerate up to 4 days. If dough rises in refrigerator, punch down.

Remove dough from refrigerator about 3 hours before serving time. Set dough aside in warm place about 1 hour. Punch dough down. Shape into rolls as desired. Place rolls in greased pans. Cover and let rise in warm draft-free area until doubled in bulk, about 1 hour. Preheat oven to 400°F. Bake for 15 to 20 minutes or until golden brown. Remove from pans; place on wire racks. Brush with butter. Makes about 48 rolls.

**Note:** If not refrigerating, allow dough to rise in bowl. Punch dough down and shape into rolls. Cover and let rise until doubled in bulk, about 1 hour. Bake as directed.

## Refrigerator Yeast Biscuits

*This no-knead dough can be kept in the refrigerator for several days and baked at your convenience.*

   1 package active dry yeast
   ½ cup warm water (105°F to 115°F)
   5 cups Martha White Self-Rising
     Flour
   3 tablespoons sugar
   ⅔ cup vegetable oil
   2 cups buttermilk

Dissolve yeast in measuring cup with warm water. Stir together flour and sugar in large mixing bowl. Add oil, buttermilk and dissolved yeast; blend thoroughly. Cover and refrigerate overnight or up to 3 days. To prepare, preheat oven to 375°F. Remove dough from refrigerator. Turn out onto floured board or pastry cloth. Roll out about ½-inch thick. Cut with floured 3-inch cutter. Place rounds on lightly greased baking sheet with sides lightly touching. Bake for 20 to 22 minutes or until golden brown. Remove from baking sheets and serve hot. Makes about 20 biscuits.

## Cheese Rolls

*Soft and tasty, a perfect complement to baked ham.*

   1 package active dry yeast
   1 cup warm water (105°F to 115°F)
   1 tablespoon sugar
   1½ teaspoons salt
   2 tablespoons vegetable oil
   1 egg, lightly beaten

   2 cups (8 ounces) grated sharp
     Cheddar cheese
   3 to 3½ cups Martha White
     All-Purpose Flour
   Vegetable oil

Dissolve yeast in large mixing bowl with warm water. Add sugar, salt, 2 tablespoons oil, egg and cheese; blend thoroughly. Add flour one cup at a time, beating vigorously until soft dough is formed. Turn out onto floured board or pastry cloth. Cover dough with bowl and let rest for 10 minutes. Knead just until dough is easy to handle, 2 to 3 minutes. Place dough in large greased bowl; turn once to grease top. Cover and let rise in warm draft-free area until doubled in bulk, about 40 minutes. Punch dough down. Shape into cloverleaf rolls (see page 89). Place in greased muffin cups. Brush rolls with oil. Let rise in warm draft-free area until doubled in bulk, about 30 minutes. Preheat oven to 375°F. Bake for 12 to 15 minutes or until golden brown. Remove from pans immediately and serve hot. Makes about 24 rolls.

## Beaten Batter Rolls

*Beaten batters require no kneading—the rolls have a light texture.*

   ½ cup milk
   ½ cup water
   ¼ cup vegetable oil
   3 to 3¼ cups Martha White
     All-Purpose Flour
   1 package active dry yeast
   ¼ cup sugar
   1 teaspoon salt
   2 eggs

Heat milk, water and oil in saucepan until very warm (120°F to 130°F). Stir together 1 cup flour, yeast, sugar and salt in large mixing bowl. Add heated mixture and eggs. Beat with electric mixer on high speed for 2 minutes or 300 strokes by hand. Add 1 cup flour and beat on medium speed for 1 minute or 150 strokes by hand. Stir in enough remaining flour to make a thick batter. Cover and let rise in warm draft-free area until doubled in bulk, about 1 hour. Stir batter down. Spoon batter into greased muffin pans, filling each cup about ¾ full. Let rise in warm draft-free area until doubled in bulk, about 30 minutes. Preheat oven to 375°F. Bake for 20 to 25 minutes or until golden brown. Remove from pans immediately and serve hot. Makes about 20 rolls.

## Pizza

*From plain cheese to one with the works, create your specialty from the suggested toppings.*

    Pizza Dough, following
1 can (8 ounces) tomato sauce
1 can (6 ounces) tomato paste
½ teaspoon salt
1 teaspoon Worcestershire sauce
1 teaspoon garlic salt
2 to 3 drops hot pepper sauce
1 teaspoon oregano leaves
¼ teaspoon ground thyme
    Suggested Toppings: browned ground beef or sausage, pepperoni, mushrooms, green pepper, olives, onions or other desired toppings

2 cups (8 ounces) grated mozzarella cheese

Prepare Pizza Dough as directed. Preheat oven to 400°F. Divide dough in half. On floured board or pastry cloth, roll each half into an 11-inch circle. Place rounds on greased 12-inch pizza pans or baking sheets; crimp edges. Combine tomato sauce, tomato paste, salt, Worcestershire sauce, garlic salt, hot pepper sauce, oregano and thyme in mixing bowl; blend thoroughly. Spread mixture over dough to within ½-inch of edge. Sprinkle with desired toppings and cheese. Bake on lowest oven rack for 20 to 25 minutes or until crust is golden brown. Makes 2 large pizzas.

### Pizza Dough

1 package active dry yeast
¾ cup plus 1 tablespoon warm water (105°F to 115°F)
2 cups Martha White All-Purpose Flour
1 teaspoon salt
2 tablespoons vegetable shortening

Dissolve yeast in measuring cup with warm water. Stir together flour and salt in large mixing bowl. Cut shortening into flour with pastry blender or two knives until mixture resembles coarse crumbs. Stir in dissolved yeast. Turn out onto lightly floured board or pastry cloth and knead just until smooth. Place dough in large greased bowl; turn once to grease top. Cover and let rise in warm draft-free area until doubled in bulk, about 1 hour. Punch dough down.

# GRITS

To the Southerner, grits are a matter of loyalty.

To those who move or travel to the South, grits are an education.

Since the purpose of all good books should be to educate as well as entertain, we offer this quick course in grits. Read carefully. You will be tested.

**History:** Americans have been eating grits for more than 380 years. And while the exact origin of grits is uncertain, Southern historians claim grits as America's first food, shared by the Native Americans with the starving settlers at Jamestown in 1607.

**English:** The word *grits* has its own grammar and can be used with either a plural or singular verb (examples: Grits are my favorite food. Grits is a favorite food of Southerners.) The word itself is believed to have come from the Old English "grytt," which means bran and has been used since at least the end of the 18th century.

**Science:** Grits are a refinement of corn. From the heart of the dried corn kernel comes hominy which has been hulled, washed and boiled. If the kernel is ground into very fine particles, it's cornmeal. And when it's ground to a gritty consistency it's, well, grits.

**Economics:** More than 600 million pounds of grits are consumed by Americans each year—that's nearly three pounds of grits for every man, woman and child in the country. The cost of one serving of grits is approximately 2½ cents.

**Health and nutrition:** Grits contain no salt or fat and are a good source of carbohydrates. Many grits are enriched with iron and B vitamins. And when combined with meat, cheese or beans, they form a complete protein-filled meal.

**Home economics:** Grits preparation takes patience. If grits are undercooked, they become watery. The longer grits are cooked, the creamier they are. If you're in a hurry, use quick grits which cook in about five minutes and have no added salt.

In their purest form, grits are usually consumed with a dab of butter and a dash of salt and pepper. But for fancy fixing, cheese, hot peppers or even tomatoes can convert this everyday dish into something special. Even this morning's leftover grits can dress up for evening as fried cheese party bits or sliced grits with cheese or tomato sauce.

And now it's time for a real test—stir up some grits for your family or friends and see what kind of grade they give you.

Jalapeño Cheese Grits Casserole (page 98)

## First Prize Grits Casserole

*"Best of the Show" at the 1988 World Grits Festival in St. George, South Carolina.*

4 cups water
1 teaspoon salt
1 cup Jim Dandy Quick Grits
1 pound (16 ounces) sausage
½ cup chopped green pepper
½ cup chopped onion
½ cup chopped celery

1 can (10¾ ounces) cream of celery soup
1 cup (4 ounces) grated sharp Cheddar cheese

Preheat oven to 375°F. Grease a 2-quart baking dish. Bring water and salt to a boil in large saucepan. Slowly stir in grits. Cover, reduce heat and cook for 5 minutes, stirring occasionally. Sauté sausage, pepper, onion and celery to-

## ★ Grandpa Jones ★

Louis Marshall Jones is just about everyone's favorite grandpa. Known chiefly during the past 20 years for his comedy roles on "Hee Haw," Jones is also one of the world's finest traditional five-string banjo play-ers. When Martha White needed a spokesman for its Trail Blazer dog food, the company naturally turned to Grandpa. After all, his rendition of "Ol' Rattler" has become the highest tribute to a hunting hound.

## CHEESE GRITS CASSEROLE

4 cups water
1 teaspoon salt
1 cup Jim Dandy Quick Grits
1½ cups (6 ounces) grated sharp Cheddar cheese, divided
½ cup (1 stick) butter or margarine
4 eggs, lightly beaten
1 cup milk

¼ teaspoon cayenne pepper

Preheat oven to 350°F. Grease a 2-quart baking dish. Bring water and salt to a boil in large saucepan. Slowly stir in grits. Cover, reduce heat and cook for 5 minutes, stirring occasionally. Remove pan from heat.

Stir in one cup cheese and butter until melted. Add eggs, milk and pepper; blend well. Pour mixture into prepared dish. Sprinkle with remaining cheese. Bake for 1 hour or until cheese is golden brown. Cool for 10 minutes before serving. Makes 6 to 8 servings.

gether in large skillet until sausage is browned and vegetables are tender; drain. Add sausage mixture to grits; stir to blend. Pour mixture into prepared dish. Spread soup over grits mixture and sprinkle evenly with cheese. Bake for 30 to 35 minutes or until cheese is golden brown. Cool for 10 minutes before serving. Makes 6 to 8 servings.

## Fried Grits Slices

*An old-fashioned way to turn leftover grits into a breakfast specialty.*

    4 cups water
    1 teaspoon salt
    1 cup Jim Dandy Quick Grits
        Martha White Self-Rising or
        All-Purpose Flour
        Vegetable oil or shortening for
        frying

Grease an 8½x4½x2½-inch loaf pan. Bring water and salt to a boil in large saucepan. Slowly stir in grits. Cover, reduce heat and cook for 5 minutes, stirring occasionally. Pour cooked grits into prepared pan. Cool; cover and refrigerate for 2 hours or until firm. In large skillet, heat ¼-inch deep oil over medium heat until a drop of water sizzles when dropped in skillet. Turn chilled grits out of loaf pan onto cutting board. Cut into ½-inch slices. Coat slices on all sides with flour. Fry slices on one side until golden brown; turn and fry on other side until golden brown. Drain on paper towels. These are best served warm. Makes about 16 slices.

## Fried Sausage Grits Slices

*For a down-home country lunch, serve with green beans, summer squash and tomatoes fresh from the garden.*

    1 recipe Fried Grits Slices
    ½ pound (8 ounces) sausage,
        browned and drained

Prepare Fried Grits Slices as directed; except—stir sausage into hot grits mixture before pouring into greased loaf pan. Continue preparation as directed. Makes about 16 slices.

### GRITS-LOVER'S PRAYER

**O**ur Father, watchin' my kitchen,
Please help me understand
Why some folks just don't take to
    grits
Like I know you planned.

Perhaps it's 'cause they missed out—
Through no fault of their own,
Their mamas served 'em oatmeal
'Til they were nearly grown.

For that I cannot blame them
And since it's not too late,
I pray some good soul finds them
And puts grits upon their plate.

I'm sure there are grits in heaven
And angels are eatin' right.
But there are no grits below us
'Cept those burned black as night.

## Creole Grits Casserole

*Fresh and colorful Creole sauce bakes over a layer of sliced grits.*

    4 cups water
    1 teaspoon salt
    1 cup Jim Dandy Quick Grits
    1 cup chopped celery
    1 medium onion, chopped
    1 medium green pepper, chopped
    ¼ cup (½ stick) butter or margarine
    1 can (14½ ounces) tomatoes,
      chopped and undrained
    1 cup ketchup
    1 can (2½ to 3 ounces) sliced
      mushrooms, drained
    1 teaspoon oregano
    ½ cup (2 ounces) grated Parmesan
      cheese
    ¼ cup (½ stick) butter or margarine,
      melted

Country breakfast, featuring Grits

Drizzle with ¼ cup melted butter. Bake for 35 to 40 minutes or until hot and bubbly. Cool for 10 minutes before serving. Makes 6 to 8 servings.

Grease an 8½x4½x2½-inch loaf pan. Bring water and salt to a boil in large saucepan. Slowly stir in grits. Cover, reduce heat and cook for 5 minutes, stirring occasionally. Pour grits into prepared pan. Cool; cover and refrigerate for 2 hours or until firm. In large skillet, sauté celery, onion and green pepper in ¼ cup butter until tender. Stir in tomatoes, ketchup, mushrooms and oregano. Simmer for 15 minutes, uncovered, stirring occasionally. Preheat oven to 350°F. Grease a 13x9x2-inch baking dish. Turn chilled grits out of loaf pan onto cutting board. Cut into ½-inch slices. In prepared baking dish, arrange slices in two rows, overlapping slightly. Pour Creole mixture over grits and sprinkle with Parmesan cheese.

## Jalapeño Cheese Grits Casserole

*A creamy casserole with a south-of-the-border kick.*

    4 cups water
    1 teaspoon salt
    1 cup Jim Dandy Quick Grits
    2 cups (8 ounces) grated sharp
      Cheddar cheese
    1 roll (6 ounces) jalapeño cheese
    ½ cup (1 stick) butter or margarine
    3 eggs, lightly beaten
    2 tablespoons chopped jalapeño
      pepper
    1 tablespoon Worcestershire sauce
      Paprika

Preheat oven to 350°F. Grease a 2-quart baking dish. Bring water and salt to a boil in large saucepan. Slowly stir in grits. Cover, reduce heat and cook for 5 minutes, stirring occasionally. Remove pan from heat. Stir in cheeses and butter until melted. Add eggs, jalapeño pepper and Worcestershire sauce; blend well. Pour mixture into prepared dish. Sprinkle with paprika as desired. Bake for 40 to 45 minutes or until set. Cool for 10 minutes before serving. Makes 6 to 8 servings.

# The World Celebrates Grits

Each spring a sleepy little town in South Carolina wakes up to celebrate its favorite breakfast food—grits.

And it invites the rest of the world to join in.

Actually, the folks in St. George, South Carolina, eat grits any time of the day and claim to be the "Grits Capital of the World." The community has also found creative ways to honor this corn meal cousin.

Officials of the St. George World Grits Festival claim more grits are consumed in the South Carolina low country than anywhere else in the world. And no one has ever stepped forward to dispute this fact.

St. George's three-day festival held in April has attracted more than 25,000 visitors each year since 1986 and places emphasis on family fun, featuring a multitude of events designed to appeal to visitors of all ages.

Festival-goers can watch grits being ground from corn at an authentic mill, enter their favorite recipes in the Martha White Grits Cooking Contest and test their endurance and gastronomic capacity at the Grits Eating Contest.

There are grits dinners and a grits parade, and the queen of grits makes an appearance.

As far as the eye can see, there are grits-lovers proudly wearing the world-famous official World Grits Festival T-shirt and eagerly anticipating the next year's celebration.

# *Sausage Cheese Grits Casserole

*For a change of pace, transform grits, a Southern breakfast favorite, into a hearty supper casserole.*

    4 cups water
    ½ teaspoon salt
    1 cup Jim Dandy Quick Grits
    1½ cups (6 ounces) grated sharp
        Cheddar cheese, divided
    ¼ cup (½ stick) butter or margarine
    4 eggs, lightly beaten
    ½ cup milk
    1 pound (16 ounces) sausage,
        browned and drained

Preheat oven to 350°F. Grease a 3-quart baking dish. Bring water and salt to a boil in large saucepan. Slowly stir in grits. Cover, reduce heat and cook for 5 minutes, stirring occasionally. Remove pan from heat. Stir in 1 cup cheese and butter until melted. Add eggs, milk and sausage; blend well. Pour mixture into prepared dish. Sprinkle with remaining cheese. Bake for 1 hour or until cheese is golden brown. Cool for 10 minutes before serving. Makes 6 to 8 servings.

# Garlic Cheese Grits Casserole

*Just a hint of garlic accents this popular creamy casserole.*

    4 cups water
    1 teaspoon salt
    1 cup Jim Dandy Quick Grits

    2 cups (8 ounces) grated sharp
        Cheddar cheese
    1 roll (6 ounces) garlic cheese
    ½ cup (1 stick) butter or margarine
    3 eggs, lightly beaten
    1 tablespoon Worcestershire sauce
        Paprika

Preheat oven to 350°F. Grease a 2-quart baking dish. Bring water and salt to a boil in large saucepan. Slowly stir in grits. Cover, reduce heat and cook for 5 minutes, stirring occasionally. Remove pan from heat. Stir in cheeses and butter until melted. Add eggs and Worcestershire sauce; blend well. Pour mixture into prepared dish. Sprinkle with paprika as desired. Bake for 40 to 45 minutes or until set. Cool for 10 minutes before serving. Makes 6 to 8 servings.

# Fried Cheese Grits Party Bites

*For a unique appetizer, serve with a variety of dipping sauces.*

    4 cups water
    1 teaspoon salt
    1 cup Jim Dandy Quick Grits
    1 cup (4 ounces) grated sharp
        Cheddar cheese
    1 egg, lightly beaten
    ¼ teaspoon paprika
    ¼ teaspoon hot pepper sauce
        Vegetable oil or shortening for
            deep frying
        Martha White Self-Rising or
            All-Purpose Flour

Grease a shallow 2-quart baking dish. Bring water and salt to a boil in large saucepan. Slowly stir in grits. Cover, reduce heat and cook for 5 minutes, stirring occasionally. Remove pan from heat. Stir in cheese until melted. Add egg, paprika and hot pepper sauce; blend well. Pour grits mixture into prepared dish. Cool; cover and chill for 2 hours or until firm. In heavy saucepan or electric fryer, heat 2 to 3 inches of oil over medium-high heat to 375°F. Cut chilled grits into 1-inch cubes. Coat cubes on all sides with flour. Fry cubes until golden brown and floating on top of oil. Drain on paper towels. These are best served warm. Makes about 40 appetizers.

## Italian Grits Casserole

*Inspired by the classic Italian polenta.*

> 4 cups water
> 1 teaspoon salt
> 1 cup Jim Dandy Quick Grits
> 1 jar (26 ounces) pasta sauce
> 1 cup (4 ounces) grated mozzarella cheese

Grease an 8½x4½x2½-inch loaf pan. Bring water and salt to a boil in large saucepan. Slowly stir in grits. Cover, reduce heat and cook for 5 minutes, stirring occasionally. Pour grits into prepared pan. Cool; cover and refrigerate for 2 hours or until firm. Preheat oven to 350°F. Grease a 13x9x2-inch baking dish. Turn chilled grits out of loaf pan onto cutting board. Cut into ½-inch slices. In prepared baking dish, arrange slices in two rows, overlapping slices slightly. Pour pasta sauce over grits and sprinkle with cheese. Bake for 40 to 45 minutes or until hot and bubbly. Cool for 10 minutes before serving. Makes 6 to 8 servings.

## Dandy Swiss Grits Bake

*First-prize winner at the 1989 World Grits Festival in St. George, South Carolina.*

> 2 cups milk
> 1 cup (4 ounces) grated Swiss cheese
> ½ cup Jim Dandy Quick Grits
> ¼ cup (½ stick) butter or margarine
> ½ teaspoon salt
> ⅛ teaspoon pepper
> ¼ cup grated Parmesan cheese

Preheat oven to 350°F. Grease a 1-quart baking dish. Bring milk to a boil in large saucepan over medium heat; add cheese and stir until melted. Add grits; cook and stir until mixture is thickened. Remove pan from heat. Add butter, salt and pepper; beat with electric mixer on high speed for three minutes. Pour mixture into prepared dish; sprinkle with Parmesan cheese. Bake for 30 to 35 minutes or until golden brown and bubbly. Cool for 5 minutes before serving. Makes 4 to 6 servings.

# Main Dishes and Side Dishes

"All things are ready, come to the feast!
Come, for the table now is spread;
Ye famishing, ye weary,
Come, and thou shalt be richly fed."
—Hymn by Charlotte G. Homer
and W. A. Ogden

Regular Sunday observances in the South don't end with the final strains of the closing hymn or after the last "Amen" has been solemnly spoken from the pulpit. Sunday dinner* is also an important part of weekly thanksgiving.

Finally, the extra leaves are added to the table, the good Sunday linen tablecloth is spread and the meal begins with the scrape of chairs scooted up to the table and a prayer of sincere thanks.

The food begins its slow journey around the table in the time-honored ritual of passing. The clatter of silverware in the serving bowl is the sincerest form of applause.

Dinner rolls neatly arranged on grandma's favorite platter are served to a youngster's plate. The stew 'n' biscuits floating in an heirloom soup tureen makes the rounds. There are vegetables freshly picked from the garden or liberated from the captivity of last summer's canning. Eyeglasses fog over from the steam of passing heaping plates of mashed potatoes, dumplings, green beans, potato soup, fresh corn on the cob and plantation pie.

But the heart of Sunday dinner has always been meat. And that is why the long oak dining room table is anchored at each end with a heaping platter of ham and fried chicken.

Settlers of the South brought with them the pig, who foraged for himself and in return graced the dinner table as succulent smoked ham, spicy sausages and tender chops.

Right behind the pig comes poultry. Killing the old hen an hour or two before dinner was once a time-honored practice. Dusted with flour or white corn meal, golden fried chicken is an enduring hallmark of the South.

Catfish was once hooked in nearby ponds and cleaned by its captors. Today's cooks can catch farm-raised catfish in the convenience of their neighborhood supermarket.

Dishes continue circling the table a second and a third time. Eventually all that remains is the soft center of the cornbread, enough chicken for a cold supper and a bit of gravy.

Full and satisfied. That's the taste of heaven as preached by Sunday dinner.

---

*In the South, dinner is the meal you eat around noontime, as opposed to the meal which you eat in the evening, which is referred to as supper.

---

[ *103* ]

Chicken Casserole Supreme (page 110)

# Old-Fashioned Chicken and Dumplings

*Honest country cooking—choose drop or rolled dumplings to cook in the savory chicken broth.*

> 1 broiler-fryer chicken (2½ to 3 pounds)
> 2 quarts (8 cups) water
> 1 large onion, peeled and cut in half
> 1 large carrot, peeled and cut in half
> 1 large celery stalk, cut in half
> 2 tablespoons butter or margarine
> 1 teaspoon salt
> ½ teaspoon pepper
> 2 cups sifted Martha White Self-Rising Flour
> ⅓ cup shortening
> ½ cup chicken broth

Place chicken, water, onion, carrot and celery in Dutch oven. Bring to a boil; cover, reduce heat and simmer one hour or until tender. Remove chicken from broth; cool both chicken and broth. Bone chicken, cutting meat into bite-size pieces. Skim fat from surface of cooled broth. Bring broth to a boil and add butter, salt and pepper. Cut shortening into flour in mixing bowl using pastry blender or two knives until mixture resembles coarse crumbs. Add broth and stir with a fork only until dough leaves sides of bowl. Prepare your choice of dumplings (below) using prepared dough.

ROLLED DUMPLINGS: Roll out dough to ⅛-inch thickness on lightly floured board or pastry cloth. Cut dough into strips or small squares. Slowly drop dumplings one at a time into boiling broth. Cover, reduce heat and simmer 15 minutes or until dumplings are done. Gently stir once or twice during cooking to prevent dumplings from sticking together. Stir chicken pieces into dumplings just before serving. Makes 10 to 12 servings.

DROP DUMPLINGS: Pat out dough to ½-inch thickness on lightly floured board or pastry cloth. Pinch off dough in small pieces. Slowly drop dumplings one at a time into boiling broth. Cover, reduce heat and simmer 15 minutes or until dumplings are done. Gently stir once or twice during cooking to prevent dumplings from sticking together. Stir chicken pieces into dumplings just before serving. Makes 10 to 12 servings.

**Note:** If using Martha White All-Purpose Flour, sift 1 tablespoon baking powder and ¾ teaspoon salt with flour.

# Chicken on Egg Bread

*A Middle Tennessee favorite—simply chicken on cornbread with a rich flavorful sauce.*

> 1 recipe Martha White's Egg Bread, following
> 1 broiler-fryer chicken (2½ to 3 pounds), cooked and cut into bite-size pieces
> 1 recipe Rich Sauce, following

Split wedges of Egg Bread and top each wedge with chicken. Pour as much Rich Sauce as desired over chicken and cornbread. Serve hot. Makes 6 to 8 servings.

## Martha White's Egg Bread

2 eggs
1½ cups milk
¼ cup vegetable oil or melted shortening
2½ cups Martha White Self-Rising Corn Meal Mix
2 teaspoons sugar

Preheat oven to 450°F. Grease a 10-inch cast-iron skillet and place in oven to heat. Beat eggs in mixing bowl. Add remaining ingredients; stir until smooth. (Batter should be creamy and pourable. If batter seems too thick, add a little more liquid.) Pour batter into prepared skillet. Bake for 20 to 25 minutes or until golden brown. Makes 6 to 8 servings.

## Rich Sauce

2 tablespoons finely chopped onion
⅓ cup (5⅓ tablespoons) butter or margarine
½ cup Martha White Self-Rising Flour
2 cups milk
1 cup chicken broth
1½ teaspoons Worcestershire sauce
1 teaspoon A-1 Steak Sauce
¼ teaspoon salt
⅛ teaspoon cayenne pepper
⅛ teaspoon nutmeg

Combine onion and butter in medium saucepan; sauté over medium heat until onion is transparent. Slowly stir in flour, stirring constantly for one minute. Gradually stir in milk and broth. Bring mixture to a boil over medium heat, stirring constantly. Boil for 1 minute, stirring constantly. Sauce should be thickened. Add remaining ingredients and blend well. Keep warm until ready to serve. Makes about 4 cups.

## CHICKEN FROM A TO Z

Chicken is one of the most popular ingredients in Southern main dishes.

Chicken is economical and easy to keep on hand because it freezes well. Following are tips on storing chicken:

♦ Uncooked chicken can be stored safely in the refrigerator for two to three days.
♦ Freeze chicken in store wrapping for up to three months. When put in freezer wrap, it can be stored for up to six months.
♦ Never stuff chicken before refrigerating or freezing it.
♦ Frozen chicken can be thawed in the refrigerator or by immersing in cold water, changing the water frequently. It can also be thawed in a microwave.
♦ To keep bacteria from forming, don't leave cooked chicken at room temperature more than 1½ hours after cooking.

Grandma's Sunday Fried Chicken and Gravy

## Grandma's Sunday Fried Chicken and Gravy

*A Southern classic served with buttermilk biscuits and cream gravy. Covering the skillet keeps the chicken moist, but it still cooks up crisp and delicious.*

  1 **cup Martha White All-Purpose Flour**
  1 **teaspoon salt**
½ **teaspoon pepper**
  1 **broiler-fryer chicken (2½ to 3 pounds), cut up**
    **Vegetable oil or shortening for frying**
1½ **cups water**
    **Cream Gravy, following**

Combine flour, salt and pepper in large plastic bag or paper sack. Rinse chicken pieces; pat dry. Drop two chicken pieces at a time into bag with seasoned flour. Shake until pieces are coated. Repeat this procedure until all pieces are coated. In large skillet, heat ½-inch deep oil over medium heat to 350°F. Fry chicken, covered, 20 to 25 minutes or until golden brown and crispy, turning pieces about every 10 minutes. Remove chicken from skillet; pour off drippings and reserve. Return chicken to skillet and add water. Cover, reduce heat and steam chicken 10 to 15 minutes. Add more water, if needed. Check for desired degree of doneness. Serve with Cream Gravy, if desired. Makes about 6 servings.

### Cream Gravy

¼ **cup drippings and browned particles from cooked chicken**
¼ **cup Martha White All-Purpose Flour***
  2 **cups milk**
    **Salt and pepper to taste**

Pour off all drippings and scrape browned particles from skillet in which chicken was fried, reserving ¼ cup drippings and brown particles. Return reserved drippings and particles to skillet. Add flour and stir to blend. Cook and stir over medium heat for about 1 minute. Gradually stir in milk. Bring mixture to a boil, stirring constantly. Simmer for 2 to 3 minutes, stirring constantly. Season to taste with salt and pepper. Serve warm with fried chicken. Makes 2½ cups.

*Seasoned flour left after coating chicken may be used.

## Lattice-Topped Turkey Bake

*Biscuit dough forms a decorative lattice top over a rich turkey casserole.*

1 can (10¾ ounces) condensed
  cream of chicken soup
1 cup milk, divided
¼ teaspoon seasoned salt
2 cups chopped cooked turkey
1 package (16 ounces) frozen mixed
  broccoli, cauliflower and carrots,
  thawed and drained
1 cup (4 ounces) grated sharp
  Cheddar cheese, divided
1 can (2.8 ounces) French-fried
  onions, divided
1 package (5½ ounces) Martha
  White BixMix
1 egg, lightly beaten

Preheat oven to 425°F. Grease a 12x8x2-inch baking dish. Stir together soup, ¾ cup milk, seasoned salt, turkey, vegetables, ½ cup cheese and ½ can onions in large mixing bowl. Pour mixture into prepared dish. Bake uncovered for 10 minutes. While mixture is baking, combine biscuit mix, egg and remaining ¼ cup milk in small bowl; stir with fork to blend. Add a little more milk if necessary to make a soft drop dough. Remove casserole from oven and drop dough by spoonfuls onto mixture to form a lattice pattern. Return to oven and bake for 20 to 25 additional minutes or until biscuits are golden brown. Remove casserole from oven and sprinkle with remaining cheese and onions. Return to oven and bake for 3 to 5 minutes or until cheese melts and onions are lightly browned. Cool for 10 minutes before serving. Makes 6 to 8 servings.

## Picnickin' Fried Chicken

*Dipping chicken pieces in buttermilk, then seasoned flour will produce a crunchy coating that stays crisp until picnic time.*

2 cups Martha White All-Purpose
  Flour
2 teaspoons salt
1 teaspoon pepper
1½ cups buttermilk
1 broiler-fryer chicken (2½ to 3
  pounds), cut up
  Vegetable oil or shortening for
  frying

Combine flour, salt and pepper in large plastic bag or paper sack. Pour buttermilk into a shallow bowl. Rinse chicken pieces; pat dry. Drop a few chicken pieces at a time into bag with seasoned flour. Shake until pieces are coated. Repeat this procedure until all pieces have been coated with flour. Dip all pieces in buttermilk. Return pieces to bag and shake in seasoned flour again. Remove chicken pieces from bag and place on waxed paper. Repeat this procedure until all pieces are coated. In large skillet, heat ½-inch deep oil over medium heat to 350°F. Fry chicken, uncovered, 25 to 30 minutes or until golden brown and crispy, turning pieces about every 10 minutes. Check for desired degree of doneness. Drain on paper towels. Makes about 6 servings.

# Bobka
# (Chicken Roll)

*Years ago this recipe was a favorite among ladies who attended demonstrations in the Martha White Kitchen. The source of the name has been long since forgotten, but not the delectable chicken-filled pastry.*

1 recipe Pastry, below
1 recipe Chicken Filling, following

Preheat oven to 375°F. Grease a baking sheet. Prepare Pastry as directed; cover and chill while making filling. Prepare Chicken Filling as directed. Divide dough in half. On lightly floured board or pastry cloth, knead each half about five times or until smooth. For each half, roll out dough to a 12x8-inch rectangle. Spread each rectangle with half of filling, spreading to within one inch of edges. Lightly roll each half up jelly-roll style, beginning with a long side. Pinch long edge to seal; fold ends under. Carefully place rolls on prepared baking sheet. Bake for 25 to 30 minutes or until lightly browned. To serve, cut rolls into 1-inch slices and serve with reserved soup mixture which has been heated. Makes 6 to 8 servings.

## Pastry

½ cup shortening
1¼ cups sifted Martha White
   Self-Rising Flour
1 egg, beaten
3 tablespoons milk

Cut shortening into flour in mixing bowl using pastry blender or two knives until mixture resembles coarse crumbs. Add egg and milk; stir with a fork only until dough leaves sides of bowl. Shape dough into a ball and leave in bowl.

## STRATEGIC MEAL PLANNING

**H**alf the effort of putting together the perfect meal is planning it. The most appetizing and attractive meals are those that include a variety of foods.

♦ Texture variety: Don't serve a meal made up of only soft foods or only crisp foods. Prepare a variety of both, such as meat, broccoli and creamed potatoes.

♦ Color variety: Try to spice up a plate with foods in a variety of colors. If you need more color in a meal, garnish with parsley and a slice of orange. Try substituting red peppers for green peppers if your meal already includes something green.

♦ Temperature variety: Supply your dinner guests with a combination of cold and hot foods. Add a cool salad or cole slaw to a hot meal.

♦ Taste variety: For variety, add a sweet fruit salad to a meal containing all spicy or tangy dishes.

### Chicken Filling

1 cup cooked, finely diced chicken
½ cup finely chopped celery
2 tablespoons chopped parsley
1 can (10¾ ounces) cream of
chicken soup, divided
1 teaspoon soy sauce
½ cup water

Combine chicken, celery, parsley, ½ can cream of chicken soup (undiluted) and soy sauce; stir until blended. Stir together remaining ½ can soup and water in another bowl and set aside to be heated and used as a sauce.

## ★ Chet Atkins ★

Because of his monumental influence as a musician, producer and record-label executive, Chet Atkins probably has been the single most significant figure in country music during the last half of the 20th century. A guitar fancier and experimenter since boyhood, Atkins ultimately developed picking styles that are still essential studies for any would-be guitar virtuoso.

### EASY PICKIN' CHICKEN PIE

3 cups cooked, diced chicken
1 package (10 ounces) frozen mixed vegetables
1 can (10¾ ounces) cream of celery soup, undiluted
1 cup chicken broth
¼ teaspoon pepper
1 cup Martha White Self-Rising Flour
1 cup milk

½ cup (1 stick) butter or margarine, melted

Preheat oven to 400°F. Grease a shallow 2-quart baking dish. Spread chicken and vegetables evenly in prepared dish. Stir together soup, broth and pepper in small mixing bowl; pour evenly over chicken mixture. Combine flour, milk and butter in separate bowl; stir until smooth. Pour flour mixture over ingredients in baking dish. Bake for 45 to 50 minutes or until golden brown. Cool for 10 minutes before serving. Makes 4 to 6 servings.

**Note:** If using Martha White All-Purpose Flour, sift 1½ teaspoons baking powder and a scant ½ teaspoon salt with flour.

Crispy Fried Fish

## Chicken Casserole Supreme

*This rich creamy chicken casserole topped with tender biscuits is the perfect choice for an informal supper with friends.*

- ½ **cup finely chopped onion**
- ½ **cup finely chopped celery**
- 1 **cup sliced small fresh mushrooms**
- ¼ **cup (½ stick) butter or margarine**
- ⅓ **cup Martha White All-Purpose Flour**
- 2 **cups chicken broth**
- 1 **cup (8 ounces) whipping cream**
- 2½ **cups cooked, diced chicken**
- ¼ **cup sliced stuffed olives**
- 2 **tablespoons minced parsley**
- ½ **teaspoon salt**
- ¼ **teaspoon pepper**
- 2 **tablespoons shortening**
- 1 **cup sifted Martha White Self-Rising Flour**
- ½ **cup less 1 tablespoon buttermilk**

Preheat oven to 400°F. Grease a 1½-quart baking dish. Combine onion, celery, mushrooms and butter in large saucepan; sauté over medium heat until vegetables are tender. Slowly stir in ⅓ cup flour, stirring constantly for one minute. Gradually stir in broth and cream. Bring mixture to a boil over medium heat, stirring constantly. Boil for 1 minute, stirring constantly. Sauce should be thickened. Add chicken, olives, parsley, salt and pepper; stir gently. Pour mixture into prepared dish. Cut shortening into 1 cup flour in small bowl using a pastry blender or two knives until mixture resembles coarse crumbs. Add buttermilk and stir with a fork only until dough leaves sides of bowl. Turn dough out onto lightly floured board or pastry cloth and knead gently 5 or 6 times. Roll out to ½-inch thickness. Cut into rounds or shapes with floured 2-inch cutter. Place rounds on top of casserole mixture. Bake for 25 to 30 minutes or until casserole is bubbly and biscuits are golden brown. Cool for 10 minutes before serving. Makes 4 to 6 servings.

## Crispy Fried Fish

*Traditional corn meal coating—especially good on catfish, crappie and bream—don't forget the hush puppies.*

- 1 **cup Martha White Self-Rising Corn Meal Mix**
- ½ **teaspoon salt**
- ¼ **teaspoon pepper**
- 1 **egg**
- 2 **tablespoons water**

1 **pound fresh or frozen fish fillets,
   cut into pieces
   Vegetable oil or shortening for
   frying**

Stir together corn meal, salt and pepper in shallow dish. Beat egg in a shallow bowl; add water and blend well. Coat fish pieces in seasoned corn meal; dip in egg mixture. Coat pieces again with seasoned corn meal. In large skillet, heat 1-inch deep oil over medium-high heat to 400°F. Fry a few pieces of fish at a time in hot oil until golden brown. Drain on paper towels. Makes 4 servings.

## Fried Fish with Crisp Potato Flake Coating

*Potato flakes provide a light coating reminiscent of the flavor of potato chips.*

1 **egg**
2 **tablespoons water**
1 **package (2 ounces) Martha White
   SpudFlakes**
1 **pound fresh or frozen fish fillets,
   cut in pieces
   Salt
   Vegetable oil or shortening for
   frying**

Beat egg in shallow bowl; add water and blend well. Empty potato flakes into shallow pan. Sprinkle fish fillets with salt as desired. Dip fillets first in egg mixture, then coat with potato flakes. In medium skillet, heat 1-inch deep oil over medium-high heat to 400°F. Fry a few pieces of fish at a time in hot oil until golden brown. Drain on paper towels. Makes 4 servings.

## Skillet Pizza

*No need to heat up the oven to have a crisp crusty pizza—just cook it in an electric skillet.*

1 **package (6½ ounces) Martha
   White Pizza Crust Mix**
1 **can (6 ounces) tomato paste**
2 **teaspoons Italian seasoning**
¼ **teaspoon salt**
1 **pound ground beef, browned and
   drained**
½ **cup chopped onion**
1 **can (2½ to 3 ounces) sliced
   mushrooms, drained
   Optional ingredients: chopped
      green pepper, pepperoni
      slices, black olive slices,
      jalapeño pepper slices**
2 **cups (8 ounces) grated mozzarella
   cheese**

Grease a cool electric skillet. Prepare pizza crust mix according to package directions. Line bottom of skillet with pizza dough. Stir together tomato paste, Italian seasoning and salt in mixing bowl; spread evenly over dough. Layer ground beef, onion, mushroom slices and any optional toppings on tomato paste mixture. Sprinkle with cheese. Cover and set temperature control to 375°F. Bake for 15 to 20 minutes or until crust is brown on bottom and cheese is melted. Remove cover and cool for 10 minutes before serving. Makes 6 to 8 servings.

## Deep Dish Pizza

*Really more of a meat pie, sure to be a hit with the teens.*

1 pound ground beef
¼ cup chopped onion
1 can (12 ounces) tomato paste
1⅓ cups water
2 teaspoons oregano
1½ teaspoons garlic salt
1 package (6½ ounces) Martha White Pizza Crust Mix
6 large slices (9 ounces) mozzarella cheese
¼ cup grated Parmesan cheese

Preheat oven to 400°F. Grease a 13x9x2-inch baking dish. Sauté ground beef and onion in large skillet until beef is browned and onion is tender; drain. Return mixture to skillet and stir in tomato paste, water, oregano and garlic salt. Simmer uncovered for 15 minutes, stirring occasionally. Prepare pizza crust mix according to package directions. Press dough into bottom and halfway up sides of prepared dish. Line crust with three slices of mozzarella cheese. Pour half of sauce mixture onto cheese. Top with remaining slices of cheese and sauce mixture. Sprinkle evenly with Parmesan cheese. Bake for 20 to 25 minutes or until bubbly. Cool for 10 minutes before serving. Makes 6 to 8 servings.

**Note:** For a thicker, chewier crust, use one package (8 ounces) Martha White Deep Pan Pizza Crust Mix.

## Chicken Garden Pizza

*A healthy alternative topped with lightly sautéed vegetables and shredded chicken.*

No-stick cooking spray
½ cup chopped onion
½ cup chopped green pepper
½ cup diced zucchini
½ cup diced eggplant
1 can (14½ ounces) whole tomatoes, drained and chopped
1 clove garlic, minced
¼ teaspoon oregano
¼ teaspoon basil
1 package (6½ ounces) Martha White Pizza Crust Mix
1 cup cooked shredded chicken
1 cup (4 ounces) grated mozzarella cheese

Preheat oven to 425°F. Coat a large skillet with cooking spray; place over medium heat until hot. Sauté onion and green pepper in skillet until tender; add zucchini and eggplant and continue to cook for 2 minutes, stirring constantly. Stir in tomatoes, garlic, oregano and basil. Cover and simmer 5 minutes; uncover and cook 15 minutes or until thickened, stirring occasionally. Coat a 12-inch pizza pan with cooking spray. Prepare pizza crust mix according to package directions; press into prepared pan. Spread vegetable sauce evenly over crust; sprinkle with chicken and cheese. Bake for 20 to 25 minutes or until crust is browned and cheese is melted. Makes one 12-inch pizza.

**Note:** For a vegetarian pizza, omit chicken.

## Vegetable Pizza Turnovers

*Green pepper, zucchini and tomatoes seasoned with Italian herbs, then folded in pizza crust is easy with pizza crust mix.*

1 tablespoon vegetable oil
½ cup chopped onion
½ cup chopped green pepper
½ cup unpeeled diced zucchini
1 can (14½ ounces) whole tomatoes, drained and chopped, juice reserved
1 clove garlic, minced
¼ teaspoon oregano
¼ teaspoon basil
1 package (8 ounces) Martha White Deep Pan Pizza Crust Mix
1 cup (4 ounces) grated mozzarella cheese
1 egg white, beaten

Coat a large skillet with oil. Sauté onion and green pepper in skillet until tender; add zucchini and continue to cook for 2 minutes, stirring constantly. Stir in tomatoes, garlic, oregano, basil and 2 tablespoons reserved juice from tomatoes. Cover and simmer 5 minutes; uncover and cook 15 to 20 minutes or until thickened, stirring occasionally. Preheat oven to 425°F. Grease a large baking sheet. Prepare pizza crust mix according to package directions. Divide dough into four equal pieces; pat each piece into a 6-inch circle. Spoon ¼ of vegetable mixture onto center of each circle; divide cheese evenly between circles. Fold each circle in half; crimp and roll edges tightly together. Brush turnovers with egg white. Bake for 12 to 15 minutes or until golden brown. Cool for a few minutes before serving. Makes 4 turnovers.

## Sausage Cheese Plantation Pie

*The focal point for a brunch buffet, just add fruit and muffins to delight your guests.*

2 tablespoons shortening
1 cup sifted Martha White Self-Rising Flour
⅓ cup milk
1 pound sausage, browned and drained
2 cups (8 ounces) grated sharp Cheddar cheese
2 cups (8 ounces) grated mozzarella cheese
6 eggs
½ cup milk
1 teaspoon oregano
¼ teaspoon pepper

Preheat oven to 350°F. Grease a 13x9x2-inch baking dish. Cut shortening into flour with pastry blender or two knives until mixture resembles coarse crumbs. Add ⅓ cup milk and stir with a fork only until dough leaves sides of bowl. Press dough into bottom of prepared dish. Sprinkle sausage and cheeses evenly over dough. Beat eggs in mixing bowl; stir in ½ cup milk, oregano and pepper. Pour egg mixture evenly over sausage and cheeses. Bake for 25 to 30 minutes or until golden brown. Cool for 10 minutes before serving. Makes 8 to 10 servings.

Richard Lindsey named his mill's best-selling product for his daughter, put her picture on the package, and the rest is history.

Preheat oven to 350°F. Partially bake prepared pastry shell 10 minutes; cool. Combine browned ground beef, mushrooms and cheese in large mixing bowl. Combine remaining ingredients in another bowl. Add to ground beef mixture; stir to blend. Pour mixture into prepared pastry shell. Bake 1 hour or until golden brown and center is set. Cool on wire rack 10 minutes before slicing. Makes 6 to 8 servings.

## Beef and Swiss Quiche

*A creamy mushroom quiche filled with ground beef and rich Swiss cheese.*

>        One 9-inch pastry shell (page 124)
> ½  pound ground beef, browned and drained
> 1  jar (4 ounces) mushroom slices, drained
> 1  cup (4 ounces) grated Swiss cheese
> 2  eggs, lightly beaten
> ½  cup milk
> 1  can (10¾ ounces) condensed cream of mushroom soup
> 2  tablespoons chopped chives
> ¼  teaspoon salt
> ⅛  teaspoon white pepper
> 2  drops hot sauce

## Quick Quiche

*Cheddar cheese and bacon gives this quiche a hearty flavor suitable for a light supper.*

> ½  cup chopped onion
> 2  tablespoons butter or margarine
> 3  eggs
> 1½  cups milk
> ½  cup Martha White BixMix
> 1  cup (4 ounces) grated sharp Cheddar cheese
> 4  strips bacon, cooked and crumbled
> ½  teaspoon dry mustard
> ¼  teaspoon salt
> ⅛  teaspoon cayenne pepper
> 1  can (2½ to 3 ounces) sliced mushrooms, drained (optional)

Preheat oven to 375°F. Grease a 9-inch quiche pan, pie pan or square baking pan. In small skillet, sauté onion in butter until transparent. Combine onion and remaining ingredients, except mushrooms, in mixing bowl. Beat with electric mixer on medium speed for about 2 minutes. Stir in mushrooms, if desired. Pour mixture into prepared pan. Bake on bottom rack of oven for 25 to 30 minutes or until knife inserted in center comes out clean. Cool for 5 minutes before serving. Makes 6 to 8 servings.

## Sausage Cornbread Bake

*Sausage, corn and cheese make this cornbread casserole a satisfying main dish.*

> 1 pound sausage
> 1 cup chopped onion
> 2 eggs
> 1½ cups Martha White Self-Rising Corn Meal Mix
> 1 can (17 ounces) cream-style corn
> ¾ cup milk
> ¼ cup vegetable oil or melted shortening
> 2 cups (8 ounces) grated sharp Cheddar cheese

Preheat oven to 425°F. Grease a 10½-inch cast-iron skillet or 2-quart baking dish. Sauté sausage and onion in medium skillet until sausage is browned and onion is tender; drain. Beat eggs in large mixing bowl. Add corn meal, corn, milk and oil; blend thoroughly. Pour half of corn meal mixture into prepared pan; sprinkle evenly with sausage mixture and cheese. Pour remaining corn meal mixture over sausage and cheese. Bake for 30 to 35 minutes or until deep golden brown. Cool for 10 minutes before serving. Makes 6 to 8 servings.

## Chili Con Cornbread

*Sure to become a family favorite, easy to prepare yet spicy and satisfying.*

> 2 cans (15 ounces each) chili, or 4 cups homemade chili
> 1 egg
> ½ cup milk
> 2 tablespoons vegetable oil or melted shortening
> 1 cup Martha White Self-Rising Corn Meal Mix
> 1 cup (4 ounces) grated sharp Cheddar cheese, divided

Preheat oven to 400°F. Grease an 8-inch square baking dish. Pour chili into prepared dish. Beat egg in mixing bowl. Stir in milk, oil, corn meal and ½ cup cheese; blend thoroughly. Pour corn meal mixture evenly over chili. Sprinkle remaining cheese over batter. Bake for 30 to 35 minutes or until golden brown. Cool for 5 minutes before serving. Makes 4 to 6 servings.

## Vegetable Beef Casserole

*A complete meal—just add a fruit accompaniment.*

1 pound ground beef
1 medium onion, chopped
3 carrots, thinly sliced
3 stalks celery, thinly sliced
1 can (8½ ounces) green peas, drained
1 can (2½ ounces) sliced mushrooms, drained
1 can (15 ounces) tomato sauce
1 teaspoon salt
¼ teaspoon pepper
2 packages (2 ounces each) Martha White SpudFlakes, prepared according to package directions*

Preheat oven to 400°F. Grease a 3-quart baking dish. Brown ground beef and onion in large skillet; drain and set aside. Cover carrots with 1 inch water in small saucepan and cook for 10 minutes; drain. Add drained carrots, celery, peas, mushrooms, tomato sauce, salt and pepper to beef mixture; stir to blend. Pour mixture into prepared dish. Drop prepared potatoes by spoonfuls onto casserole. Bake for 20 to 25 minutes or until potatoes begin to brown. Cool for 5 minutes before serving. Makes 6 to 8 servings.

*SpudFlakes require salt, 2 tablespoons butter and ½ cup milk per package.

## Mexicali Casserole

*Mexican cornbread mix baked on top of a spicy beef mixture. Serve with a crisp green salad.*

1 pound ground beef
1 package (1½ ounces) taco seasoning mix
1 can (14½ ounces) whole tomatoes, chopped and undrained
1 can (8½ ounces) whole kernel corn, drained
1 egg
⅔ cup milk
1 package (6½ ounces) Martha White Mexican Cornbread Mix

Preheat oven to 400°F. Grease a shallow 2-quart baking dish. Brown ground beef in large skillet; drain. Return beef to skillet and add taco seasoning mix, tomatoes and corn. Bring mixture to a boil over medium heat, stirring occasionally. Pour mixture into prepared dish. Beat egg in small mixing bowl. Add milk and cornbread mix; stir until smooth. Pour cornbread batter over ground beef mixture. Bake for 25 to 30 minutes or until golden brown. Cool for 10 minutes before serving. Makes 4 to 6 servings.

## Beef Supper Casserole

*Biscuit crust on the top and bottom sandwiches a cheesy ground beef filling.*

1 pound ground beef
1 cup chopped onion
1 egg
1 cup (8 ounces) dairy sour cream
¾ teaspoon salt

¼ teaspoon pepper
1 recipe Old-Fashioned Buttermilk
   Biscuits (page 12)
1 cup (4 ounces) grated sharp
   Cheddar cheese

Preheat oven to 400°F. Grease bottom of a 9-inch square baking pan. Brown ground beef in skillet; drain and reserve drippings. Sauté onion in reserved beef drippings until tender; drain. Beat egg in mixing bowl; stir in sour cream, salt and pepper. Prepare biscuits as directed; except—after kneading gently, divide dough in half. Roll out first half on lightly floured board or pastry cloth to fit dimensions of pan. Pat dough tightly into bottom of pan. Sprinkle dough evenly with ground beef. Add onion layer and pour sour cream mixture over all. Sprinkle with cheese. Repeat rolling procedure with remaining biscuit dough. Place dough on top of casserole mixture. Bake for 30 to 35 minutes or until light golden brown. Cool for 10 minutes before serving. Cut into squares to serve. Makes 6 to 8 servings.

## JUST SAY CHEESE

From bleu to American, mozzarella to Roquefort and Monterey to Cheddar, cheese is a basic ingredient in many appetizers, salads, main dishes and desserts.

♦ Cook only on low heat for a brief time when cooking with cheese. Overcooking causes cheese to become tough and stringy.
♦ Add grated cheese to a casserole as the dish comes out of the oven or microwave. The heat of the food will melt the cheese.

*Storing Cheese:*

♦ Hard cheeses such as Cheddar, Swiss and Parmesan may be kept for several weeks.
♦ Soft cheeses such as cream, cottage and brie are very perishable and should be used within a few days.
♦ Refrigerate all cheeses.
♦ Store in original wrapper; cut surfaces should be tightly covered.
♦ For the most distinct flavors, hard cheeses should be served at room temperature and soft cheeses should be served well chilled.

*Freezing Cheese:*

♦ As a rule, freezing is not recommended for cheeses because it changes the texture.
♦ If freezing is necessary, use a moistureproof wrapper to prevent evaporation.
♦ Some cheeses that may be successfully frozen are Cheddar, mozzarella, Parmesan, Swiss and provolone.
♦ Hard cheese may become crumbly with freezing, but its flavor will not be affected; use it for cooking.
♦ Thaw frozen cheese slowly in the refrigerator in the unopened package. Use as soon as possible after thawing.

## Stew 'N' Biscuits

*Keep these ingredients in the pantry for a hot and hearty meal when time is limited.*

1 can (40 ounces) beef stew
1 package (5½ ounces) Martha
    White BixMix
⅓ cup milk

Preheat oven to 425°F. Pour stew into an ungreased 2-quart baking dish. Stir together biscuit mix and milk with fork to form a soft dough. Drop dough by spoonfuls onto stew to form dumplings. Cover and bake for 15 minutes. Remove cover and bake for 20 to 25 minutes or until dumplings are browned and stew is bubbly. Makes 4 to 6 servings.

## Super Taco

*Like the ultimate taco salad piled on hot and spicy Mexican Cornbread.*

1 egg
⅓ cup milk
1 package (6½ ounces) Martha
    White Mexican Cornbread Mix
1 can (8¾ ounces) cream-style corn
2 cups (8 ounces) grated sharp
    Cheddar cheese, divided
1 pound ground beef
1 package (1¼ ounces) taco
    seasoning mix
1 cup chopped onion, divided
1½ cups shredded lettuce
1 cup chopped tomatoes
½ cup taco sauce
½ cup dairy sour cream
    Avocado slices (optional)

Preheat oven to 425°F. Grease a 10-inch cast-iron skillet and place in oven to heat. Beat egg in mixing bowl. Add milk, cornbread mix, corn and 1 cup cheese; blend thoroughly. Pour batter into prepared skillet. Bake for 20 to 25 minutes or until golden brown. In large skillet, sauté ground beef with taco seasoning mix and ½ cup onion until beef is browned and onion is tender; drain. Remove cornbread from oven and turn out onto large serving plate. Top cornbread with layers of ground beef mixture, lettuce, tomatoes, remaining onion and cheese, taco sauce and sour cream. Garnish with avocado slices, if desired. This is best when served warm. Makes 8 to 10 servings.

## Easy Creamy Broccoli Soup

*Serve hot with cheese toast.*

1 package (10 ounces) frozen
    chopped broccoli
2 cups milk
2 tablespoons butter or margarine
1 package (2 ounces) Martha White
    SpudFlakes
2 teaspoons instant minced onion
    (optional)
1 cup chicken broth
½ teaspoon salt

Prepare broccoli according to package directions, omitting salt. Place undrained broccoli in blender container. Heat milk and butter in same saucepan broccoli was cooked in (do not boil).

Super Taco

Stir in potato flakes and onion, if desired. Add potato mixture to broccoli and process briefly. Return mixture to saucepan; add broth and salt. Simmer over low heat for 10 minutes or until heated through, stirring occasionally. Makes six ½-cup servings.

**Note:** For thinner consistency, add a little more milk.

## Creamy Cheese Soup

*Instant potato flakes thicken this flavorful soup. Garnish with crisp crumbled bacon and serve with a green salad.*

3 cups milk
2 tablespoons butter or margarine

1 package (2 ounces) Martha White SpudFlakes
1¼ teaspoons instant minced onion
½ teaspoon salt
½ teaspoon seasoned salt
¼ teaspoon pepper
1½ cups (6 ounces) grated sharp Cheddar cheese
Cooked, crumbled bacon (optional)

Heat milk and butter in saucepan (do not boil). Add remaining ingredients, except bacon, in order listed; blend well. Simmer for about 10 minutes on low heat, stirring occasionally. Garnish with cooked crumbled bacon, if desired. Makes about five 1-cup servings.

## Country-Style Potato Soup

*Satisfying flavor simplified with instant potato flakes.*

   3½ **cups milk**
     3 **tablespoons butter or margarine**
     1 **package (2 ounces) Martha White SpudFlakes**
  1¼ **teaspoons instant minced onion**
    ½ **teaspoon salt**
    ½ **teaspoon celery salt**
    ¼ **teaspoon pepper**

Heat milk and butter in saucepan (do not boil). Add remaining ingredients in order listed; blend well. Simmer about 10 minutes on low heat, stirring occasionally. Makes four 1-cup servings.

## Vidalia Onion-Topped Corn Pudding

*If you like Vidalia onions, you'll love this casserole—perfect as a side dish.*

   2 **cups chopped Vidalia onions**
  ¼ **cup (½ stick) butter or margarine**
   1 **cup (8 ounces) dairy sour cream**
   2 **eggs**
   1 **can (17 ounces) cream-style corn**
  ½ **cup buttermilk**
   1 **cup Martha White Self-Rising Corn Meal Mix**
 1½ **cups (6 ounces) grated sharp Cheddar cheese, divided**
   2 **tablespoons sugar**
  ½ **teaspoon dried whole dillweed**

Preheat oven to 400°F. Grease a shallow 2-quart baking dish. Sauté onions in butter in a large skillet until tender, about 10 minutes. Remove pan from heat; stir in sour cream. Beat eggs in mixing bowl. Add corn, buttermilk, corn meal, 1 cup cheese, sugar and dillweed; blend well. Pour batter into prepared pan. Spoon onion mixture evenly over top of batter. Sprinkle with remaining ½ cup cheese. Bake for 25 to 30 minutes or until onions just begin to brown. Cool for 15 minutes before serving. Makes 6 to 8 servings.

## Fried Corn

*Not technically fried—the corn is cut from the cob and poured into a skillet containing hot drippings. Then the corn is simmered until thick and cooked.*

   6 **medium ears of corn**
 1½ **cups water**
   3 **tablespoons Martha White All-Purpose or Self-Rising Flour**
   2 **teaspoons sugar**
   1 **teaspoon salt**
  ⅛ **teaspoon pepper**
   3 **tablespoons bacon drippings or butter**

Shuck corn, pull off silks, then wash under running water, using a vegetable brush to remove remaining silks. Hold ear of corn upright in large pan or bowl and cut corn from cob, using a sharp knife. Cut off just the tips of the grain. Make a second cut down the cob to cut off remaining grain, then scrape the milk out of the cob. Repeat this procedure with all ears of corn. Add water, flour, sugar, salt and pepper; stir to blend. Melt drippings in large skillet over medium-low heat until hot. Add corn and reduce heat to low. Fry uncovered about 40 minutes or until cooked down, stirring occasionally. Serve hot. Makes 4 to 6 servings.

## Fried Okra

*A traditional part of a summer vegetable lunch. The challenge is to cook enough for pre-meal samplers and still have some left to serve.*

> 1 pound okra, cleaned
> ¾ cup Martha White Self-Rising Corn Meal Mix
> Vegetable oil or shortening for frying

Cut okra crosswise in ½-inch slices. Combine okra and corn meal in large plastic bag. Shake to coat evenly. Remove okra from bag. In large skillet, heat ¼-inch deep oil over medium heat to 350°F. Fry until crisp and golden brown, stirring occasionally. Drain on paper towels. Serve hot. Makes 4 servings.

## Fried Green Tomatoes

*When the harvest is plentiful, serve some tomatoes before they ripen. They're tart and tasty when coated with corn meal and lightly fried.*

> 5 medium green tomatoes, cleaned
> 1 package (6 ounces) Martha White Cotton Pickin' Cornbread Mix

Salt
Vegetable oil or shortening for frying

Cut tomatoes into ½-inch slices. Stir cornbread mix and desired amount of salt together in shallow pan. Coat tomato slices in cornbread mix. In large skillet, heat ¼-inch deep oil over medium heat to 350°F. Fry on one side until golden brown; turn and fry other side until golden brown. Drain on paper towels. Serve hot. Makes 6 servings.

## Fresh Corn Fritters

*These moist fried puffs of corn are an interesting addition to summer breakfast or lunch.*

> Vegetable oil or shortening for deep frying
> 1 cup corn kernels cut from the cob
> 2 tablespoons water
> 1 egg, lightly beaten
> ½ cup milk
> 1 package (5½ ounces) Martha White FlapStax

In heavy saucepan or electric fryer, heat 2 to 3 inches of oil over medium-high heat to 375°F. Combine corn and water in small saucepan. Bring mixture to a boil. Cover, reduce heat and simmer about 7 minutes or just until corn is tender; drain. Combine remaining ingredients in medium bowl. Fold in corn. Drop by teaspoonfuls into hot oil. Fry until deep golden brown. Drain on paper towels. Serve warm. Makes about 24 fritters.

# PIES AND COBBLERS

The best things in life aren't free. The most worthwhile things in this world come at a great price.

Family, friends, love and freedom—they cost each of us in terms of time and attention and personal sacrifice. That's what gives them their value.

The same is true of pie and cobbler-making. They're a labor of love that begins with picking a filling. In days gone by, picking a filling didn't mean deliberating in the aisle of the local grocery store. It meant hours of hard work in the hot fields or orchards . . . picking a filling.

Getting down on your knees to crawl through the strawberry rows, carefully avoiding the briers and chigger bites in the blackberry patch or craning your neck as you reached high for a sun-ripened peach was flavor-enhancing labor. It was all an unseen seasoning that gave the warm pie more than a wonderful taste.

In this world of quick-fix this and one-step that, the pie is the yardstick against which all truly great cooks measure themselves. In an age of frozen and instant, pie-judging contests are still competitive events at state and county fairs across the country. No two cooks bake the same pie in the same way. And no single act of cookery nets as much scrutiny and analysis.

Pie perfection is the marriage of flaky crust to a deep, rich filling.

Making a perfect pie crust doesn't come naturally. Crusts are a talent, a touch, learned from a favorite aunt or grandmother. Through these able teachers, family pie crust formulas come down through the generations just like silver candlesticks.

In the South, the choice of pie fillings reflects the march of the seasons. First come the harvests of strawberries, cherries and blackberries followed by summer peaches, crisp rhubarb and golden apples of autumn. The humble cobblers and fried pies from dried or home-canned fruits will sustain us until picking season rolls around again. And let's not forget the rich cream pies and all manner of syrup-based pies, such as pecan and chess.

The sight of an apple pie cooling just inside a half-opened, lace-curtained kitchen window might be a symbol of America, but its origins are far older than this country and at least as old as Western civilization. Historians suspect that the Romans came up with the notion of meats, fish, vegetables or fruits swaddled in a crusty pastry that we call pie.

A thick, sweet slice of pie just might be the best way to give your family a taste of ancient history.

Old-Fashioned Peach Cobbler (page 141)

## One 9-Inch Pastry Shell

*Cutting in the shortening in two stages makes this all-purpose pastry both tender and flaky.*

  1 cup sifted Martha White
     All-Purpose Flour
  ½ teaspoon salt
  ⅓ cup shortening
  2½ to 3 tablespoons cold water

Stir together flour and salt in mixing bowl. Cut in half of shortening using pastry blender or two knives until mixture is fine and mealy. Cut in remaining shortening until mixture is consistency of small peas. Sprinkle water over the mixture; stir gently with a fork until dough leaves sides of bowl. If some dry particles remain in bottom of bowl, sprinkle with about ½ teaspoon water; continue to stir with fork until particles are worked into dough. Mixture should be moist enough to form a ball but should not be sticky. Shape dough into a ball; flatten on lightly floured board or pastry cloth. Roll into circle about one inch larger than rim of pie pan. Carefully roll dough around rolling pin. Unroll into pie pan, being careful not to stretch pastry. Fit pastry into pan, trimming ½-inch beyond rim. Fold overhang under, then press to form decorative edge as desired. Makes one 9-inch pastry shell.

FOR BAKED 9-INCH PASTRY SHELL: Preheat oven to 475°F. Prick bottom of crust thoroughly with fork that has been dipped in flour. Bake 8 to 10 minutes or until light golden brown. Cool on wire rack.

## Pastry for 2-Crust Pie

  2 cups sifted Martha White
     All-Purpose Flour
  1 teaspoon salt
  ⅔ cup shortening
  4½ to 5 tablespoons cold water

Stir together flour and salt in mixing bowl. Cut in half of shortening using pastry blender or two knives until mixture is fine and mealy. Cut in remaining shortening until mixture is consistency of small peas. Sprinkle water over the mixture; stir gently with a fork until dough leaves sides of bowl. If some dry particles remain in bottom of bowl, sprinkle with about ½ teaspoon water; continue to stir with fork until particles are worked into dough. Mixture should be moist enough to form a ball but should not be sticky. Divide dough in half. Shape first half of dough into a ball; flatten on lightly floured board or pastry cloth. Roll into circle about one inch larger than rim of pie pan. Carefully roll dough around rolling pin. Unroll into pie pan, being careful not to stretch pastry. Fit pastry into pan, trimming edge even with rim of pan. For top crust, repeat procedure for bottom crust, carefully placing pastry over filling. Trim edge ½-inch beyond rim. Fold top crust edge under bottom crust, then press to form decorative edge as desired. Makes pastry for a 2-crust pie.

## Press 'N' Bake Cream Cheese Crust

*Rich and tender—no need to use your rolling pin.*

1 package (3 ounces) cream cheese, softened
½ cup (1 stick) butter or margarine, softened
1 cup sifted Martha White All-Purpose Flour

Combine cream cheese and butter in mixing bowl; beat well. Stir in flour until blended. Cover dough and refrigerate for 30 minutes. Press dough into bottom and up sides of a 9-inch pie pan. Form decorative edge as desired. Cover crust and chill until needed if not used immediately. Makes one 9-inch pie crust.

## Oil Pastry

*For one 9-inch pastry shell.*

1¼ cups sifted Martha White All-Purpose Flour
½ teaspoon salt
¼ cup vegetable oil
2 to 2½ tablespoons cold water

Stir together flour and salt in mixing bowl. Add oil; cut in with pastry blender or two knives until mixture resembles coarse crumbs. Sprinkle water over the mixture; stir gently with a fork until dough leaves sides of bowl. If some dry particles remain in bottom of bowl, sprinkle with about ½ teaspoon water; continue to stir with fork until particles are worked into dough. Mixture should be moist enough to form a ball, but should not be sticky. Shape dough into a ball; flatten on lightly floured board or pastry cloth. Roll into circle about one inch larger than rim of pie pan. Carefully roll dough around rolling pin. Unroll into pie pan, being careful not to stretch pastry. Fit pastry into pan, trimming ½-inch beyond rim. Fold overhang under, then press to form decorative edge as desired. Makes one 9-inch pastry shell.

## Meringue for One 9-Inch Pie

3 egg whites, at room temperature
½ teaspoon vanilla
¼ teaspoon cream of tartar
6 tablespoons sugar

Combine egg whites, vanilla and cream of tartar in small mixing bowl. Beat with electric mixer on medium speed until foamy and soft peaks form. Add sugar, one tablespoon at a time, beating on high speed until mixture forms stiff, glossy peaks and sugar is dissolved. Spoon meringue onto hot filling, covering the edge first. Carefully seal meringue to inner edge of crust to prevent shrinking. Spoon remaining meringue over center of filling and blend to edge of pie. Bake as directed for individual pie recipe.

# Reunions—A Feast of Family

Summertime is the season for the most distinctive of family gatherings—The Reunion.

All across the country, distant twigs of sprawling family trees harvest their curly-headed offshoots for a journey to their roots. Four generations in a single station wagon travel along rolling rural roads to a hillside family homeplace. With them they bring out-of-focus black-and-white photographs of a forgotten family wedding, their own version of great-great-grandfather's favorite tall tale and the most precious cargo of all—food.

For hundreds of miles in the protective pillow of Mama's lap, savory dishes have survived sweltering heat and back seat sibling rivalry to grace the centerpiece of all reunions—the traditional family dinner on the grounds. There, laid out on a long makeshift table set on sawhorses is a genealogy in vittles.

With your taste buds, you can trace the family tree faithfully preserved in recipes. There's great Aunt Garnet's dressed eggs and one of many unnamed cousins' fresh garden vegetables. Each family member brings her specialty, a recipe practiced and faithfully reproduced, reunion after reunion.

There are candied yams, country hams and chicken fried with a greater variety of herbs and spices than the Colonel ever imagined. As polite kin, of course, we sample every item. We serve ourselves a "gracious plenty" until our paper plate nearly folds. We might even go back for seconds, with the reminder to "leave room for dessert, y'hear?"

Who could ever forget to leave room for dessert? You'd sooner call your uncle's third wife by his first wife's name. Desserts at reunions are the classic example of the pulpit exhortation that "The greatest shall be last." In fact, they are so special they require their very own table guarded watchfully by an army of aunts. These aunts hover over the table occasionally using their wooden-handled funeral home fans to shoo a misplaced fly or child from lighting on a perfectly formed pecan pie, cobbler or tea cake.

And if you're lucky or maybe the youngest or oldest or most recently married, you'll be given the choice of leftover desserts to take home. Then, on a rainy day when family seems especially far away, you can cut yourself a sliver of pie and enjoy a delicious mouthful of reunion memories.

## Vanilla Cream Pie

*A rich velvety cream filling with chocolate, coconut and banana variations.*

⅔ cup sugar
2 tablespoons cornstarch
1 tablespoon Martha White All-Purpose Flour
¼ teaspoon salt
2¼ cups milk
3 egg yolks, lightly beaten
2 tablespoons butter or margarine
1 teaspoon vanilla
1 baked 9-inch pastry shell (page 124)
Meringue for one 9-inch pie (page 125)

Preheat oven to 350°F. Stir together sugar, cornstarch, flour and salt in medium saucepan; gradually stir in milk. Bring to a boil over medium heat, stirring constantly. Reduce heat to medium-low and cook an additional 2 minutes, stirring constantly. Remove pan from heat. Gradually stir one cup hot mixture into egg yolks; return egg mixture to saucepan. Return mixture to boil over medium-low heat and cook for 2 minutes, stirring constantly. Remove pan from heat; stir in butter and vanilla. Pour filling into pastry shell. Spread meringue on hot filling, carefully sealing to edge of crust to prevent shrinking. Bake for 12 to 15 minutes or until light golden brown. Cool on wire rack completely before serving or refrigerating. Makes 6 to 8 servings.

### Chocolate Cream Pie

Prepare Vanilla Cream Pie as directed; except—increase sugar to 1 cup and chop 2 squares (1 ounce each) unsweetened chocolate and add to dry ingredients in saucepan.

### Coconut Cream Pie

Prepare Vanilla Cream Pie as directed; except—stir 1 cup flaked coconut into custard with butter and vanilla. Sprinkle meringue with ⅓ cup flaked coconut; bake until meringue is light golden brown and coconut is toasted.

### Banana Cream Pie

Prepare Vanilla Cream Pie as directed; except—slice 2 bananas and arrange slices in bottom of baked pastry shell. Pour filling over bananas.

## Fudge Pie

1½ cups sugar
¼ cup cocoa
3 eggs, lightly beaten
½ cup (1 stick) butter or margarine, melted
2 teaspoons vanilla
1 unbaked 9-inch pastry shell (page 124)

Preheat oven to 350°F. Stir together sugar and cocoa in mixing bowl. Add eggs, butter and vanilla; blend well. Pour mixture into pastry shell. Bake 25 to 30 minutes or until set. Do not overbake. May be served warm. Makes one 9-inch pie.

**Note:** For a less sweet pie, add only 1¼ cups sugar to recipe.

## Key Lime Pie

*A refreshing Southern favorite.*

    3 egg yolks
    1 can (14 ounces) sweetened
       condensed milk
  ½ cup lime juice
      Green food coloring (optional)
    1 baked 9-inch pastry shell
      (page 124)
      Meringue for one 9-inch pie
      (page 125)

Preheat oven to 350°F. Beat egg yolks in medium bowl. Stir in condensed milk, lime juice and a few drops of food coloring, if desired. Pour filling into pastry shell. Spread meringue on filling, carefully sealing to edge of crust to prevent shrinking. Bake for 12 to 15 minutes or until light golden brown. Cool on wire rack. Chill before serving. Makes 6 to 8 servings.

## Apple Pie

*Crisp cooking apples retain their shape during baking and give this all-American favorite a tart flavor.*

  ¾ cup sugar
    2 tablespoons Martha White
      All-Purpose Flour
  ½ teaspoon cinnamon
  ⅛ teaspoon nutmeg
    6 cups (2 pounds) peeled, thinly-
      sliced tart cooking apples
      Pastry for 2-crust pie (page 124)
    1 tablespoon butter

Preheat oven to 375°F. Stir together sugar, flour, cinnamon and nutmeg in large bowl. Add apples and toss gently to coat. Spread apple mixture in pastry shell. Dot with butter. Adjust top pastry; seal and form decorative edge as desired. Cut slits in top crust so steam can escape. Cover edge of pie with aluminum foil. Bake for 25 minutes. Remove foil and bake for an additional 20 to 25 minutes or until crust is golden brown. Cool completely on wire rack. Makes 6 to 8 servings.

## Blue Ribbon Cherry Pie

*A prize winner anytime.*

    1 cup sugar
    3 tablespoons cornstarch
  ⅛ teaspoon salt
    1 can (16 ounces) pitted tart red
      cherries, drained, reserving ½ cup
      juice

¼ teaspoon red food coloring
1 tablespoon butter or margarine
¼ teaspoon almond extract
  Pastry for 2-crust pie (page 124)

1 teaspoon vanilla
¾ cup chopped pecans
  Whipped cream, ice cream,
  chocolate sauce, slivered almonds
  or maraschino cherries, if desired

Stir together sugar, cornstarch and salt in medium saucepan; gradually stir in cherries, reserved juice and food coloring. Bring to a boil over medium heat, stirring constantly. Reduce heat to low and cook 1 minute, stirring constantly. Remove pan from heat; stir in butter and almond extract. Set aside until cool. Preheat oven to 425°F. Prepare bottom crust of pastry as directed. Roll top crust out as directed. Cut top crust into ½-inch wide strips with floured knife or pastry wheel. Pour cooled filling into pastry shell. Weave strips of crust to form a lattice top. Seal and form decorative edge as desired. Bake for 10 minutes. Reduce oven temperature to 350°F and bake for 30 to 35 minutes or until crust is golden brown and filling begins to bubble. Cool completely on wire rack. Makes 6 to 8 servings.

## Fudge Brownie Pie

*This rich crustless pie may be baked in a microwave or conventional oven.*

½ cup (1 stick) butter or margarine
2 squares (1 ounce each)
  unsweetened chocolate
1 cup sugar
2 eggs
¾ cup Martha White Self-Rising
  Flour

Grease a 10-inch glass pie pan or 9-inch glass deep pie pan. Combine butter and chocolate in microwave-safe bowl. Microwave on MEDIUM for 2 to 3 minutes or until melted, stirring occasionally. Stir in remaining ingredients in order listed; blend well. Pour into prepared pan. Place pan on inverted saucer. Microwave on MEDIUM-HIGH for 3 to 5 minutes, rotating dish ¼ turn every 2 minutes. Microwave on HIGH for 2 to 4 minutes or until center is almost done, rotating dish ¼ turn after half the time. Let dish stand directly on towel-covered countertop for 10 minutes to complete cooking. Cool for an additional 10 to 15 minutes before serving. Cut in wedges and serve with desired toppings. Makes 4 to 6 servings.

CONVENTIONAL OVEN: Preheat oven to 350°F. (Preheat oven to 325°F if using a glass pie pan.) Grease a 10-inch glass or metal pie pan or 9-inch glass or metal deep dish pie pan. Melt butter and chocolate in saucepan over low heat. Stir in remaining ingredients in order listed. Pour batter into prepared pan. Bake for 25 to 30 minutes or until brownies begin to pull away from sides of pan. Cool in pan on wire rack.

**Note:** If using Martha White All-Purpose Flour, sift 1 teaspoon baking powder and ½ teaspoon salt with flour.

## Black-Bottom Pie

*A classic, featuring a rich chocolate cream layer on the bottom, topped with a light, airy vanilla custard.*

½ cup sugar
1½ tablespoons cornstarch
2 cups milk
4 egg yolks, lightly beaten
1½ squares (1½ ounces) semisweet
  chocolate, melted
1 teaspoon vanilla
1 baked 9-inch pastry shell
  (page 124)
1 tablespoon unflavored gelatin
2 tablespoons water
4 egg whites
¼ teaspoon cream of tartar
½ cup sugar
2 teaspoons brandy extract
  Whipped cream (optional)

Stir together ½ cup sugar and cornstarch in medium saucepan; gradually stir in milk. Bring to a boil over medium heat, stirring constantly. Reduce heat to medium-low and cook for an additional 2 minutes, stirring constantly. Remove pan from heat. Gradually stir one cup hot mixture into egg yolks; return egg mixture to saucepan. Return mixture to a boil over medium-low heat and cook for 2 minutes, stirring constantly. Remove pan from heat. Add chocolate and vanilla to one cup of custard. Pour chocolate custard into pie shell; chill. Soften gelatin in water; stir into remaining hot custard and chill. Combine egg whites and cream of tartar in small mixing bowl. Beat with electric mixer on medium speed until foamy and soft peaks form. Add remaining sugar one tablespoon at a time, beating at high speed until mixture forms stiff glossy peaks and sugar is dissolved. Fold meringue into cold gelatin-custard mixture. Stir in brandy extract. Spread meringue mixture over chocolate layer and chill. Serve with whipped cream, if desired. Makes 6 to 8 servings.

## Swiss Chocolate Pie

*Adding marshmallows to the hot filling makes this pie light enough for a hot summer evening.*

1 cup sugar
½ cup Martha White All-Purpose
  Flour
¼ teaspoon salt
2 cups milk
2 squares (1 ounce each)
  unsweetened chocolate
12 large marshmallows
2 tablespoons butter or margarine
1 teaspoon vanilla

1 baked 9-inch pastry shell
(page 124)
Whipped cream (optional)

Stir together sugar, flour and salt in medium saucepan; gradually stir in milk. Bring to a boil over medium heat, stirring constantly. Reduce heat to medium-low and cook for an additional 2 minutes, stirring constantly. Add chocolate and marshmallows; cook until melted. Remove pan from heat. Stir in butter and vanilla; cool. Pour filling into pastry shell. Refrigerate until ready to serve. Top with whipped cream, if desired. Makes 6 to 8 servings.

## Georgia Boy's Peanut Butter Pie

*A rich vanilla cream pie with a Southern flair—the peanut butter crumb mixture is sprinkled in the bottom of the pie and on top of the meringue.*

½ cup sifted confectioners' sugar
¼ cup crunchy peanut butter
1 baked 9-inch pastry shell
(page 124)
⅔ cup sugar
2 tablespoons cornstarch
1 tablespoon Martha White
All-Purpose Flour
¼ teaspoon salt
2¼ cups milk
3 egg yolks, lightly beaten
1 tablespoon butter or margarine
1 teaspoon vanilla
Meringue for one 9-inch pie
(page 125)

Preheat oven to 350°F. Combine confectioners' sugar and peanut butter in small bowl. Sprinkle half the peanut butter mixture on bottom of pastry shell. Stir together sugar, cornstarch, flour and salt in medium saucepan; gradually stir in milk. Bring to a boil over medium heat, stirring constantly. Reduce heat to medium-low and cook for an additional 2 minutes, stirring constantly. Remove pan from heat. Gradually stir one cup hot mixture into egg yolks; return egg mixture to saucepan. Return mixture to a boil over medium-low heat and cook for 2 minutes, stirring constantly. Remove pan from heat; stir in butter and vanilla. Pour filling over peanut butter mixture in pastry shell. Spread meringue on hot filling, carefully sealing to edge of crust to prevent shrinking. Sprinkle remaining peanut butter mixture over meringue. Bake for 12 to 15 minutes or until light golden brown. Cool completely on wire rack before serving or refrigerating. Makes 6 to 8 servings.

## Dorothy's Caramel Pie

*The basic cooking technique of caramelizing sugar gives the pie filling its characteristic flavor.*

1¾ cups sugar, divided
½ cup sifted Martha White
  Self-Rising Flour
3 egg yolks
2 cups milk
2 tablespoons butter or margarine
1 teaspoon vanilla
1 baked 9-inch pastry shell
  (page 124)
Meringue for one 9-inch pie
  (page 125)

Preheat oven to 350°F. Stir together ¾ cup sugar and flour in medium saucepan. Beat egg yolks in small bowl; stir in milk. Gradually stir milk mixture into sugar and flour. Bring to a boil over medium heat, stirring constantly. Reduce heat to medium-low and cook an additional 2 minutes, stirring constantly. Remove pan from heat and set aside. Pour remaining 1 cup sugar into heavy skillet. Cook over medium heat until sugar melts and liquid is golden brown, stirring constantly with a wooden spoon. Stir carmelized sugar rapidly into custard. Return mixture to a boil over medium-low heat and cook 2 minutes, stirring constantly. Remove pan from heat. Stir in butter and vanilla. Pour filling into pastry shell. Spread meringue on hot filling, carefully sealing to edge of crust to prevent shrinking. Bake for 12 to 15 minutes or until light golden brown. Cool on wire rack completely before serving or refrigerating. Makes 6 to 8 servings.

## Strawberry Cream Cheese Pie

*A flavor that is the essence of springtime.*

1 quart strawberries, divided
1 cup sugar
¼ cup cornstarch
1 package (3 ounces) cream cheese,
  softened
2 teaspoons milk
1 baked 9-inch pastry shell
  (page 124)
Whipped cream (optional)

Wash, cap and drain strawberries. Mash 2 cups strawberries in medium bowl; strain juice and add water if necessary to make 1½ cups of juice. Stir together sugar and cornstarch in medium saucepan; gradually stir in strawberry juice. Bring to a boil over medium heat, stirring constantly. Reduce heat to medium-low and cook for an additional 2 minutes, stirring constantly; cool to lukewarm. Soften cream cheese by blending with milk and carefully spread over bottom of pastry shell. Top with remaining whole berries. Pour cooled juice mixture over berries and chill. Serve with whipped cream, if desired. Makes 6 to 8 servings.

## Fresh Strawberry Pie

*Reminiscent of the famous restaurant version. Sure to be a springtime favorite.*

1 cup sugar
6 tablespoons cornstarch

1 cup water
4 tablespoons strawberry-flavored gelatin
1 pint whole strawberries
1 baked 9-inch pastry shell (page 124)
Whipped cream (optional)

Stir together sugar and cornstarch in medium saucepan; gradually stir in water. Bring to a boil over medium heat, stirring constantly. Reduce heat to medium-low and cook for an additional 2 minutes, stirring constantly. Mixture should be thickened and clear. Remove from heat. Stir in gelatin until dissolved; cool to lukewarm. Wash, cap and drain strawberries. Arrange in single layer in bottom of pastry shell. Carefully pour cooled gelatin mixture over berries. Chill for several hours before serving. Serve with whipped cream, if desired. Makes 6 to 8 servings.

## Pecan Pie

*Originally reserved for those blessed with a grove of pecan trees—now a delicacy available to all.*

4 eggs
1 cup sugar
1 cup light corn syrup
½ cup (1 stick) butter or margarine, melted
1 teaspoon vanilla
1 cup pecan halves
1 unbaked 9-inch pastry shell (page 124)

Preheat oven to 350°F. Beat eggs in mixing bowl. Add sugar, corn syrup, butter and vanilla; blend well. Stir in pecans. Pour filling into pastry shell. Bake for 45 to 50 minutes or until knife inserted one inch from center comes out clean. Cover outer edges with foil to prevent overbrowning, if necessary. Do not overbake. Pie will continue to set as it cools. Cool on wire rack. Makes 6 to 8 servings.

## Miss Martha's Chess Pie

*The story goes that the name "chess" was derived from the description, "its 'just' pie" denoting the simple ingredients.*

1⅓ cups sugar
⅓ cup (5⅓ tablespoons) butter or margarine, softened
3 eggs
⅓ cup milk
1 teaspoon vanilla
1 teaspoon vinegar
1 tablespoon Martha White Self-Rising Corn Meal Mix
1 unbaked 9-inch pastry shell (page 124)

Preheat oven to 350°F. Cream sugar and butter together in mixing bowl. Add eggs one at a time, beating well after each addition. Add milk, vanilla, vinegar and corn meal; beat until blended. Pour filling into pastry shell. Bake for 40 to 45 minutes or until knife inserted one inch from center comes out clean. Do not overbake. Pie will continue to set as it cools. Cool on wire rack. Makes 6 to 8 servings.

## Pumpkin Chess Pie

*Try this combination of favorite pies for a holiday get-together.*

1⅓ cups sugar
6 tablespoons (¾ stick) butter or margarine, softened
1 cup canned pumpkin
¼ cup plus 2 tablespoons half-and-half
2 eggs
1 teaspoon vanilla
4 teaspoons Martha White Self-Rising Corn Meal Mix
½ teaspoon salt
½ teaspoon cinnamon
¼ teaspoon ginger
¼ teaspoon nutmeg
¼ teaspoon cloves
1 Press 'N' Bake Cream Cheese Crust (page 124)
Whipped cream (optional)

Preheat oven to 350°F. Cream sugar and butter together in mixing bowl with electric mixer until light and fluffy. Add remaining ingredients except crust and whipped cream; beat until well blended. Pour filling into pastry shell. Bake for 45 to 50 minutes or until knife inserted one inch from center comes out clean. Do not overbake. Pie will continue to set as it cools. Cool on wire rack. This pie is good served chilled and topped with whipped cream. Makes 6 to 8 servings.

## Chocolate Pecan Pie

*A pecan and chocolate chip temptation.*

3 eggs
1 cup sugar
¾ cup light corn syrup

¼ cup (½ stick) butter or margarine, melted
1 teaspoon vanilla
½ cup semisweet chocolate morsels
½ cup chopped pecans
1 unbaked 9-inch pastry shell (page 124)
Pecan halves (optional)

Preheat oven to 350°F. Beat eggs in mixing bowl. Add sugar, corn syrup, butter and vanilla; blend well. Stir in chocolate morsels and pecans. Pour filling into pastry shell. Arrange extra pecan halves on top, if desired. Bake for 45 to 50 minutes or until knife inserted one inch from center comes out clean. Do not overbake. Pie will continue to set as it cools. Cool on wire rack. Makes 6 to 8 servings.

## *Buttermilk Pie

*A little buttermilk lends a subtle tart flavor to this old-fashioned favorite.*

1¼ cups sugar
2 tablespoons Martha White Self-Rising Corn Meal Mix
3 eggs, lightly beaten
½ cup (1 stick) butter or margarine, melted
⅓ cup buttermilk
1 teaspoon vanilla
1 unbaked 9-inch pastry shell (page 124)

Preheat oven to 350°F. Stir together sugar and corn meal in mixing bowl.

Add eggs, butter, buttermilk and vanilla; blend well. Pour filling into pastry shell. Bake for 40 to 45 minutes or until knife inserted one inch from center comes out clean. Do not overbake. Pie will continue to set as it cools. Cool on wire rack. Makes 6 to 8 servings.

**Note:** Buttermilk Pie is wonderful when baked in a Press 'N' Bake Cream Cheese Crust (page 125). This pie is also delicious refrigerated and served cold.

## Old-Fashioned Egg Custard Pie

*Smooth and creamy, the ingredients are always on hand.*

1 unbaked 9-inch pastry shell (page 124)
4 eggs
2¼ cups milk
⅔ cup sugar
1 teaspoon vanilla
¼ teaspoon salt
Nutmeg

Preheat oven to 400°F. Bake prepared pastry shell for 5 minutes (do not prick). Cool on wire rack. Beat eggs in mixing bowl. Add milk, sugar, vanilla and salt; blend well. Pour filling into pastry shell; sprinkle with nutmeg as desired. Bake for 15 minutes. Reduce oven temperature to 325°F. Bake for 35 to 40 minutes or until knife inserted one inch from center comes out clean. Do not overbake. Cool on wire rack. Makes 6 to 8 servings.

*One of Martha White Test Kitchen's ten all-time favorite recipes.

# and now... A Message from Our Sponsor

◆

"Now you bake right (Ah Ha)—
With Martha White (Yes, Ma'am).
Goodness gracious, good and light,
Martha White.
For the finest biscuits ever wuz—
Get Martha White Self-Rising Flour,
The one all-purpose flour,
Martha White Self-Rising Flour has got Hot Rize."

It's rare for folks to enjoy a commercial . . . much less request one. But audiences everywhere, from Carnegie Hall to Tokyo, have requested the famous Martha White bluegrass jingle.

Written in the early 1950s, Martha White's popular theme song was penned for just $100 by the late Pat Twitty of Nashville. The song was immortalized by early Martha White spokesmen and Grand Ole Opry stars Earl Scruggs and Lester Flatt and is preserved on their Carnegie Hall album.

Over the years, the theme's lyrics have been adapted to advertise cornbread, cakes and pies, but it's snappy bluegrass rhythms and cheerful banjo twang have remained the same. And it continues to entertain.

## Cool and Easy Lemon Pie

*Sensational combination—tart lemon filling in a cookie-like crust that's easy to make with a muffin mix.*

1 package (7 ounces) Martha White
  Bran Muffin Mix
1 cup chopped pecans
6 tablespoons (¾ stick) butter or
  margarine, melted
1 can (14 ounces) sweetened
  condensed milk
1 can (6 ounces) frozen lemonade
  concentrate, thawed
1 carton (4 ounces) frozen whipped
  topping, softened

Preheat oven to 350°F. Combine muffin mix, pecans and butter in mixing bowl; crumble ½ cup into square baking pan. Press remaining crust mixture into a 9-inch pie pan. Bake both crust and crumbled mixture for 10 to 12 minutes or until lightly browned. Remove both from oven. Stir crumbled mixture to break into fine crumbs. Completely cool both crust and crumbs on wire racks. Combine sweetened condensed milk and lemonade in mixing bowl; fold in whipped topping. Pour filling into prepared crust. Sprinkle crumbs over pie. Chill several hours or overnight. Makes 6 to 8 servings.

# *Lemon Meringue Pie

*A refreshing ending to a spicy meal.*

        1½ cups sugar
         ⅓ cup plus 1 tablespoon cornstarch
         ¼ teaspoon salt
        1½ cups water
          3 egg yolks, lightly beaten
         ½ cup lemon juice
          3 tablespoons butter or margarine
          2 teaspoons grated lemon peel
          2 drops yellow food color (optional)
          1 baked 9-inch pastry shell
             (page 124)
            Meringue for one 9-inch pie
             (page 125)

Preheat oven to 350°F. Stir together sugar, cornstarch and salt in medium saucepan; gradually stir in water. Bring to a boil over medium heat, stirring constantly. Reduce heat to medium-low and cook an additional 2 minutes, stirring constantly. Remove pan from heat. Gradually stir one cup hot mixture into egg yolks; return egg mixture to saucepan. Return mixture to boil over medium-low heat and cook 2 minutes, stirring constantly. Remove pan from heat; stir in lemon juice, butter, lemon peel and food color, if desired. Pour filling into pastry shell. Spread meringue on hot filling, carefully sealing to edge of crust to prevent shrinking. Bake for 12 to 15 minutes or until light golden brown. Cool on wire rack completely before serving or refrigerating. Makes 6 to 8 servings.

## FRUIT FOR THOUGHT

Everyone's heard that Eve tempted Adam with one, and we all know that one a day will keep the doctor away, but how much do you really know about apples?

There are three types of apples—eating, all-purpose and cooking. When choosing an apple, consider what you will use it for. Red Delicious is a good apple just for eating. It is sweet, juicy and crisp. The Golden Delicious is the best all-purpose apple because it holds its shape when cooked and darkens slowly. Jonathans, Granny Smiths and Winesaps are the best choice for baking because of their mildly tart flavor and their firm flesh which holds its shape when cooked.

When cooking with apples, remember these helpful tips:

♦ About three medium apples make one pound.
♦ One pound of apples, when diced, will yield about three cups.
♦ It takes about two pounds of apples to make one 9-inch pie.
♦ To prevent the cut surface of an apple from browning, dip in a citrus juice (lemon or orange), salt water or an anti-browning agent.
♦ Store apples in a crisper in the refrigerator. This retains their quality, juiciness and crispness.

*One of Martha White Test Kitchen's ten all-time favorite recipes.

## French Coconut Pie

*The coconut rises to the top and bakes crisp and golden brown.*

1½ cups sugar
3 eggs, lightly beaten
½ cup (1 stick) butter or margarine, melted
1 tablespoon lemon juice
1 teaspoon vanilla
1 can (3½ ounces) flaked coconut (about 1 cup)
1 unbaked 9-inch pastry shell (page 124)

Preheat oven to 350°F. Combine sugar, eggs, butter, lemon juice and vanilla in mixing bowl; blend until smooth. Stir in coconut. Pour filling into pastry shell. Bake for 40 to 45 minutes or until knife inserted one inch from center comes out clean. Do not overbake. Cool on wire rack. Makes 6 to 8 servings.

## Lemon Rub Pie

*A little lemon juice and grated peel add zest to this chess-like pie.*

1¾ cups sugar
2 tablespoons Martha White Self-Rising Corn Meal Mix
1 tablespoon Martha White Self-Rising Flour
4 eggs
¼ cup (½ stick) butter or margarine, melted
¼ cup milk
¼ cup lemon juice

2 tablespoons grated lemon peel
1 unbaked 9-inch pastry shell (page 124)

Preheat oven to 375°F. Stir together sugar, corn meal and flour in mixing bowl. Add eggs, butter, milk, lemon juice and lemon peel; beat with electric mixer on medium speed until blended and smooth. Pour filling into pastry shell. Bake for 35 to 40 minutes or until knife inserted one inch from center comes out clean and top is very brown. Do not overbake. Cool on wire rack. Makes 6 to 8 servings.

## Old South Sweet Potato Pie

*An old-fashioned Southern favorite for the holiday dinner table.*

1⅓ cups sugar
⅓ cup (5⅓ tablespoons) butter or margarine, softened
3 eggs
1 can (17 ounces) sweet potatoes, drained and mashed
⅓ cup milk
1 teaspoon vanilla
½ teaspoon cinnamon
½ teaspoon nutmeg
¼ teaspoon salt
1 unbaked 9-inch pastry shell (page 124)

Preheat oven to 350°F. Cream sugar and butter together in mixing bowl. Add eggs one at a time, beating well after each addition. Add sweet potatoes, milk, vanilla, cinnamon, nutmeg and salt; beat until well blended. Pour filling into pastry shell. Bake for 40 to 45 minutes or until knife inserted one inch from center comes out clean. Do not overbake. Pie will continue to set as it cools. Cool on wire rack. Makes 6 to 8 servings.

## Traditional Pumpkin Pie

*Thanksgiving dinner wouldn't be complete without at least one of these pies on the sideboard.*

    2 eggs
    1 can (16 ounces) solid-pack
       pumpkin
    ¾ cup sugar
    1¾ teaspoons pumpkin pie spice
    ½ teaspoon salt
    1 can (12 to 13 ounces) evaporated
       milk or 1½ cups half-and-half
    1 unbaked 9-inch pastry shell with
       high fluted edges (page 124)
    Whipped cream (optional)

Preheat oven to 425°F. Beat eggs in mixing bowl. Add pumpkin, sugar, spice, salt and milk; blend until smooth. Pour filling into pastry shell. Bake for 15 minutes. Reduce oven temperature to 350°F. Bake for 40 to 45 minutes or until knife inserted one inch from center comes out clean. Do not overbake. Cool on wire rack. Serve with whipped cream, if desired. Makes 6 to 8 servings.

Lemon Rub Pie

# *Mom's Apple Cobbler

*Far from ordinary, this cobbler has swirls of chopped apples in rich biscuit dough and bakes up moist and tender with a crisp crust.*

½ cup (1 stick) butter or margarine
2 cups sugar
2 cups water
½ cup shortening
1½ cups sifted Martha White
    Self-Rising Flour
⅓ cup milk
2 cups peeled, finely chopped
    apples
1 teaspoon cinnamon
    Cream or ice cream (optional)

Preheat oven to 350°F. Melt butter in a 13x9x2-inch glass or metal baking dish. Heat sugar and water in medium saucepan until sugar dissolves; set aside. Cut shortening into flour with pastry blender or two knives until mixture resembles coarse crumbs. Add milk and stir with a fork only until dough leaves sides of bowl. Turn dough out onto lightly floured board or pastry cloth; knead gently just until smooth. Roll out to a 12x10x¼-inch rectangle. Stir together apples and cinnamon in mixing bowl. Sprinkle apples evenly over dough. Roll up jelly-roll style, beginning with a long side. Press edges to seal. Cut into 16 slices, each about ½ inch thick. Arrange slices in pan with melted butter. Pour sugar syrup carefully around and over rolls. (This looks like too much liquid, but the crust will absorb it.) Bake for 40 to 45 minutes or until golden brown. Cool for 15 minutes before serving. Serve warm with cream or ice cream, if desired. Makes 8 to 10 servings.

**Note:** If using Martha White All-Purpose Flour, sift 2 teaspoons baking powder and ½ teaspoon salt with flour.

# Easy Peach Cobbler

*Baked in a conventional or microwave oven, this easy dessert is a treat served warm with ice cream.*

1 can (21 ounces) peach pie filling
¼ cup chopped pecans
½ cup Martha White BixMix
2 tablespoons brown sugar
2 tablespoons milk
2 tablespoons cold butter or
    margarine, chopped
½ teaspoon vanilla
1 tablespoon granulated sugar
¼ teaspoon cinnamon
    Ice cream (optional)

Spread pie filling in a shallow ungreased 1- to 2-quart baking dish; sprinkle with pecans. Place dish on inverted saucer. Microwave on HIGH for 4 to 5 minutes or until bubbly, stirring after half the time. Combine biscuit mix, brown sugar, milk, butter and vanilla; blend well. Drop dough by spoonfuls onto pie filling to form six dumplings. Stir together sugar and cinnamon; sprinkle over dumplings. Microwave on HIGH for 3 to 5 minutes or until dumplings are almost dry, rotating dish ¼ turn every 2 minutes. Remove from oven and set dish directly on towel-covered countertop for 5 min-

*One of Martha White Test Kitchen's ten all-time favorite recipes.

utes to complete cooking. Serve warm with ice cream, if desired. Makes 4 to 6 servings.

**For Conventional Oven:**
Spread pie filling in baking dish; sprinkle with pecans. Drop dough onto pie filling to form six dumplings; sprinkle with sugar and cinnamon mixture. Bake uncovered at 400°F for 18 to 20 minutes.

## Old-Fashioned Peach Cobbler

*Pre-baked strips of flaky pastry are layered with the peach filling—the result is perfection.*

**Pastry:**

> 4 cups sifted Martha White All-Purpose Flour
> 1¼ teaspoons salt
> 1⅓ cups shortening
> ⅔ cup water

Preheat oven to 400°F. Stir together flour and salt in mixing bowl. Cut in half of shortening using pastry blender or two knives until mixture is fine and mealy. Cut in remaining shortening until mixture is consistency of small peas. Sprinkle water over the mixture; stir gently with a fork until dough leaves sides of bowl. Mixture should be moist enough to form a ball but should not be sticky. Press dough into a smooth ball. Divide dough into thirds. On lightly floured board or pastry cloth, roll out a third of the dough as thinly as possible, about ⅛-inch thick. Cut into 3x1-inch strips with floured knife or pastry wheel. Place strips on ungreased baking sheet. Bake for 8 minutes or until lightly browned. Cool on wire rack. Cover remaining dough. Prepare filling as directed.

**Filling:**

> 2 cups sugar
> 3 tablespoons Martha White All-Purpose Flour
> 7 cups (about 3 pounds) sliced fresh or frozen peaches
> 1 cup water
> ½ teaspoon almond extract
> ½ cup (1 stick) butter or margarine, divided

Reduce oven temperature to 375°F. Grease a 13x9x2-inch baking dish. Stir together sugar and flour. Add peaches, water and almond extract; stir to blend. Roll out half of the remaining dough in shape of baking dish, about ⅛-inch thick. Fit pastry into bottom and up sides of dish leaving a 1-inch overhang. Spoon half of filling into pastry shell. Dot with half the butter. Scatter baked pastry strips over filling. Spoon remaining filling over pastry strips. Dot with remaining butter. Roll out remaining dough in shape of baking dish, about ⅛-inch thick. Cut into ¾-inch wide strips with floured knife or pastry wheel. Weave strips of crust to form a lattice top. Seal and form decorative edge as desired. Bake for 50 to 60 minutes or until crust is golden brown and filling begins to bubble. Cool on wire rack. Makes 8 to 10 servings.

## Company Cobbler

*Keep frozen strawberries and a muffin mix on hand and be ready for unexpected guests.*

> 2 packages (10 ounces each) frozen sweetened strawberries, thawed
> ½ cup sugar
> 2 tablespoons cornstarch
> 3 tablespoons butter or margarine
> 1 package (7 ounces) Martha White Strawberry Muffin Mix
> ½ cup milk

Preheat oven to 425°F. Grease a shallow 2-quart baking dish. Spread strawberries evenly in prepared dish. Stir together sugar and cornstarch in small mixing bowl; sprinkle over strawberries. Dot with butter. Combine muffin mix and milk in small mixing bowl; stir just until blended. Spoon batter evenly over strawberry mixture. Bake for 20 to 25 minutes or until golden brown and bubbly. Cool on wire rack. Makes 6 to 8 servings.

## Superfast Blueberry Cobbler

*The easy batter cooks up through the berries to form a buttery-rich crust. Good enough for company.*

> ½ cup (1 stick) butter or margarine
> 1 cup sifted Martha White Self-Rising Flour
> ¾ cup sugar, divided
> ¾ cup milk
> 2 cups fresh blueberries
> ½ cup water

Preheat oven to 350°F. Melt butter in a shallow 1½-quart baking dish. Combine flour, ¼ cup sugar and milk in mixing bowl; stir to blend. Pour batter evenly over melted butter. Stir together berries, remaining ½ cup sugar and water; spoon evenly over batter. Do not stir. Bake for 45 to 50 minutes or until golden brown and bubbly. Makes 4 to 6 servings.

## Easy Cherry Cobbler

*This dumpling-topped cobbler is convenient to prepare using pie filling and biscuit mix.*

> 2 cans (21 ounces each) cherry pie filling
> 1 package (5½ ounces) Martha White BixMix
> 1 tablespoon sugar
> ¼ cup milk
> ¼ cup (½ stick) butter or margarine, melted

Preheat oven to 400°F. Grease a shallow 2-quart baking dish. Pour pie filling

Mom's Apple Cobbler (page 140)

into prepared dish. Combine remaining ingredients in mixing bowl; stir to form soft dough. Drop dough by spoonfuls onto pie filling to form dumplings. Cover with lid or foil. Bake for 20 minutes. Remove cover and bake for an additional 12 to 15 minutes or until golden brown and bubbly. Cool on wire rack. Makes 4 to 6 servings.

## Cherry Turnovers

*Easy to make with a rich biscuit dough and cherry pie filling—serve warm topped with more warm pie filling.*

> 2 cups sifted Martha White
>    Self-Rising Flour
> 3 tablespoons sugar
> ⅓ cup (5⅓ tablespoons) butter or
>    margarine, softened
> 1 egg
>    About ½ cup milk
> 1 can (21 ounces) cherry pie filling

Preheat oven to 450°F. Lightly grease baking sheet. Stir together flour and sugar in mixing bowl. Cut butter into flour mixture with pastry blender or two knives until mixture resembles coarse crumbs. Beat egg in measuring cup; add enough milk to make ⅔ cup liquid. Add milk mixture to flour mixture and stir with a fork only until dough leaves sides of bowl. Turn dough out onto lightly floured board or pastry cloth; knead gently just until smooth. Roll dough out to a 16x12x⅛-inch rectangle. Cut into twelve 4-inch squares. Place squares on prepared baking sheet. Spoon about 1 tablespoon pie filling into center of each square. Fold opposite corner over, forming a triangle. Press edges together using floured fork; prick tops with fork to vent. Bake for 10 to 12 minutes or until golden brown. Heat remaining filling and spoon over warm turnovers. Makes 12 turnovers.

**Note:** If using Martha White All-Purpose Flour, sift 1 tablespoon baking powder and ¾ teaspoon salt with flour.

### CANNED FRUITS MAKE EASY COBBLERS

**A**re you in the mood for a cobbler and there's no fresh fruit in season? The answer is canned fruit.

Water-packed fruits and canned pie fillings are the best choices for quick cobblers. Here are some things to keep in mind when using canned fruits in cobblers:

- Be sure to drain water-packed fruits unless the recipe calls for water. If so, drain the juice into a measuring cup and add enough water to make the amount called for in the recipe.
- Water-packed fruits are soft—handle with care.
- Pie filling is a convenient cobbler ingredient if a sweet, thick cobbler is what you desire. All the preparation has been done—you just pour it into a baking dish, add a topping or crust and bake.

# Blackberry Roll

*This rich pastry, rolled jelly-roll style, has a crisp crust and oozes with blackberry filling.*

**Pastry:**

>     2 cups sifted Martha White
>       All-Purpose Flour
>     2 teaspoons sugar
>     1 teaspoon salt
>     ½ cup (1 stick) butter or margarine,
>       softened
>     1 egg, beaten
>     ¼ cup milk

Stir together flour, sugar and salt in mixing bowl. Cut in butter with pastry blender or two knives until mixture resembles coarse crumbs. Add egg and milk; stir gently with a fork only until dough leaves sides of bowl. Press dough into a smooth ball. Divide in half; cover and set aside. Prepare filling.

**Filling:**

>     2 cups sugar
>     3 tablespoons flour
>     6 cups (about 2 pounds) fresh or
>       frozen blackberries
>     ½ cup (1 stick) butter or margarine,
>       divided
>     2 cups water
>     2 tablespoons sugar

Preheat oven to 375°F. Grease a 13x9x2-inch baking dish. Stir together 2 cups sugar and flour in mixing bowl; carefully fold in berries. On lightly floured board or pastry cloth, roll out half of prepared dough to a 14x10-inch rectangle. Spread half of berry mixture to within two inches of edges. Dot with half the butter. Roll up jelly-roll style, beginning with a long side. Fold ends under and carefully place roll in prepared dish. Repeat this procedure with remaining dough and berries. Cut several slits in top of each roll. Pour water into dish around rolls; sprinkle rolls with 2 tablespoons sugar. Bake for 60 to 65 minutes or until golden brown and bubbly. Makes 8 to 10 servings.

# Apple Good

*Spicy apples covered with a crisp, buttery oatmeal topping—a comforting dessert for a cold winter night.*

>     1 cup granulated sugar
>     2 tablespoons Martha White All-
>       Purpose Flour
>     ½ teaspoon cinnamon
>     6 cups peeled, chopped apples
>     ¾ cup quick-cooking or old-
>       fashioned oats
>     ¾ cup sifted Martha White
>       All-Purpose Flour
>     ¾ cup firmly packed brown sugar
>     ½ cup chopped pecans
>     ½ cup (1 stick) butter or margarine,
>       softened

Preheat oven to 350°F. Grease an 8-inch square baking pan. Stir together sugar, 2 tablespoons flour and cinnamon in large bowl. Add apples and stir gently to coat. Pour mixture into prepared pan. Combine oats, ¾ cup flour, brown sugar, pecans and butter in mixing bowl; use fingers to blend. Sprinkle crumb mixture evenly over apples.

Bake for 40 to 45 minutes or until golden brown and bubbly. Makes 4 to 6 servings.

## Apple-Mallow Crisp

*Memories of special dinners at Grandma's will come rushing back after just one spoonful.*

> 4 cups peeled, sliced tart apples
> ¼ cup raisins
> ¼ cup water
> ¾ cup Martha White All-Purpose Flour
> ½ cup sugar
> 1 teaspoon cinnamon
> ¼ teaspoon salt
> ½ cup (1 stick) butter or margarine, softened
> 1½ cups miniature marshmallows
> Vanilla ice cream (optional)

Preheat oven to 350°F. Grease a shallow 2-quart baking dish. Spread apples and raisins evenly in bottom of prepared dish; pour in water. Stir together flour, sugar, cinnamon and salt in mixing bowl. Cut butter into flour mixture using a pastry blender or two knives until mixture resembles coarse crumbs. Sprinkle crumb mixture evenly over apple mixture. Bake for 35 to 40 minutes or until light golden brown and bubbly. Remove pan from oven; move rack to highest position and turn on broiler. Sprinkle marshmallows evenly over hot mixture. Return to oven and broil for 1 minute or until marshmallows are light golden brown. Serve warm with vanilla ice cream, if desired. Makes 6 to 8 servings.

### BEAT THE HEAT WITH HOMEMADE ICE CREAM

It's difficult to think of a fun-filled summer day that isn't capped off with a bowl of fresh homemade ice cream. It's as American as baseball and apple pie.

♦ Cool the ice cream mixture before churning.

♦ It is okay to prepare an ice cream mixture for churning a day or two ahead of time—but wait to add the fruit until ready to freeze.

♦ Ice cream expands during freezing—fill freezer only ⅔ full to prevent spillover.

The texture of the ice cream is determined by the temperature of the salted ice used to freeze the mixture.

♦ Ice cream too soft? Add a little more rock salt to the crushed ice in the freezer.

♦ Ice cream too hard? Too much rock salt was added. Be sure and measure for best results (about 20 pounds of ice to 3 or 4 cups of rock salt is best for a 1-gallon freezer).

♦ Homemade ice cream will keep 1 to 2 months in the freezer.

♦ Do not refreeze partially thawed ice cream. A coarse, icy texture will result.

♦ Store the ice cream in plastic containers—not the freezing canister.

## PRETTY AS A PEACH

Luscious fresh peaches are probably best enjoyed just as they are. But as your imagination goes to work, envision an old-fashioned peach cobbler, homemade peach ice cream and a juicy peach shortcake.

Here are some tips on how to pick the best peaches:

♦ Best quality peaches are bright, velvety and fresh in appearance.
♦ The red blush does not necessarily mean the peach is ripe; the blush varies with the variety of peach.
♦ To pick a ripe peach, look for a creamy to golden background color and look for one that "gives" lightly to gentle pressure when held in your hand.
♦ Don't pinch or poke peaches to test for ripeness; they bruise easily.

*Preparation and Serving:*

♦ To peel peaches easily, dip them in boiling water for about 15 seconds, then run under cold water; pull off skins.
♦ To prevent browning of peeled or cut peaches that are not to be used immediately, sprinkle them with lemon juice or an anti-browning liquid.
♦ Peaches are classified as either freestone or cling peaches. The fruit of freestone varieties is easily removed from around the pit or seed.

## Old-Fashioned Fried Peach Pies

*Southern cooks traditionally made their fried pies with the tart apples or peaches dried after the summer harvest.*

> 1 package (7 ounces) dried peaches, chopped
> 2 cups water
> 1 cup sugar
> ¼ cup (½ stick) butter or margarine
> 1 tablespoon lemon juice
> ½ teaspoon cinnamon
> ¼ teaspoon almond extract
> 1 recipe Pastry for 2-Crust Pie (page 124)
> Vegetable oil or shortening for frying
> Confectioners' sugar (optional)

Combine peaches, water and sugar in large saucepan. Bring to a boil over medium heat. Cover, reduce heat to low and simmer for 1 hour and 30 minutes or until tender. Mash thoroughly. Stir in butter, lemon juice, cinnamon and almond extract; cool completely. Prepare pastry as directed; except—after kneading gently, divide dough into 10 equal pieces. Roll each piece into a 6-inch circle. Spoon 2 level tablespoons of filling into center of each circle. Fold top half of circle over bottom half, moistening edges very lightly to seal. Crimp edges with floured fork. In large skillet, heat ¼-inch deep oil over medium high heat to 375°F. Fry pies on one side until golden brown; turn and fry on other side. Drain on paper towels. Cool slightly before serving—filling will be hot. Sprinkle generously with

Old-Fashioned Fried Peach Pies

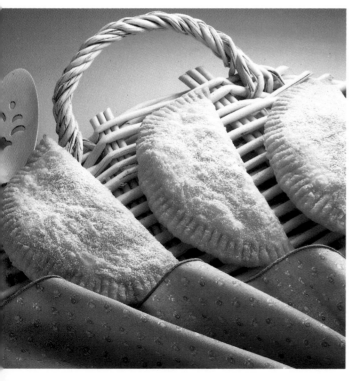

confectioners' sugar, if desired. These are best when served warm. Makes 10 pies.

## Teatime Tassies

*Tiny pecan tarts for an afternoon tea or holiday open house.*

> 1 package (3 ounces) cream cheese, softened
> ½ cup (1 stick) butter or margarine, softened
> 1 cup sifted Martha White All-Purpose Flour
> 1 egg
> ¾ cup firmly packed light brown sugar
> 1 tablespoon butter, melted
> 1 teaspoon vanilla
> ¼ teaspoon salt
> ¾ cup chopped pecans

Combine cream cheese and ½ cup butter in mixing bowl; beat well. Stir in flour until blended. Cover dough and refrigerate for 30 minutes. To prepare filling, beat egg in mixing bowl. Stir in remaining ingredients in order listed, mixing well after each addition. Preheat oven to 325°F. Remove dough from refrigerator; divide into 24 equal pieces. Press dough pieces into bottom and up sides of ungreased miniature 1⅞x⅞-inch muffin cups. Divide filling evenly among cups. Bake for 25 to 30 minutes or until crust is light golden brown. Cool in pans for 10 minutes. Carefully remove tassies from muffin cups with knife blade. Cool on wire rack. Makes 24 tassies.

Little Miss Martha demonstrates her high and light baking in this early television commercial for Martha White Corn Meal.

## Oven-Fried Apple Pies

*An updated version using pizza crust mix. These are baked, not fried.*

> 2 packages (6½ ounces each) Martha White Pizza Crust Mix
> ½ cup plus 2 tablespoons water
> ¼ cup (½ stick) butter or margarine, melted
> Dried Apple Filling, following
> Melted butter or margarine

Preheat oven to 400°F. Grease a large baking sheet. Combine pizza crust mix, water and butter in mixing bowl; stir to blend. Turn dough out onto lightly floured board or pastry cloth; knead gently just until smooth. Divide dough in half. Divide each half into 8 pieces. Roll each piece into a 5-inch circle. Spoon 1 heaping tablespoon of filling into center of each circle. Fold top half of circle over bottom half, moistening edges very lightly to seal. Crimp edges with a floured fork. Pierce top of pie with fork several times to vent. Place on prepared baking sheet. Bake for 15 to 17 minutes or until golden brown. Brush with melted butter. Cool slightly before serving—filling will be hot. These are best when served warm. Makes 16 pies.

### Dried Apple Filling

> 1 package (6 ounces) dried apples
> 2 cups water
> 1 cup sugar
> ¼ cup (½ stick) butter or margarine, melted
> 1 tablespoon lemon juice
> ½ teaspoon cinnamon
> ½ teaspoon nutmeg

Combine apples, water and sugar in large saucepan. Bring to a boil over medium heat. Cover, reduce heat to low and simmer for 1 hour or until tender. Mash thoroughly. Stir in butter, lemon juice, cinnamon and nutmeg; cool completely.

# Apple Dumplings

*Filled with sliced tart apples, these envelopes of rich pastry are laced with the goodness of cinnamon, nutmeg and butter.*

2 cups sugar
2 cups water
¼ cup (½ stick) butter or margarine
¼ teaspoon cinnamon
¼ teaspoon nutmeg
2 cups sifted Martha White All-Purpose Flour
1 teaspoon baking powder
1 teaspoon salt
¾ cup shortening
½ cup milk
3 medium Granny Smith apples, peeled and sliced
¼ cup sugar
1 teaspoon cinnamon
Vanilla ice cream (optional)

Combine sugar, water, butter, cinnamon and nutmeg in large saucepan. Cook over medium heat until sugar is dissolved and butter is melted, stirring occasionally. Do not boil. Remove from heat. Preheat oven to 350°F. Grease a 13x9x2-inch baking pan. Stir together flour, baking powder and salt in mixing bowl. Cut shortening into flour mixture with pastry blender or two knives until mixture resembles coarse crumbs. Add milk and stir with a fork only until dough leaves sides of bowl. Turn dough out onto lightly floured board or pastry cloth; knead gently just until smooth. Roll out to an 18x12x⅛-inch rectangle. Cut dough into six 6-inch squares. Toss sliced apples with sugar and cinnamon in large bowl. Divide apples evenly between pastry squares, piling apples in center of each square. Lightly moisten edges of dumplings with water; bring all four corners to center, pinching all edges to seal. Carefully place dumplings in prepared pan. Pour prepared sugar syrup around dumplings. Bake for 50 minutes or until golden brown. Serve warm with vanilla ice cream, if desired. Makes 6 dumplings.

# CAKES

It had to be whispered only once: "Be still . . . the cake will fall." Screen doors would magically cease their slamming, the porch swing would stop and the household's thundering herds of children would go out to play on tiptoes.

The power of this simple six-word phrase was in both its warning and its promise.

Its warning, along with the furrowed brow that accompanied it, suggested that somehow the cake's fall was linked to your own. In kitchen theology, the hereafter was only one fallen angel food cake away.

But the promise was far more powerful than any threat of punishment. "Be still . . . the cake will fall" conjured up images of cloud-soft coconut cakes so tall and light they almost floated . . . moist pound cakes so heavy with eggs and sugar they satisfied the deepest hunger in a soul.

It was the promise that a cake was in the making. And with cake always came lots of other good things.

Cake, of course, always followed the best meal. No self-respecting Southern cook would think of tarnishing a pure, snow-white cake with a common meal of tomato sandwiches.

Cake sometimes graced the plate with an equally tantalizing sidekick . . . fresh homemade ice cream. The ice cream recipe called for a considerable amount of cranking, but it provided a sore arm with just desserts.

And once a year there'd always be a cake ablaze with candles, a monument etched in icing to mark a birthday . . . hopefully, your own. Larger families meant more cakes per year, but smaller families meant more cake per person. No matter what size family you came from, the cake equation always added up to your advantage.

For fanciness, holidays took the cake. Fruitcakes at Christmas, heart-shaped cakes at Valentine's Day and bunny cakes at Easter designated the passing of special days with good taste.

Cake also served to sweeten our joys and lessen our sorrows. Just as a three-tiered wedding cake signaled the beginning of a new life together, a foil-covered sheet cake baked to comfort a grieving family marked the end of a life.

But perhaps the best tasting cake was the unexpected one. You came home, opened the door and there it sat on the counter . . . for no reason at all.

Cake for cake's sake.

Old-Fashioned Jam Cake with Caramel Glaze (page 158)

# Lane Cake

*The creation of a South Alabama family, distinguished by a rich raisin pecan filling that goes between the layers and on top of the cake.*

⅓ cup (5⅓ tablespoons) butter or margarine, softened
⅓ cup shortening
1¾ cups sugar
½ teaspoon vanilla
½ teaspoon lemon extract
2½ cups sifted Martha White Self-Rising Flour
⅔ cup milk
8 eggs, separated
1¼ cups sugar
½ cup (1 stick) butter or margarine
1 cup chopped pecans
1 cup raisins
¼ teaspoon salt
⅓ cup orange juice

Preheat oven to 350°F. Grease and flour two 9-inch round baking pans or two 8-inch square baking pans. Cream butter, shortening and sugar together in mixing bowl until light and fluffy. Blend in vanilla and lemon extracts. Add flour alternately with milk to creamed mixture, beginning and ending with flour. Beat egg whites in mixing bowl until stiff; gently fold into batter. Pour batter into prepared pans. Bake for 30 minutes or until cake begins to pull away from sides of pan and toothpick inserted in center comes out clean. Cool in pans for 10 minutes; remove from pans and cool on wire racks. Beat egg yolks lightly in small bowl. Combine beaten egg yolks, sugar and butter in medium saucepan. Cook over medium heat, stirring constantly, for 5 minutes or until sugar is dissolved and mixture is slightly thickened. (Do not overcook—mixture should be transparent.) Remove from heat and stir in remaining ingredients; cool completely. Spread one third of mixture between layers. Pour remaining two-thirds over top layer, letting some drizzle down sides of cake. Makes 12 to 15 servings.

# Appalachian Stack Cake

*An honest mountain original, thin spicy cake layers are stacked with tart dried apple filling—best made several days in advance.*

1 cup shortening
¾ cup molasses
¾ cup sugar
2 eggs
¼ cup buttermilk
6 cups sifted Martha White All-Purpose Flour
1 teaspoon baking soda
1 teaspoon cinnamon
1 teaspoon nutmeg
1 teaspoon ginger
Dried Apple Filling, following

Preheat oven to 350°. Cream shortening, molasses and sugar together in large mixing bowl until light and fluffy. Add eggs; beat well. Blend in buttermilk. Sift flour, soda, cinnamon, nutmeg and ginger together. Add dry ingredients to creamed mixture; beat well. Divide dough into ten equal portions. Draw an 8-inch circle (use outline of 8-inch round baking pan) on waxed paper. Roll out one portion of dough to fit circle. Slide dough and waxed paper onto baking sheet. Bake for 12 to 14 minutes or until golden brown. Slide rounds off baking sheet; remove waxed paper while still warm and place on wire racks to cool. Repeat procedure with remaining portions of dough. Stack cool layers on serving plate, spreading dried apple filling between layers. Do not spread filling over top layer. Cover tightly and store several days before serving for moistest cake and best flavor. Makes 12 to 15 servings.

### Dried Apple Filling

    8 cups dried apples
    5⅓ cups water
    1 cup sugar
    ¾ teaspoon cinnamon
    ½ teaspoon nutmeg

Combine apples, water and sugar in large saucepan. Bring to a boil over medium heat. Cover, reduce heat to low and simmer 30 minutes or until tender. Mash thoroughly. Stir in cinnamon and nutmeg; cool completely.

## Apple Dapple Cake

*Apples, coconut, dates and pecans combine to make a delicious alternative to a holiday fruit cake.*

    3 eggs
    2 cups sugar
    1 cup vegetable oil or melted
      shortening

    2 teaspoons vanilla
    3 cups sifted Martha White
      Self-Rising Flour
    1 teaspoon cinnamon
    3 cups peeled, chopped apples
    2 cups flaked coconut
    1 cup chopped dates
    1 cup chopped pecans
      Caramel Topping, below

Preheat oven to 325°F. Grease and flour a 10-inch tube pan. Beat eggs in mixing bowl. Add sugar, oil and vanilla; blend thoroughly. Stir in flour and cinnamon until well blended. Stir in apples, coconut, dates and pecans. Spoon batter into prepared pan. Bake for 1 hour and 30 minutes or until toothpick inserted one inch from edge comes out clean. Remove from oven and pour hot Caramel Topping over hot cake. Cool cake completely in pan on wire rack. Remove from pan, cover tightly and chill for easier slicing. Makes 12 to 15 servings.

**Note:** If using Martha White All-Purpose Flour, sift 1 teaspoon soda and 1 teaspoon salt with flour.

### Caramel Topping

    1 cup firmly packed brown sugar
    ½ cup (1 stick) butter or margarine
    ½ cup milk

Combine all ingredients in medium saucepan. Bring to a boil over medium heat, stirring constantly. Boil 2 minutes, stirring constantly.

## Heart Cake

*Create a sweetheart of a cake using square and round pans.*

> 1 recipe Easy Yellow Cake
> (page 160)
> Strawberry Frosting, following

Prepare Easy Yellow Cake as directed, except—pour batter into the following greased and floured baking pans: One 8-inch square and one 8-inch round or one 9-inch square and one 9-inch round. Bake as directed. After layers are cool, cut round layer in half. Place square layer on large tray as shown and place each half of the round layer on an adjoining side to form a heart shape, trimming ends of round layer to fit, if necessary. Frost with Strawberry Frosting. Makes 12 to 15 servings.

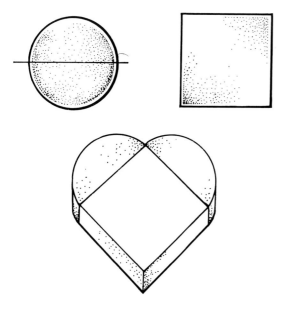

### Strawberry Frosting

> ¼ cup (½ stick) butter or margarine, softened
> 4 cups sifted confectioners' sugar (about 1 pound)
> 1 package (10 ounces) frozen sweetened strawberries, thawed

Cream butter and sugar together in mixing bowl until light and fluffy. Drain strawberries, reserving juice. Blend strawberries into creamed mixture, adding reserved juice as needed to achieve desired spreading consistency.

## Fresh Coconut Cake

*A traditional holiday favorite made the old-fashioned way—with fresh grated coconut and coconut milk poured over the baked layers.*

> 2½ cups sifted Martha White All-Purpose Flour
> 3½ teaspoons baking powder
> 1 teaspoon salt
> 1½ cups sugar
> ¾ cup shortening
> 1 cup milk, divided
> 1½ teaspoons vanilla
> 5 egg whites
> 1 fresh coconut, drained (reserving milk), peeled and grated
> White Cloud Icing, following

Preheat oven to 350°F. Grease and flour two 9-inch round baking pans or two 8-inch square baking pans. Sift flour,

Heart Cake with Strawberry Frosting

baking powder and salt together into mixing bowl. Add sugar, shortening, ¾ cup milk and vanilla to flour mixture. Beat with electric mixer on low speed for 30 seconds, scraping bowl constantly. Turn mixer to medium speed and beat for 2 minutes, scraping bowl often. Add remaining ¼ cup milk and egg whites. Beat on high speed for 2 minutes, scraping bowl often. Pour batter into prepared pans. Bake for 30 to 35 minutes or until cake begins to pull away from sides of pan and toothpick inserted in center comes out clean. Cool in pans for 10 minutes; remove from pans and cool completely on wire racks. Punch holes in surface of layers with toothpick and pour reserved coconut milk over layers. Spread White Cloud Icing between layers. Spread sides and top of cake with remaining icing. Sprinkle top and sides of cake with generous amounts of grated coconut. This is best if covered loosely and stored in a cool place for one day before serving. Makes 12 to 15 servings.

## White Cloud Icing

- 1½ cups sugar
- ¼ teaspoon cream of tartar
- ⅛ teaspoon salt
- ⅓ cup water
- 3 egg whites, at room temperature
- 1 teaspoon vanilla

Combine sugar, cream of tartar, salt and water in heavy medium-size saucepan. Cook over medium heat, stirring constantly until clear. Cook without stirring to soft-ball stage (240°F). Beat egg whites in large metal or glass mixing bowl until soft peaks form. Continue beating and gradually pour in hot syrup mixture. Blend in vanilla and continue beating until stiff peaks form and icing is thick enough to spread.

## Christmas Tree Cake

*Let the kids decorate this holiday cut-out.*

   1 recipe Easy Yellow Cake (page
     160)
   1 recipe Creamy Butter Icing,
     following
  12 peppermint sticks
     Green crystal sugars
     Red candies

Cut cooled cake as shown in diagram.
Arrange cake pieces A and B to form a
triangle equal to cake piece C on one
tray. Place cake piece C on another tray.
Frost both cakes with Creamy Butter
Icing, making strokes through frosting
to resemble tree branches. Sprinkle
cakes with green sugar. Insert 6 peppermint sticks in end of each cake to make
tree trunks. Decorate with red candies
to make ornaments for the trees. Makes
2 cakes.

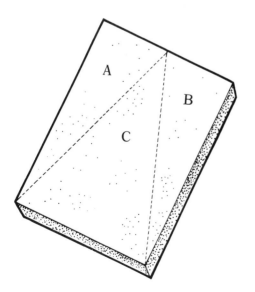

### Creamy Butter Icing

   3 cups sifted confectioners' sugar
  ⅓ cup butter or margarine, softened
   3 tablespoons milk
 1½ teaspoons vanilla

Combine all ingredients; blend until
smooth.

## Banana Sheet Cake

*Bananas that are too ripe to eat are perfect
for baking. They make this cake moist and
flavorful.*

Use recipe for Banana Cake with Chocolate Whipped Cream recipe (page 161).
Prepare batter as directed, except—
pour batter into a greased and floured
13x9x2-inch baking pan. Bake at 350°F
for 50 to 55 minutes or until cake begins to pull away from sides of pan and
toothpick inserted in center comes out
clean. Cool in pan on wire rack. Spread
with Banana Frosting, below. Makes 12
to 15 servings.

### Banana Frosting

  ¼ cup (½ stick) butter or margarine,
     softened
  ½ cup mashed ripe banana
     (about 1 large)
   1 teaspoon lemon juice
   4 cups sifted confectioners' sugar
     (about 1 pound)

Cream butter in mixing bowl until
fluffy. Stir in banana and lemon juice.
Gradually beat in sugar until frosting is
of spreading consistency.

# What Does It Mean When It Says . . .

In cake baking, there are certain phrases in recipes that can be confusing to the inexperienced cook, as well as the seasoned one.

These terms describe a procedure or method that usually affects the outcome of the finished product. Here are some simplified explanations of the more common phrases.

What does it mean when it says . . .

- *Grease and flour the pan?* Use a pastry brush, paper towel or waxed paper to apply vegetable shortening evenly and generously to bottom and sides of pan. (Do not use oil, butter or margarine to grease pans.) Add a little flour to greased pan and shake to coat bottom and sides. Invert pan and tap gently to remove excess flour.

- *Add liquid and dry ingredients alternately?* To keep the creamed mixture light and fluffy, the remaining ingredients are added a little at a time. Beginning and ending with the dry ingredients, a small amount of the flour mixture is added and blended in. Then a small amount of the liquid ingredient is added and blended in. This continues until both ingredients are used. This keeps the batter light and airy.

- *Cool on a wire rack?* Racks raise the food up off the counter and allow air to circulate around the cake. The cake cools much faster and no moisture forms on the bottom. Wire racks are recommended because they are heatproof and serve many purposes. When a recipe recommends cooling in pan, remove cake from oven and place pan on wire rack. Other recipes will recommend cooling in pan for a few minutes before turning out to cool completely. In this case, remove cake from oven and place pan on wire rack for recommended time. Loosen edges of cake gently. Invert another rack over the pan. Invert as a unit; cake should fall out of pan onto rack. Remove pan. Replace inverted rack over cake bottom and invert as a unit again so that the top side is up. Remove top rack. Let cake cool completely before frosting.

## Carrot Pineapple Nut Cake

*Moist and rich topped with cream cheese icing—take to a family gathering and get rave reviews.*

4 eggs
2 cups sugar
1½ cups vegetable oil or melted shortening
2 cups sifted Martha White Self-Rising Flour
2 teaspoons cinnamon
2 cups finely grated carrots
1 can (8¼ ounces) crushed pineapple, undrained
¾ cup chopped pecans
Cream Cheese Frosting, following
Ground nutmeg (optional)

Preheat oven to 325°F. Grease and flour a 13x9x2-inch baking pan. Beat eggs in large mixing bowl. Add sugar and oil; beat until well blended. Stir in flour and cinnamon; blend thoroughly. Stir in carrots, undrained pineapple and pecans. Pour batter into prepared pan. Bake for 55 to 60 minutes or until cake begins to pull away from sides of pan and toothpick inserted in center comes out clean. Cool in pan on wire rack. Spread with Cream Cheese Frosting. Sprinkle with nutmeg, if desired. Makes 12 to 15 servings.

**Note:** If using Martha White All-Purpose Flour, sift 1 tablespoon baking powder and ¾ teaspoon salt with flour.

**Cream Cheese Frosting**

1 package (8 ounces) cream cheese, softened
½ cup (1 stick) butter or margarine, softened
4 cups sifted confectioners' sugar (about 1 pound)
2 teaspoons vanilla

Beat cream cheese and butter together in mixing bowl. Gradually stir in sugar until smooth. Add vanilla; blend thoroughly.

## Old-Fashioned Jam Cake

*Scaled down to make two layers and topped with an easy caramel glaze, this holiday favorite is just as good as Grandma's.*

½ cup (1 stick) butter or margarine, softened
1 cup sugar
3 eggs
½ teaspoon vanilla
1½ cups sifted Martha White All-Purpose Flour
½ teaspoon allspice

½ teaspoon cinnamon
½ teaspoon cloves
½ teaspoon baking soda
¼ teaspoon salt
½ cup buttermilk
1 cup blackberry jam
½ cup strawberry preserves
½ cup raisins
½ cup chopped black walnuts
  Caramel Glaze, following
  Thin orange wedges (optional)
  Light brown sugar (optional)

Carrot Pineapple Nut Cake

Preheat oven to 325°F. Grease bottoms of two 8-inch square or two 8-inch round cake pans. Line bottoms of pans with waxed paper. Grease and flour waxed paper and sides of pans. Cream butter and sugar together in mixing bowl until light and fluffy. Add eggs one at a time, beating well after each addition. Blend in vanilla. Sift flour, spices, soda and salt together in medium bowl. Add flour mixture, buttermilk, jam and preserves to creamed mixture. Beat with electric mixer on medium speed for 2 minutes, scraping bowl often. Stir in raisins and walnuts. Pour batter into prepared pans. Bake for 45 to 50 minutes or until cake begins to pull away from sides of pan and toothpick inserted in center comes out clean. Cool in pans for 10 minutes; remove from pans and cool completely on wire racks. Place one layer on serving plate; pour about ⅓ of warm Caramel Glaze over layer. Top with remaining layer and pour remainder of glaze over surface of cake. Garnish with thin orange wedges sprinkled with brown sugar just before serving, if desired. For best results, cover tightly and store for two days to one week before slicing. Do not refrigerate; however, the cake may be frozen. Makes 12 to 15 servings.

**Note:** Old-Fashioned Jam Cake may be prepared in a greased and floured 13x9x2-inch baking pan (do not use waxed paper). Cool cake in pan on wire rack and pour glaze over surface.

### Caramel Glaze

¼ cup (½ stick) butter or margarine
½ cup firmly packed dark brown
  sugar
¼ cup milk
2 cups sifted confectioners' sugar
1 teaspoon vanilla

Melt butter in saucepan over medium-low heat. Stir in brown sugar. Cook and stir 2 minutes. Add milk and continue cooking until mixture boils, stirring constantly. Remove from heat; gradually stir in confectioners' sugar. Blend in vanilla. If glaze gets too thick, add a little more milk.

# First Prize Chocolate Cake

*This moist chocolate layer cake with rich chocolate icing will make any occasion a celebration.*

½ cup (1 stick) butter or margarine
4 squares (1 ounce each)
  unsweetened chocolate
2 eggs
1¾ cups buttermilk
2 teaspoons vanilla
2½ cups sifted Martha White
  Self-Rising Flour
2 cups sugar
  Dark Chocolate Frosting,
  following

Preheat oven to 350°F. Grease and flour two 8-inch square baking pans or two 9-inch round baking pans. Combine butter and chocolate in small saucepan. Melt over low heat; remove pan from heat and set mixture aside to cool. Beat eggs in mixing bowl with electric mixer for about 2 minutes on medium speed. Blend in buttermilk and vanilla. Add flour and sugar to buttermilk mixture; beat until well blended. Stir in chocolate mixture. Pour batter into prepared pans. Bake for 30 to 35 minutes or until cake begins to pull away from sides of pan and toothpick inserted in center comes out clean. Cool in pans for 10 minutes; remove from pans and cool completely on wire racks. Spread Dark Chocolate Frosting between layers. Spread sides and top of cake with remaining frosting. Makes 12 to 15 servings.

**Note:** If using Martha White All-Purpose Flour, sift 3¾ teaspoons baking powder and 1 teaspoon salt with flour.

## Dark Chocolate Frosting

½ cup (1 stick) butter or margarine
4 squares (1 ounce each)
  unsweetened chocolate
4 cups sifted confectioners' sugar
  (about 1 pound)
½ cup evaporated milk
¼ teaspoon salt
2 teaspoons vanilla

Combine butter and chocolate in medium saucepan. Melt over low heat; remove pan from heat. Gradually blend in sugar, milk, salt and vanilla. Beat until smooth.

# Easy Yellow Cake

*All ingredients go in the bowl together for easy mixing. This versatile cake may be served frosted or plain when accompanied by fresh fruit or a sauce.*

2 cups sifted Martha White
  All-Purpose Flour
2 teaspoons baking powder
¾ teaspoon salt
1½ cups sugar
⅓ cup shortening
⅓ cup (5⅓ tablespoons) butter or
  margarine, softened
¾ cup milk
1 teaspoon vanilla
3 eggs

Preheat oven to 350°F. Grease and flour a 13x9x2-inch baking pan. Sift flour, baking powder and salt together into mixing bowl. Add remaining ingredients to flour mixture. Beat with electric mixer on low speed for 30 seconds, scraping bowl constantly. Turn mixer to high speed and beat for 3 minutes, scraping bowl often. Pour batter into prepared pan. Bake for 25 to 30 minutes or until cake begins to pull away from sides of pan and toothpick inserted in center comes out clean. Cool in pan on wire rack and serve as desired. Makes 12 to 15 servings.

## Banana Cake with Chocolate Whipped Cream

*Easy-to-make chocolate whipped cream is a delectable complement to this moist banana cake.*

    1 cup shortening
    2 cups sugar
    3 eggs
    2 cups mashed bananas
      (about 4 large)
    1 teaspoon vanilla
    3 cups sifted Martha White
      All-Purpose Flour
    1 teaspoon baking soda
    1 teaspoon salt
    ½ cup buttermilk
    1 cup chopped pecans
      Chocolate Whipped Cream,
        following
    2 medium bananas
      Lemon juice
    ½ cup coarsely chopped pecans

Preheat oven to 350°F. Grease and flour two 8-inch square or two 9-inch round baking pans. Cream shortening and sugar together in mixing bowl until light and fluffy. Add eggs one at a time, beating well after each addition. Blend in bananas and vanilla. Sift flour, soda and salt together; add to creamed mixture alternately with buttermilk, beginning and ending with flour mixture. Stir in 1 cup pecans. Pour batter into prepared pans. Bake for 30 to 35 minutes or until cake begins to pull away from sides of pan and toothpick inserted in center comes out clean. Cool in pans for 10 minutes; remove from pans and cool on wire racks. Place bottom layer on serving plate; spread with half of the Chocolate Whipped Cream. Slice bananas and dip slices in lemon juice. Place half of the banana slices in a ring around edge of bottom layer. Cover with top layer of cake; spread with remaining Chocolate Whipped Cream. Garnish with remaining banana slices and ½ cup chopped pecans. Keep refrigerated until serving time. Makes 12 to 15 servings.

### Chocolate Whipped Cream

    1 cup semisweet or milk chocolate
      morsels
    1 cup (8 ounces) whipping cream

Melt chocolate morsels in small saucepan over low heat; set aside to cool. In chilled mixing bowl using electric mixer on high speed, whip cream until stiff. Gently fold in cooled chocolate until blended.

Banana Cake with Chocolate Whipped Cream (page 161)

## Orange Cake

*A filling made with orange juice and peel lends a special touch to this holiday favorite.*

¾ cup (1½ sticks) butter or
    margarine, softened
1¼ cups sugar
 8 egg yolks
 1 teaspoon vanilla
 ½ teaspoon orange extract
 2 cups sifted Martha White
    All-Purpose Flour
 1 teaspoon baking powder
 ¼ teaspoon baking soda
 ¼ teaspoon salt
 ¾ cup buttermilk
    Orange Filling, following
    Cream Cheese Icing, following

Preheat oven to 350°F. Grease and flour two 9-inch round baking pans or two 8-inch square baking pans. Cream butter and sugar together in mixing bowl until light and fluffy. Add egg yolks one at a time, beating well after each addition. Blend in vanilla and orange extracts. Sift flour, baking powder, soda and salt together; add to creamed mixture alternately with buttermilk, beginning and ending with flour mixture. Mix well after each addition. Pour batter into prepared pans. Bake for 30 minutes or until cake begins to pull away from sides of pan and toothpick inserted in center comes out clean. Cool in pans for 10 minutes; remove from pans and cool on wire racks. Spread Orange Filling between layers. Spread sides and top of cake with Cream Cheese Icing. Makes 12 to 15 servings.

**Note:** Orange Cake may be prepared in a greased and floured 13x9x2-inch cake pan. Bake as directed. Omit Orange Filling and spread with Cream Cheese Icing.

### Orange Filling

¾ cup sugar
 3 tablespoons cornstarch
 ¼ teaspoon salt
 ⅔ cup water
 ½ cup orange juice
 1 tablespoon grated orange peel
 2 tablespoons butter or margarine

Combine sugar, cornstarch, salt, water, orange juice and orange peel in saucepan. Bring to a boil, stirring constantly; cook 1 minute. Remove from heat and stir in butter. Chill before spreading between cake layers.

## Cream Cheese Icing

    2 packages (3 ounces each) cream
      cheese, softened
    ¼ cup (½ stick) butter or margarine,
      softened
    4 cups sifted confectioners' sugar
      (about 1 pound)
    ½ teaspoon orange extract
    1 teaspoon grated orange peel

Beat cream cheese and butter together in mixing bowl. Gradually stir in sugar until smooth. Add orange extract and orange peel; blend thoroughly.

## German Chocolate Cake

*The combination of delicate sweet chocolate and coconut topping have made this cake a classic.*

    1 package (4 ounces) German sweet
      chocolate
    ½ cup water
    1 cup (2 sticks) butter or margarine,
      softened
    2 cups sugar
    4 eggs
    1 teaspoon vanilla
    2½ cups sifted Martha White
      Self-Rising Flour
    1 cup milk
      German Coconut Topping,
        following

Preheat oven to 350°F. Grease and flour three 9-inch round baking pans. Combine chocolate and water in small saucepan. Melt over low heat, stirring to blend. Remove pan from heat and set mixture aside to cool. Cream butter and sugar together in mixing bowl until light and fluffy. Add eggs one at a time, beating well after each addition. Blend in vanilla. Add flour to creamed mixture alternately with milk, beginning and ending with flour. Mix well after each addition. Stir in melted chocolate mixture. Pour batter into prepared pans. Bake for 40 to 45 minutes or until cake begins to pull away from sides of pan and toothpick inserted in center comes out clean. Cool in pans for 10 minutes. Remove from pans and cool on wire racks. Spread German Coconut Topping between layers and on top of cake. Makes 12 to 15 servings.

**Note:** If using Martha White All-Purpose Flour, sift 1 tablespoon plus ¾ teaspoon baking powder and 1 teaspoon salt with flour.

## German Coconut Topping

    1 cup sugar
    1 cup evaporated milk
    ½ cup (1 stick) butter or margarine
    3 egg yolks
    1 can (3½ ounces) flaked coconut
      (about 1 cup)
    1 cup chopped pecans
    1 teaspoon vanilla

Combine sugar, milk, butter and egg yolks in medium saucepan. Cook and stir over medium heat for 12 minutes, or until thickened. Stir in coconut, pecans and vanilla. Beat with electric mixer on medium speed until thick enough to spread.

## CAKE SECRETS AND SHORTCUTS

**H**ere are a few cake-related secrets:

♦ To cut a sheet cake neatly, use a two-foot piece of sewing thread. Hold thread tightly stretched and draw the straight thread down through the cake.

♦ Cakes do best if baked in the size pan recommended in the recipe. However, if the correct pan is not available or a special shaped pan is to be used, fill pans only half full of batter.

♦ Shiny metal pans make a tender cake with a light brown crust because the pan reflects the heat. If you have dark pans, reduce oven temperature 25 degrees.

♦ Place pans in the middle of the oven for even browning. Layer pans should not touch and there should be at least one inch of space all the way around pans.

♦ Store plain cakes or cakes frosted with butter-cream type frosting in a cake keeper or under an inverted bowl. Refrigerate cakes with whipped cream or cream cheese frosting. Cakes with fluffy cooked frosting should be eaten the same day they are made.

♦ Plain or butter-cream frosted cakes freeze well. Unfrosted cakes will keep 4 to 6 months in the freezer; frosted cakes will keep 2 to 3 months. Freezing cakes with cooked frosting is not recommended.

# Aunt E.C.'s Pound Cake

*The original pound cake derived its name from the ingredients used to prepare it—a pound each of butter, sugar, eggs and flour. This version uses those same simple ingredients.*

    2 cups (4 sticks) butter or
      margarine, softened
    3½ cups sugar
    10 large or 12 small eggs
    4 cups sifted Martha White
      All-Purpose Flour

Preheat oven to 325°F. Grease and flour a 10-inch tube pan. Cream butter and sugar together in large mixing bowl until light and fluffy. Add eggs one at a time, beating well after each addition. Gradually add flour, beating until well blended. Spoon batter into prepared pan. Bake for 1 hour and 40 minutes or until toothpick inserted one inch from edge comes out clean. Cool in pan for 10 minutes; turn out onto wire rack and cool completely. Makes 12 to 15 servings.

# Chocolate Pound Cake

*A pound cake that's chocolate—irresistible.*

    1 cup (2 sticks) butter or margarine,
      softened
    ½ cup shortening
    3 cups sugar
    5 eggs
    1½ teaspoons vanilla
    3 cups sifted Martha White
      All-Purpose Flour
    ½ cup cocoa

½ teaspoon salt
½ teaspoon baking powder
½ cup milk

Preheat oven to 325°F. Grease and flour a 10-inch tube pan. Cream butter, shortening and sugar together in mixing bowl until light and fluffy. Add eggs one at a time, beating well after each addition. Blend in vanilla. Sift flour, cocoa, salt and baking powder together; add to creamed mixture alternately with milk, beginning and ending with flour mixture. Mix well after each addition. Spoon batter into prepared pan. Bake for 1 hour and 30 minutes or until toothpick inserted one inch from edge comes out clean. Cool in pan for 10 minutes; turn out onto wire rack and cool completely. Makes 12 to 15 servings.

## Chocolate Chocolate Chip Pound Cake

*A chocolate lover's dream—chocolate pound cake with chocolate morsels—drizzled with a chocolate glaze.*

½ cup (1 stick) butter or margarine, softened
½ cup shortening
2 cups sugar
6 eggs
1 teaspoon vanilla
3 cups sifted Martha White All-Purpose Flour
½ teaspoon salt
¼ teaspoon baking soda
1 cup (8 ounces) dairy sour cream
1 package (6 ounces) semisweet chocolate morsels

1 package (4 ounces) German sweet chocolate, melted
Shiny Chocolate glaze, below

Preheat oven to 325°F. Grease and flour a 10-inch tube pan or 12-cup bundt pan. Cream butter, shortening and sugar together in mixing bowl until light and fluffy. Add eggs one at a time, beating well after each addition. Blend in vanilla. Sift flour, salt and soda together; add to creamed mixture alternately with sour cream, beginning and ending with flour mixture. Mix well after each addition. Stir in chocolate morsels and melted chocolate. Spoon batter into prepared pan. Bake for 1 hour and 15 minutes or until toothpick inserted one inch from edge comes out clean. Cool in pan for 5 minutes; turn out onto wire rack and cool completely. Drizzle with Shiny Chocolate Glaze. Makes 12 to 15 servings.

### Shiny Chocolate Glaze

¼ cup (½ stick) butter or margarine
2 squares (1 ounce each) semisweet chocolate
⅓ cup sugar
¼ cup milk
2 teaspoons cornstarch
1 teaspoon vanilla

Combine butter and chocolate in small saucepan. Melt over low heat, stirring often. Add sugar and blend well. Stir milk into cornstarch until dissolved; add to chocolate mixture. Bring to a boil over medium heat, stirring constantly. Cook and stir 2 minutes longer. Remove from heat; blend in vanilla.

## Brown Sugar Pound Cake

*This cake has a homespun flavor enhanced by a caramel glaze.*

>    1 cup (2 sticks) butter or margarine, softened
> ½ cup shortening
> 2¼ cups firmly packed light brown sugar (about 1 pound)
> ½ cup granulated sugar
>    5 eggs
>    2 teaspoons vanilla
>    3 cups sifted Martha White All-Purpose Flour
> ½ teaspoon baking powder
> ¼ teaspoon salt
>    1 cup milk
>    1 cup chopped pecans
>       Caramel Glaze, below

Preheat oven to 350°F. Grease and flour a 10-inch tube pan. Cream butter, shortening and sugars together in mixing bowl until light and fluffy. Add eggs one at a time, beating well after each addition. Blend in vanilla. Sift flour, baking powder and salt together; add to creamed mixture alternately with milk, beginning and ending with flour mixture. Mix well after each addition. Stir in pecans. Spoon batter into prepared pan. Bake for 1 hour and 15 minutes or until toothpick inserted one inch from edge comes out clean. Cool in pan for 10 minutes; turn out onto wire rack and cool completely. Drizzle with Caramel Glaze, if desired. Makes 12 to 15 servings.

**Caramel Glaze**

> ¼ cup (½ stick) butter or margarine
> ½ cup firmly packed brown sugar
> ¼ cup milk
>    2 cups sifted confectioners' sugar
>    1 teaspoon vanilla

Melt butter in small saucepan over medium-low heat. Stir in brown sugar; cook for 2 minutes, stirring constantly. Add milk and continue cooking until mixture boils, stirring constantly. Remove from heat; gradually stir in confectioners' sugar. Add vanilla; stir until smooth.

## *Cream Cheese Pound Cake

*The richness of cream cheese makes this moist cake so delectable, it's wonderful served plain.*

> 1½ cups (3 sticks) butter or margarine, softened
>    1 package (8 ounces) cream cheese, softened
>    3 cups sugar
>    6 eggs
> 1½ teaspoons vanilla
>    3 cups sifted Martha White All-Purpose Flour
> ¼ teaspoon salt
>       Confectioners' sugar (optional)

Preheat oven to 325°F. Grease and flour a 10-inch tube pan or 12-cup bundt pan. Beat butter and cream cheese together in mixing bowl until well blended. Add sugar to mixture and cream until light and fluffy. Add eggs one at a time, beating well after each addition. Blend in vanilla. Sift flour

*One of Martha White Test Kitchen's ten all-time favorite recipes.

Cream Cheese Pound Cake

and salt together; blend into creamed mixture. Spoon batter into prepared pan. Bake for 1 hour and 15 minutes or until toothpick inserted one inch from edge comes out clean. Cool in pan for 5 minutes; turn out onto wire rack and cool completely. Dust with confectioners' sugar, if desired. Makes 12 to 15 servings.

## Sour Cream Pound Cake

*Beautifully textured, moist and rich—you may not be able to wait for it to cool.*

    1 **cup (2 sticks) butter or margarine, softened**
    3 **cups sugar**
    6 **eggs**
    2 **teaspoons vanilla**
    ½ **teaspoon almond extract**
    3 **cups sifted Martha White All-Purpose Flour**

    ¼ **teaspoon salt**
    ¼ **teaspoon baking soda**
    1 **cup (8 ounces) dairy sour cream**
    **Confectioners' sugar (optional)**

Preheat oven to 325°F. Grease and flour a 10-inch tube pan or 12-cup bundt pan. Cream butter and sugar together in mixing bowl until light and fluffy. Add eggs one at a time, beating well after each addition. Blend in vanilla and almond extracts. Sift flour, salt and soda together; add to creamed mixture alternately with sour cream, beginning and ending with flour mixture. Mix well after each addition. Spoon batter into prepared pan. Bake for 1 hour and 15 minutes or until toothpick inserted one inch from edge comes out clean. Cool in pan for 10 minutes; turn out onto wire rack and cool completely. Dust with confectioners' sugar, if desired. Makes 12 to 15 servings.

## Almond Butter-Crusted Pound Cake

*When turned out of the pan, the buttery almond crust becomes a golden top layer on this elegant little loaf cake.*

**Crust:**

⅓ cup (5⅓ tablespoons) butter or margarine, softened
½ cup firmly packed light brown sugar
½ cup Martha White All-Purpose Flour
1 cup blanched slivered almonds, toasted and chopped*

Grease a 9x5x3-inch loaf pan. Cream butter and sugar together in mixing bowl until light and fluffy. Stir in flour and almonds; blend thoroughly. Press mixture evenly into bottom of prepared pan.

*To toast almonds, spread on baking sheet. Bake for 8 minutes at 325°F.

**Cake:**

⅓ cup (5⅓ tablespoons) butter or margarine, softened
1 package (3 ounces) cream cheese, softened
½ cup sugar
2 eggs
2 teaspoons vanilla
1 cup sifted Martha White All-Purpose Flour
½ teaspoon baking powder
¼ teaspoon salt
¼ cup milk

Preheat oven to 325°F. Cream butter, cream cheese and sugar together in mixing bowl until light and fluffy. Add eggs one at a time, beating well after each addition. Blend in vanilla. Sift flour, baking powder and salt together; add to creamed mixture alternately with milk, beginning and ending with flour mixture. Mix well after each addition. Pour batter over crust in pan. Bake for 1 hour or until toothpick inserted in center comes out clean. Cool in pan for 10 minutes. Turn out onto wire rack, crust side up, and cool completely. Makes 10 to 12 servings.

## Old-Fashioned Buttermilk Pound Cake

*A light-textured pound cake—good served with seasonal fresh fruit.*

½ cup (1 stick) butter or margarine
½ cup shortening
2 cups sugar
5 eggs
2½ teaspoons vanilla
3 cups sifted Martha White All-Purpose Flour
½ teaspoon salt
½ teaspoon baking powder
½ teaspoon baking soda
1 cup buttermilk

Preheat oven to 325°F. Grease and flour a 10-inch tube pan. Cream butter, shortening and sugar together in mixing bowl until light and fluffy. Add eggs one at a time, beating well after each addition. Blend in vanilla. Sift flour, salt, baking powder and soda together;

add to creamed mixture alternately with buttermilk, beginning and ending with flour mixture. Mix well after each addition. Spoon batter into prepared pan. Bake for 1 hour and 15 minutes or until toothpick inserted one inch from edge comes out clean. Cool in pan for 10 minutes; turn out onto wire rack and cool completely. Makes 12 to 15 servings.

## ★ Tennessee Ernie Ford ★

Tennessee Ernie Ford is one of America's most beloved performers. He has entertained overseas as well as across the United States with his music and homespun humor. Sales on his religious albums have surpassed 20 million copies. His 1955 recording of "Sixteen Tons" is a classic and has sold more than four million copies. A native of East Tennessee, Ford has been a spokesperson for Martha White since 1970.

### MAMA FORD'S APPLESAUCE CAKE

- 3 cups boiling water
- 1 pound seedless raisins
- 5 cups sifted Martha White All-Purpose Flour
- 2 teaspoons baking soda
- 1 teaspoon baking powder
- 1 tablespoon cinnamon
- 1 teaspoon cloves
- ½ teaspoon salt
- 1 cup (2 sticks) butter or margarine, softened
- 3 cups firmly packed light brown sugar
- 2 cups applesauce
- 1 cup chopped black walnuts

Preheat oven to 325°F. Grease and flour a 10-inch tube pan. Pour boiling water over raisins in medium bowl; let stand while mixing cake, stirring occasionally. Sift flour, soda, baking powder, cinnamon, cloves and salt together in large bowl. In large mixing bowl, cream butter until fluffy. Add brown sugar and applesauce; beat until smooth and light. Gradually blend in flour mixture and mix just until no dry ingredients are visible. Drain raisins. Fold raisins and walnuts into batter. Spoon batter into prepared pan. Bake for 1 hour and 45 minutes or until toothpick inserted one inch from edge comes out clean. Cool cake completely in pan. Remove cooled cake from pan and wrap tightly. This cake is best if allowed to sit several days before slicing. Makes 12 to 15 servings.

# Sugar Plum Pudding

*An old-fashioned prune cake—moist and spicy with a buttermilk glaze.*

  2 cups sifted Martha White
    Self-Rising Flour
1½ cups sugar
  1 teaspoon allspice
  1 teaspoon cinnamon
  1 teaspoon nutmeg
  3 eggs
  1 cup buttermilk
  ¾ cup vegetable oil
  1 teaspoon vanilla
  1 cup finely chopped cooked prunes
  1 cup chopped pecans
    Glaze, below

Preheat oven to 325°F. Grease and flour a 13x9x2-inch baking pan. Sift flour, sugar, allspice, cinnamon and nutmeg together into large mixing bowl. Beat eggs in separate bowl; stir in buttermilk, oil and vanilla. Add buttermilk mixture to dry ingredients, stirring just until blended. Add prunes and pecans; blend thoroughly. Pour batter into prepared pan. Bake for 35 to 40 minutes or until cake begins to pull away from sides of pan. Pour hot Glaze over hot cake. Cool in pan on wire rack. Makes 12 to 15 servings.

**Note:** If using Martha White All-Purpose Flour, sift 1 tablespoon baking powder and ¾ teaspoon salt with flour.

### Glaze

½ cup (1 stick) butter or margarine
1 cup sugar
½ cup buttermilk
1 tablespoon light corn syrup
1 teaspoon vanilla

Combine all ingredients in medium saucepan. Bring to a boil over medium heat, stirring constantly, until butter is melted.

# Spiced Pound Cake

*Just a touch of mace or nutmeg for an old-fashioned flavor—wonderful served with fresh summer peaches.*

1½ cups (3 sticks) butter or
    margarine, softened
  4 cups sifted confectioners' sugar
    (about 1 pound)
  6 eggs
  1 teaspoon vanilla
  ½ teaspoon almond extract
3½ cups sifted Martha White
    All-Purpose Flour
  ¼ teaspoon mace or nutmeg
  ¼ teaspoon salt
  ⅔ cup milk

Preheat oven to 325°F. Grease and flour a 10-inch tube pan or 12-cup bundt pan. Cream butter and sugar together in mixing bowl until light and fluffy. Add eggs one at a time, beating well after each addition. Blend in vanilla and almond extracts. Sift flour, mace or nutmeg and salt together; add to creamed mixture alternately with milk, beginning and ending with flour mixture. Mix well after each addition. Spoon batter into prepared pan. Bake for 1 hour and 15 minutes or until toothpick inserted one inch from edge comes out clean. Cool in pan for 10 minutes; turn out onto wire rack and cool completely. Makes 12 to 15 servings.

## Chess Cake

*Don't be surprised—this cake will rise and fall, producing a moist pudding-like consistency.*

 1 cup (2 sticks) butter or margarine
 1 pound (16 ounces) brown sugar
 ¾ cup granulated sugar
 1½ teaspoons vanilla
 4 eggs, lightly beaten
 2 cups sifted Martha White
    Self-Rising Flour

 1 cup chopped pecans
  Confectioners' sugar

Preheat oven to 350°F. Grease and flour a 13x9x2-inch baking pan. Melt butter in large saucepan over low heat; remove pan from heat. Stir in remaining ingredients, except confectioners' sugar, in order listed; mix well after each addition. Spread batter in prepared pan. Bake for 35 to 40 minutes or until cake begins to pull away from sides of pan. Cool in pan on wire rack for 10 minutes. Sift confectioners' sugar over top. Cool completely and cut into squares. Makes 12 to 15 servings.

**Note:** If using Martha White All-Purpose Flour, sift 2 teaspoons baking powder and ¼ teaspoon salt with flour.

## Cream of Coconut Cake

*This contemporary version of the traditional holiday favorite uses fresh frozen coconut, cream of coconut and whipped topping.*

>2½ cups sifted Martha White
>     Self-Rising Flour
>1½ cups sugar
>  ¾ cup shortening
>   1 cup milk
>1½ teaspoons vanilla
>   5 egg whites
>2½ cups (9 ounces) fresh frozen
>     coconut, divided
>   1 can (8½ ounces) cream of coconut
>   1 container (12 ounces) frozen
>     whipped topping, thawed

Preheat oven to 350°F. Grease a 13x9x2-inch baking pan. Combine flour, sugar, shortening, milk, vanilla, egg whites and 1 cup coconut in large mixing bowl. Beat with electric mixer for 2 minutes on low speed, scraping bowl often. Turn mixer to medium-high speed and beat 2 minutes, scraping

bowl occasionally. Pour batter into prepared pan. Bake for 35 to 40 minutes or until cake begins to pull away from sides of pan and toothpick inserted in center comes out clean. Cool in pan on wire rack for 10 minutes. Punch holes in cake with toothpick. Pour cream of coconut evenly over surface of cake. Cool cake completely. Spread with whipped topping; sprinkle with remaining 1½ cups coconut. Cover and chill for 3 hours before serving. Makes 12 to 15 servings.

**Note:** If using Martha White All-Purpose Flour, sift 3½ teaspoons baking powder and 1 teaspoon salt with flour.

## Mississippi Mud Cake

*Make this chocolate cake for a family celebration.*

>   1 cup shortening
>1½ cups sugar
>   4 eggs
>   2 teaspoons vanilla
>1½ cups sifted Martha White
>     All-Purpose Flour
>  ⅓ cup cocoa
>  ½ teaspoon salt
>   1 cup chopped pecans
>   2 cups miniature marshmallows
>     Mississippi Mud Icing,
>        following

Preheat oven to 325°F. Grease and flour a 13x9x2-inch baking pan. Cream shortening and sugar together in mixing bowl until light and fluffy. Add eggs one at a time, beating well after each addition. Blend in vanilla. Sift flour, cocoa and salt together; add to creamed mixture and blend thoroughly. Stir in pecans. Pour batter into prepared pan. Bake for 35 to 40 minutes or until cake begins to pull away from sides of pan and toothpick inserted in center comes out clean. Remove pan from oven and sprinkle marshmallows evenly over cake. Return to oven for 10 minutes or until marshmallows are melted. Cool in pan on wire rack. Spread with Mississippi Mud Icing. Chill before cutting into squares. Makes 12 to 15 servings.

### Mississippi Mud Icing

    1 cup (2 sticks) butter or margarine, melted
   ⅓ cup cocoa
   ½ cup evaporated milk
   4 cups sifted confectioners' sugar (about 1 pound)
   1 teaspoon vanilla
   ½ cup chopped pecans

Combine butter and cocoa in mixing bowl; add evaporated milk. Gradually stir in sugar; beat until smooth. Stir in vanilla and pecans; blend thoroughly.

## Easy Chocolate Sheet Cake

*A hint of cinnamon adds flair to this moist cake.*

   ½ cup buttermilk
   1 teaspoon baking soda
   ½ cup (1 stick) butter or margarine
   1 cup water
   ½ cup vegetable oil or melted shortening
   ¼ cup cocoa
   2 eggs, lightly beaten
   1 teaspoon vanilla
   2 cups sifted Martha White All-Purpose Flour
   2 cups sugar
   1 teaspoon cinnamon
   Chocolate Frosting, below

Preheat oven to 400°F. Grease and flour a 13x9x2-inch baking pan. Stir together buttermilk and soda in measuring cup or small bowl and reserve for later use. Combine butter, water, oil and cocoa in medium saucepan; bring to a boil over medium heat, stirring to melt butter. Remove pan from heat and stir in buttermilk mixture. Add eggs and vanilla; blend thoroughly. Stir in flour, sugar and cinnamon until blended. Pour batter into prepared pan. Bake for 15 to 20 minutes or until cake begins to pull away from sides of pan and toothpick inserted in center comes out clean. Cool in pan on wire rack. Spread with Chocolate Frosting. Makes 12 to 15 servings.

### Chocolate Frosting

   ½ cup (1 stick) butter or margarine
   ¼ cup milk
   ¼ cup cocoa
   4 cups sifted confectioners' sugar (about 1 pound)
   1 teaspoon vanilla

Combine butter, milk and cocoa in medium saucepan. Bring to a boil over medium heat, stirring to melt butter. Remove from heat; gradually stir in sugar and vanilla. Stir until smooth.

## Pineapple Upside-Down Cake

*A traditional favorite of all ages.*

¼ cup (½ stick) butter or margarine
½ cup firmly packed brown sugar
6 slices canned pineapple in heavy syrup, drained; syrup reserved
6 maraschino cherries
35 pecan halves
1½ cups sifted Martha White Self-Rising Flour
1 cup granulated sugar
½ cup vegetable oil
1 egg
1 teaspoon vanilla
Whipped cream (optional)

Preheat oven to 350°F. Melt butter in oven in a 10-inch cast-iron skillet. Stir brown sugar and 1 tablespoon reserved pineapple syrup into melted butter; spread evenly in pan. Arrange pineapple slices in bottom of pan. Place a cherry in center of each pineapple ring. Arrange pecans, rounded sides down, in and around pineapple; set aside. Pour remaining reserved pineapple syrup into measuring cup; add enough water to make ½ cup; pour into large mixing bowl. Add flour, sugar, oil, egg and vanilla. Beat with electric mixer on low speed for 2 minutes, or until well blended. Spoon batter over pineapple and pecans. Bake for 35 to 40 minutes or until toothpick inserted in center comes out clean. Cool in pan for 5 minutes. Turn out onto large serving plate. Serve warm topped with whipped cream, if desired. Makes 6 to 8 servings.

**Note:** If using Martha White All-Purpose Flour, sift 1¾ teaspoons baking powder and ½ teaspoon salt with flour.

## Fresh Apple Nut Cake

*Made with vegetable oil, this cake is easy to stir together and bakes up moist and spicy.*

2 eggs
1 cup vegetable oil
1¾ cups sugar
2½ cups sifted Martha White Self-Rising Flour
3 cups peeled chopped apples
1 cup chopped pecans
1 teaspoon cinnamon
1 teaspoon vanilla
Cream Cheese Icing, following

Preheat oven to 300°F. Grease a 13x9x2-inch baking pan. Beat eggs in mixing bowl. Add oil and sugar; beat well. Add remaining ingredients, except Icing; blend thoroughly. Pour batter into prepared pan. Bake for 1 hour and 10 minutes or until cake begins to pull away from sides of pan. Cool in pan on wire rack. Spread with Cream Cheese Icing. Makes 12 to 15 servings.

**Note:** If using Martha White All-Purpose Flour, sift 1 teaspoon salt, 1 teaspoon baking powder and 1 teaspoon baking soda with flour.

### Cream Cheese Icing

> 2 packages (3 ounces each) cream cheese, softened
> ¼ cup (½ stick) butter or margarine, softened
> 4 cups sifted confectioners' sugar (about 1 pound)
> 2 teaspoons vanilla

Beat cream cheese and butter together until light and fluffy. Gradually beat in sugar until smooth. Add vanilla and blend thoroughly.

## Highland Oatmeal Cake

*Homey whole grain goodness, topped with a broiled coconut mixture.*

> 1½ cups boiling water
> 1 cup quick-cooking oats
> 2 eggs
> ½ cup vegetable oil
> 1 cup granulated sugar
> 1 cup firmly packed brown sugar
> 1½ cups sifted Martha White Self-Rising Flour
> 1 teaspoon cinnamon
> ½ cup raisins (optional)
> Coconut Topping, below

Preheat oven to 350°F. Grease and flour a 13x9x2-inch baking pan. Pour boiling water over oats; stir and set aside. Beat eggs in mixing bowl. Add oil, sugar and brown sugar; blend thoroughly. Stir in flour and cinnamon until well blended. Stir in oats; add raisins, if desired. Pour batter into prepared pan. Bake for 25 to 30 minutes or until golden brown and toothpick inserted in center comes out clean. Spread Coconut Topping over hot cake. Heat under broiler until topping browns. Be careful not to burn topping. Makes 12 to 15 servings.

**Note:** If using Martha White All-Purpose Flour, sift 2¼ teaspoons baking powder and ½ teaspoon salt with flour.

### Coconut Topping

> ½ cup (1 stick) butter or margarine, melted
> 1 cup firmly packed brown sugar
> ⅓ cup milk
> 1 teaspoon vanilla
> 1 cup flaked coconut
> ½ cup chopped pecans

Combine all ingredients in order listed; blend well.

## Texas Fruitcake

*Like a pound cake with candied cherries, coconut and pecans throughout.*

1½ cups (3 sticks) butter, softened (no substitute)
2 cups sugar
6 eggs
4¼ cups sifted Martha White All-Purpose Flour, divided
2 teaspoons baking powder
½ teaspoon salt
½ cup orange juice
1 pound (16 ounces) candied cherries, halved
1 can (7 ounces) flaked coconut
1½ cups broken pecans

Preheat oven to 225°F. Grease and flour a 10-inch tube pan. Cream butter and sugar together in large mixing bowl until light and fluffy. Add eggs one at a time, beating well after each addition. Sift 4 cups flour, baking powder and salt together; add to creamed mixture alternately with orange juice, beginning and ending with flour mixture. Mix well after each addition. Combine cherries, coconut, pecans and remaining ¼ cup flour in medium bowl; toss lightly to coat. Stir fruit and nut mixture into batter; blend well. Spoon batter into prepared pan. Bake for 4 hours or until cake begins to pull away from sides of pan and toothpick inserted one inch from edge comes out clean. Cool completely in pan on wire rack. Remove from pan when cool. Makes 12 to 15 servings.

# Macaroon Cake

*A beautifully textured, rich cake, blending the flavors of coconut and almond for a special holiday taste.*

6 eggs, separated
1 cup shortening
½ cup (1 stick) butter or margarine, softened
3 cups sugar
½ teaspoon almond extract
½ teaspoon coconut extract
3 cups sifted Martha White All-Purpose Flour
¼ teaspoon salt
1 cup milk
1 can (7 ounces) flaked coconut
Confectioners' sugar

Preheat oven to 300°F. Grease and flour a 10-inch tube pan. Beat egg whites in mixing bowl until soft peaks form. In large mixing bowl, cream shortening and butter until blended. Add sugar and beat until light and fluffy. Add egg yolks one at a time, beating well after each addition. Blend in extracts. Stir flour and salt together; add to creamed mixture alternately with milk, beginning and ending with flour mixture. Stir in coconut. Fold in beaten egg whites. Spoon batter into prepared pan. Bake for 1 hour and 45 minutes or until toothpick inserted one inch from edge comes out clean. Cool in pan for 15 minutes; turn out onto wire rack and cool completely. Sift confectioners' sugar over top. Makes 12 to 15 servings.

# COOKIES

A faded saltine tin, an empty coffee can, a chipped crock, a floral-pattern flour canister, a porcelain pink pig dressed as an old-timey pharmacist—the family cookie jar is cloaked in a variety of clever disguises.

But no matter how creative its costume, the cookie jar never stays full for long.

Cookies are the "good for you" reward at the end of a meal. Cookies are power, and the child lucky enough to find that Mom has packed a few in his lunchbox controls the bidding in the lunchroom. Cookies and a cold glass of milk waiting at the kitchen table are a loving welcome home after a hard day at school. Cookies are a sweet reminder of home to the lonely college freshman who finds a tin of his favorites nestled among a change of clean socks from Mom. Cookies are children's first creation, their first part in the act of baking, from sampling sugary dough to standing on a chair at the counter and decorating tiny buttery cutouts with bright icings and sparkles. And cookies are, as every child somehow knows, the preferred food of Santa Claus and his reindeer.

Cookies are for children only . . .

whatever their age. And the cookie jar is a kind of snack-time watering hole, visited daily by family members looking to see what's new.

Cookies aren't a uniquely Southern food. But they are dearly loved by most Southerners and so are viewed as an important part of Southern culture by the people of the region. Some claim that the cookie is a natural expression of the historical abundance of sugar cane in Southern states such as Louisiana. Some say cookies are a social food that found a comfortable place resting on the refreshment table at cotillions, balls and pageants. And some say, in the days before television, cookies were an easy way to entertain the swarm of children buzzing around a hot and dangerous plantation kitchen.

Like Southerners, the cookie is comfortable in any social context—formal or casual.

Cookies dress up well as Tea Cakes or Party Pecan Balls for a June bridal shower or christening. They also mingle comfortably with a simple glass of lemonade, munched to the easy sway of the front porch swing.

In cookie jar: Oatmeal Chocolate Chip Cookies (page 194); on platter, clockwise from top: Peanut Butter Chocolate Kisses (page 196). Thumbprints (page 196), Apricot Bars (page 190), Stuffed Monkeys (page 200), Date Nut Bars (page 187), Party Pecan Balls (page 198)

## Fudgey Microwave Brownies

*Brownies bake well in the microwave. Shielding the corners of the baking dish with small triangles of foil is safe and prevents the corners from overbaking.*

½ cup (1 stick) butter or margarine
2 squares (1 ounce each) unsweetened chocolate
1 cup sugar
2 eggs
¾ cup Martha White Self-Rising Flour
1 teaspoon vanilla
¾ cup chopped pecans

Grease an 8-inch square baking dish or other shallow 1½- to 2-quart microwave-safe baking dish. Combine butter and chocolate in microwave-safe bowl. Microwave on MEDIUM for 2 to 3 minutes or until melted, stirring occasionally. Stir in remaining ingredients in order listed; blend well. Pour batter into prepared dish. Cover corners of dish with foil triangles. Place dish on inverted saucer. Microwave on MEDIUM-HIGH for 3 to 5 minutes, rotating dish ¼ turn every 2 minutes. Remove foil and microwave on HIGH for 2 to 4 minutes or until center is almost done, rotating dish ¼ turn after half the time. Remove dish; stand directly on towel-covered countertop 10 minutes to complete cooking. Cool an additional 10 to 15 minutes before cutting into 2-inch squares. Makes 16 squares.

**Note:** If using Martha White All-Purpose Flour, sift 1 teaspoon baking powder and ½ teaspoon salt with flour.

## Scotchies

*Rich butterscotch flavor with the texture of a brownie.*

½ cup (1 stick) butter or margarine
1¼ cups firmly packed light brown sugar
2 eggs
1 cup Martha White Self-Rising Flour
1 teaspoon vanilla
1 cup chopped pecans

Preheat oven to 350°F. Grease a 9-inch square baking pan. Melt butter in large saucepan over low heat; remove from heat. Stir in remaining ingredients in order listed, mixing well after each addition. Spread batter in prepared pan. Bake for 25 to 30 minutes or until golden brown and beginning to slightly pull away from sides of pan. Cool in pan on wire rack. Cut into 2-inch squares. Makes 16 squares.

**Note:** If using Martha White All-Purpose Flour, sift 1½ teaspoons baking powder and ½ teaspoon salt with flour.

## Saucepan Brownies

*Just melt the chocolate and butter in a saucepan, then stir in remaining ingredients—so fudgey and easy, these brownies will become a family favorite.*

½ cup (1 stick) butter or margarine
2 squares (1 ounce each) unsweetened chocolate

1 cup sugar
2 eggs
¾ cup Martha White
   Self-Rising Flour
1 teaspoon vanilla
¾ cup chopped pecans

Preheat oven to 350°F. Grease a 9-inch square baking pan. Melt butter and chocolate in large saucepan over low heat; remove from heat. Stir in remaining ingredients in order listed, mixing well after each addition. Spread batter in prepared pan. Bake for 25 to 30 minutes or until beginning to slightly pull away from sides of pan. Cool in pan on wire rack. Cut into 2-inch squares. Makes 16 squares.

**Note:** If using Martha White All-Purpose Flour, sift 1 teaspoon baking powder and ½ teaspoon salt with flour.

## Marbled Cream Cheese Brownies

*Brownies made with German chocolate and swirled with a cheesecake-like layer—pretty enough for a party.*

### Brownie Layer:

1 package (4 ounces) German sweet
   chocolate
6 tablespoons (¾ stick) butter or
   margarine
¾ cup sugar

2 eggs, lightly beaten
⅔ cup Martha White
   Self-Rising Flour
1 teaspoon vanilla
½ cup chopped pecans

### Cream Cheese Layer:

1 package (3 ounces) cream cheese,
   softened
2 tablespoons butter or margarine,
   softened
¼ cup sugar
1 egg, lightly beaten
1 tablespoon Martha White
   All-Purpose or Self-Rising Flour
½ teaspoon vanilla

Preheat oven to 350°F. Grease a 9-inch square baking pan. For brownie layer, melt chocolate and butter in large saucepan over low heat; remove from heat. Stir in remaining brownie layer ingredients in order listed, mixing well after each addition. Spread brownie batter in prepared pan. For cream cheese layer, beat cream cheese and butter together in mixing bowl. Stir in remaining ingredients in order listed, mixing well after each addition. Spoon cream cheese mixture over brownie batter and swirl together gently with a knife. Bake for 35 to 40 minutes or until cream cheese swirls are light golden brown. Cool in pan on wire rack. Cut into 2-inch squares. Makes 16 squares.

**Note:** If using Martha White All-Purpose Flour, sift 1¼ teaspoons baking powder and ¼ teaspoon salt with flour for brownie layer.

Peanut Butter Brownies

Pour cherry pie filling over cream cheese. Chill for 1 hour or until cream cheese is firm. Cut into 2½-inch squares and garnish with whipped topping. Sprinkle chocolate shavings over whipped topping for added color, if desired. Makes 9 squares.

**Note:** Martha White Chewy Fudge Brownie Mix (10¼ ounces) requires 1 egg and 3 tablespoons vegetable oil for preparation.

## Black Forest Brownies

*A convenient brownie mix topped with cream cheese and cherry pie filling is fancy enough for company.*

> 1 package (10¼ ounces) Martha White Chewy Fudge Brownie Mix
> 1 package (8 ounces) cream cheese, softened
> 1 can (21 ounces) cherry pie filling
> Frozen whipped topping, thawed
> Chocolate shavings (optional)

Prepare and bake brownie mix according to package directions. Cool completely on wire rack. Spread softened cream cheese over cooled brownies.

## Lunchbox Brownies

*Made easy with chocolate morsels and sweetened condensed milk, they'll disappear before you know it.*

> ½ cup (1 stick) butter or margarine
> 1 package (6 ounces) semisweet chocolate morsels
> 1 can (14 ounces) sweetened condensed milk
> 1 egg, lightly beaten
> 1 teaspoon vanilla
> 1½ cups Martha White Self-Rising Flour
> ½ cup pecans (optional)

Preheat oven to 350°F. Grease a 9-inch square pan. Melt butter and chocolate morsels in large saucepan over low heat; remove from heat. Stir in remaining ingredients in order listed, mixing well after each addition. Spread batter in prepared pan. Bake for 25 to 30 minutes or until brownies begin to slightly pull away from sides of pan. Cool in pan on wire rack. Cut into 2-inch squares. Makes 16 squares.

**Note:** If using Martha White All-Purpose Flour, sift 2 teaspoons baking powder and ¾ teaspoon salt with flour.

## Peanut Butter Brownies

*Moist peanut butter squares with chocolate morsels stirred into the batter.*

- ⅓ cup (5⅓ tablespoons) butter or margarine
- ½ cup granulated sugar
- ½ cup firmly packed light brown sugar
- 2 eggs
- ½ cup crunchy or smooth peanut butter
- 1 cup Martha White Self-Rising Flour
- ½ teaspoon vanilla
- 1 package (6 ounces) semisweet chocolate morsels

Preheat oven to 350°F. Grease a 9-inch square baking pan. Melt butter in large saucepan over low heat; remove from heat. Stir in remaining ingredients in order listed, mixing well after each addition. Spread batter in prepared pan. Bake for 30 to 35 minutes or until golden brown. Cool in pan on wire rack. Cut into 2-inch squares. Makes 16 squares.

**Note:** If using Martha White All-Purpose Flour, sift 1½ teaspoons baking powder and ½ teaspoon salt with flour.

## Sour Cream Banana Bars

*Almost like little banana cakes—sour cream in the batter adds rich flavor.*

- ½ cup (1 stick) butter or margarine
- 1½ cups sugar
- 2 eggs
- 1 cup (8 ounces) dairy sour cream
- 1½ cups mashed ripe bananas (about 3 medium)
- 2 teaspoons vanilla
- 2 cups Martha White Self-Rising Flour Confectioners' Glaze, below

Preheat oven to 350°F. Grease bottom of a 15x10x1-inch jelly roll pan or two 9-inch square baking pans. Melt butter in large saucepan over low heat; remove from heat. Stir in remaining ingredients, except Glaze, in order listed. Spread batter in prepared pan(s). Bake for 20 to 25 minutes or until golden brown. Cool in pan on wire rack. Drizzle with Confectioners' Glaze. Cut into 2x1-inch bars. Makes about 60 bars.

**Note:** If using Martha White All-Purpose Flour, sift 1 tablespoon baking powder and ¾ teaspoon salt with flour.

### Confectioners' Glaze

- ¼ cup (½ stick) butter or margarine, melted
- 2 cups sifted confectioners' sugar
- 3 tablespoons milk

Combine ingredients in order listed in mixing bowl; stir until smooth.

# The Ultimate Bar Cookie

*This tempting cookie is easy to prepare using a brownie mix for the base.*

1 package (18 ounces) Martha
   White Chewy Fudge Brownie Mix
⅓ cup vegetable oil
⅓ cup water
1 egg, lightly beaten
1 package (6 ounces) butterscotch
   morsels
1 package (6 ounces) semisweet
   chocolate morsels
1 cup flaked coconut
1 cup chopped pecans
1 can (14 ounces) sweetened
   condensed milk

Preheat oven to 350°F. Grease bottom of a 13x9x2-inch baking pan. Combine brownie mix, oil, water and egg in mixing bowl; stir to blend, about 50 strokes. Spread batter in prepared pan. Sprinkle evenly with butterscotch and chocolate morsels, coconut and pecans. Pour condensed milk over entire mixture and spread carefully. Bake for 40 to 45 minutes or until coconut turns golden brown. Cool in pan on wire rack. Cut into 2x1-inch bars. Makes 48 bars.

# Cheesecake Bars

*A rich cream cheese mixture baked over a buttery crust will please the most discriminating taste.*

⅓ cup (5⅓ tablespoons) butter or
   margarine, softened

⅓ cup firmly packed brown sugar
1 cup Martha White
   All-Purpose Flour
½ cup chopped pecans
1 package (8 ounces) cream cheese,
   softened
¼ cup granulated sugar
1 egg
2 tablespoons milk
1 tablespoon lemon juice
½ teaspoon vanilla

Preheat oven to 350°F. Cream butter and brown sugar together in mixing bowl until light and fluffy. Stir in flour and pecans. Reserve 1 cup of this crumb mixture for topping. Press remaining crumb mixture into bottom of an ungreased 8-inch square baking pan. Bake for 12 to 15 minutes. Cool on wire rack. Beat cream cheese and sugar together in mixing bowl. Add egg, milk, lemon juice and vanilla; beat until smooth. Spread cream cheese mixture over cooled crust. Sprinkle evenly with reserved crumbs. Bake for 25 to 30 minutes or until light golden brown. Cool in pan on wire rack. Cut into 2x1-inch bars. Store in refrigerator. Makes 32 bars.

# Granola Bars

*A good lunch box or after-school snack.*

½ cup (1 stick) butter or margarine
½ cup firmly packed brown sugar
¼ cup honey
1 egg
1 cup Martha White
   All-Purpose Flour

½ teaspoon cinnamon
½ teaspoon baking soda
¼ teaspoon salt
1 cup quick-cooking oats
½ cup flaked coconut
½ cup chopped pecans

Preheat oven to 350°F. Grease a 13x9x2-inch baking pan. Melt butter in large saucepan over low heat; remove from heat. Stir in remaining ingredients in order listed, mixing well after each addition. (Mixture will be thick.) Press into prepared pan. Bake for 18 to 20 minutes or until golden brown. Cool in pan on wire rack. Cut into 2x1-inch bars. Makes about 60 bars.

## Sea Island Bars

*An irresistible combination of coconut, pecans and chocolate morsels stirred into an easy-to-mix brown sugar batter.*

½ cup (1 stick) butter or margarine
½ cup granulated sugar
⅓ cup firmly packed brown sugar
2 tablespoons water
1 cup Martha White
  Self-Rising Flour
1 egg
1 teaspoon vanilla
½ cup chopped pecans
½ cup flaked coconut
1 package (6 ounces) semisweet
  chocolate morsels

Preheat oven to 350°F. Grease a 9-inch square baking pan. Melt butter in large saucepan over low heat; remove from heat. Stir in remaining ingredients in order listed, mixing well after each addition. Spread batter in prepared pan. Bake for 25 to 30 minutes or until golden brown. Cool in pan on wire rack. Cut into 2x1-inch bars. Makes 32 bars.

**Note:** If using Martha White All-Purpose Flour, sift 1½ teaspoons baking powder and ½ teaspoon salt with flour.

## Oatmeal Squares

*Moist and cake-like with old-fashioned ingredients—a good lunch box treat.*

½ cup (1 stick) butter or margarine
1 cup sugar
2 eggs
¾ cup Martha White
  Self-Rising Flour
1 teaspoon cinnamon
1 teaspoon vanilla
¾ cup quick-cooking oats
¾ cup chopped pecans or raisins

Preheat oven to 350°F. Grease a 9-inch square baking pan. Melt butter in large saucepan over low heat; remove from heat. Stir in remaining ingredients in order listed, mixing well after each addition. Spread batter in prepared pan. Bake for 25 to 30 minutes or until golden brown. Cool in pan on wire rack. Cut into 2-inch squares. Makes 16 squares.

**Note:** If using Martha White All-Purpose Flour, sift 1 teaspoon baking powder and ½ teaspoon salt with flour.

Buttery Sugar Cookies (page 199), Iced Lemon Butter Bars

## Strawberry Bars

*Little buttery bars filled with strawberry preserves.*

> 1 cup (2 sticks) butter or margarine, softened
> 1 cup sugar
> 2 egg yolks
> 2 cups Martha White All-Purpose Flour
> ½ teaspoon salt
> 1 cup chopped pecans
> ½ cup strawberry jam

Preheat oven to 325°F. Grease a 9-inch square baking pan. Cream butter and sugar together in mixing bowl until light and fluffy. Add egg yolks; beat well. Stir in flour, salt and pecans. Press half of cookie mixture into prepared pan. Spread evenly with jam. Cover with remaining cookie mixture. Bake for 40 to 45 minutes or until golden brown. Cool in pan on wire rack. Cut into 2x1-inch bars. Makes 32 bars.

## Iced Lemon Butter Bars

*A delightfully refreshing finale to a light summer luncheon.*

> 1⅓ cups sifted Martha White All-Purpose Flour
> ½ cup (1 stick) butter or margarine, softened
> 1 cup sugar, divided
> 2 eggs
> 2 tablespoons Martha White All-Purpose Flour

**2 tablespoons lemon juice**
**1 teaspoon grated lemon peel**
**Confectioners' sugar**

Preheat oven to 350°F. Combine 1⅓ cups flour, butter and ¼ cup sugar in mixing bowl; stir until blended. Press dough into ungreased 9-inch square baking pan. Bake for 20 to 25 minutes or until light golden brown. Combine eggs, remaining ¾ cup sugar, 2 tablespoons flour, lemon juice and peel in mixing bowl; blend thoroughly. Pour over partially baked crust. Bake for 20 to 22 minutes or until light golden brown around the edges and filling is set. Cool in pan on wire rack for 10 minutes. Sift confectioners' sugar over top. Cool completely and cut into 2x1-inch bars. Makes 32 bars.

## Oats and Apple Trail Bars

*A natural-tasting snack bar that will be a welcome after-school treat with a glass of milk.*

**1 package (7 ounces) Martha White Apple Cinnamon Muffin Mix**
**⅓ cup quick-cooking oats**
**¼ cup (½ stick) butter or margarine, melted**
**¼ cup chopped pecans**
**2 tablespoons brown sugar**
**2 tablespoons honey**

Preheat oven to 350°F. Combine all ingredients in order listed; blend well. Press mixture into ungreased 9-inch square baking pan. Bake for 20 to 25 minutes or until golden brown. Cool 5 minutes; cut into 2x1-inch bars while warm. Makes 32 bars.

## Date Nut Bars

*Bake in advance and freeze to serve at a holiday open house.*

**¼ cup (½ stick) butter or margarine**
**½ cup sugar**
**1 egg**
**½ cup Martha White Self-Rising Flour**
**1 teaspoon vanilla**
**1 package (8 ounces) chopped dates**
**1 cup chopped pecans**
**Confectioners' Glaze (optional)***

Preheat oven to 350°F. Grease a 9-inch square baking pan. Melt butter in large saucepan over low heat; remove from heat. Stir in remaining ingredients, except confectioners' sugar, in order listed, mixing well after each addition. Spread batter in prepared pan. Bake for 25 to 30 minutes or until golden brown. Cool in pan on wire rack for 10 minutes. Sift confectioners' sugar over top. Cool completely and cut into 2x1-inch bars. Makes 32 bars.

*Bars may be drizzled with Confectioners' Glaze, if desired. Combine 1 cup sifted confectioners' sugar, 3 tablespoons milk and ¼ teaspoon vanilla in small bowl. Beat until smooth.

**Note:** If using Martha White All-Purpose Flour, sift ¾ teaspoon baking powder and ¼ teaspoon salt with flour.

## Holiday Fruit Squares

*Perfect for holiday entertaining—made with lots of candied fruit, nuts and dates.*

2 eggs
1 cup sifted confectioners' sugar
⅓ cup (5⅓ tablespoons) butter or margarine, melted
¾ cup sifted Martha White Self-Rising Flour, divided
1 cup chopped pecans
1 cup chopped dates
¾ cup chopped candied fruit
Confectioners' Glaze, below

Preheat oven to 325°F. Grease a 9-inch square baking pan. Beat eggs in mixing bowl until light. Gradually add sugar and butter; beat well. Combine ½ cup flour with pecans, dates and fruit in large bowl; blend well. Add remaining ¼ cup flour to creamed mixture; beat well. Stir in fruit and nut mixture. Pour batter into prepared pan. Bake for 30 to 35 minutes or until golden brown and center springs back when lightly touched. Cool in pan on wire rack 5 minutes. Drizzle with Confectioners' Glaze. Cool completely and cut into 2-inch squares. Makes 16 squares.

**Note:** If using Martha White All-Purpose Flour, sift 1¼ teaspoons baking powder and ½ teaspoon salt with flour.

### Confectioners' Glaze

½ cup sifted confectioners' sugar
2 teaspoons hot water
¼ teaspoon almond extract

Combine all ingredients in small bowl; stir until smooth. Add more hot water if thinner glaze is desired.

## Mincemeat Bran Bars

*Mincemeat and sweetened condensed milk add flavor and richness to this bar cookie made from a muffin mix. Don't forget these during the holidays.*

2 packages (7 ounces each) Martha White Bran Muffin Mix
½ cup chopped pecans
1 cup mincemeat
1 can (14 ounces) sweetened condensed milk
Confectioners' Glaze, below
Pecan halves

Preheat oven to 350°F. Grease a 13x9x2-inch baking pan. Stir together muffin mix and chopped pecans in mixing bowl. Add mincemeat and condensed milk; blend well. Spread batter in prepared pan. Bake for 25 to 30 minutes or until beginning to slightly pull away from sides of pan. Cool in pan on wire rack for 5 minutes; drizzle with Confectioners' Glaze. Decorate with pecan halves as desired. Cool completely and cut into 2x1-inch bars. Makes 32 bars.

### Confectioners' Glaze

1 cup sifted confectioners' sugar
2 tablespoons milk

Combine ingredients in small bowl; stir until smooth.

Performers gather around the microphone during the portion of the Grand Ole Opry sponsored by Martha White.

## Danish Raspberry Bars

*A traditional Scandinavian favorite, these crisp bar cookies are layered with raspberry preserves.*

> 1½ cups sifted Martha White
>    All-Purpose Flour
> 1½ cups quick-cooking oats
>  ½ cup granulated sugar
>  ½ cup firmly packed brown sugar
>  ½ teaspoon baking powder
>  ¾ cup (1½ sticks) butter or
>    margarine, melted
>  ¾ cup red raspberry preserves
>  ¼ cup chopped blanched
>    almonds
>    Confectioners' sugar

Preheat oven to 375°F. Stir together flour, oats, sugars and baking powder in mixing bowl. Add butter; stir to blend. Press about ⅔ of mixture into bottom of an ungreased 9-inch square baking pan. Spread evenly with preserves. Add almonds to remaining oat mixture; mixture will be crumbly. Sprinkle evenly over preserves; pat down lightly. Bake for 30 to 35 minutes or until golden brown. Cool in pan on wire rack for 5 minutes. Dust with confectioners' sugar. Cool completely. Cut into 2x1-inch bars. Makes 32 bars.

## Crispy Bran Bars

*A crispy, buttery bar cookie—easy to prepare using a muffin mix.*

> 1 package (7 ounces) Martha White
>    Bran Muffin Mix
> 1 cup chopped pecans
> ¼ cup firmly packed brown sugar
> ¼ cup quick-cooking oats
> ½ teaspoon cinnamon
> ½ cup (1 stick) butter or margarine,
>    melted

Preheat oven to 325°F. Grease an 8- or 9-inch square baking pan. Combine all ingredients in mixing bowl in order listed; blend well. Press mixture evenly into prepared pan. Bake for 30 to 35 minutes or until golden brown. Cool in pan on wire rack. Cut into 2x1-inch bars. Makes 32 bars.

# Apricot Bars

*Tart dried apricot filling sandwiched between buttery layers of cookie dough. Pack in decorative tins for a memorable gift.*

1 cup (2 sticks) butter or margarine, softened
1 cup sugar
2 egg yolks
2 cups sifted Martha White All-Purpose Flour
½ teaspoon salt
1 cup chopped pecans
Apricot Filling, below
Dried apricots, thinly sliced (optional)

Preheat oven to 325°F. Grease a 9-inch square baking pan. Cream butter and sugar together in mixing bowl until light and fluffy. Add egg yolks; beat well. Stir in flour, salt and pecans. Press half of cookie mixture into prepared pan. Spread evenly with cooled Apricot Filling. Cover with remaining cookie mixture. Bake for 50 to 55 minutes or until golden brown. Cool in pan on wire rack. Cut into 2x1-inch bars. Garnish bars with apricot slices, if desired. Makes 32 bars.

### Apricot Filling

½ cup finely chopped dried apricots
½ cup water
⅓ cup sugar
½ teaspoon vanilla

Combine apricots and water in small saucepan. Cover and cook 20 minutes over medium-low heat. Add sugar; cook uncovered until thick. Cool slightly; stir in vanilla. Cool completely before spreading.

**Note:** For a decorative touch, dip apricot slices in melted semisweet chocolate morsels, if desired.

# Pecan Pie Squares

*Irresistible—like little squares of pecan pie with the added pleasure of a sweet buttery crust.*

**Crust:**

2 cups sifted Martha White All-Purpose Flour
¼ cup sugar
½ teaspoon salt
½ cup (1 stick) butter or margarine, melted

**Filling:**

3 eggs, lightly beaten
1 cup sugar
1 cup light corn syrup
2 tablespoons butter or margarine, melted
1 teaspoon vanilla
2 cups chopped pecans

Preheat oven to 350°F. Grease a 13x9x2-inch baking pan. Combine crust ingredients in mixing bowl; blend with electric mixer on medium speed until mixture resembles corn meal. Press crust mixture firmly and evenly into prepared pan. Bake for 20 minutes or until very light golden brown. Combine filling ingredients in mixing bowl in order listed, blending well after each addition. Pour filling over baked crust; return to oven. Bake for 25 to 28 minutes or until filling is set. Cool completely on wire rack before cutting into 2-inch squares. Makes 24 squares.

### Chocolate Pecan Pie Squares

Follow directions for Pecan Pie Squares; except—after final baking, remove pan from oven and place on wire rack. Sprinkle hot filling with one bag (12 ounces) milk chocolate morsels. Set aside for 5 minutes; spread chocolate layer evenly over filling with spatula or back of spoon.

## Chewy Mincemeat Bars

*If you like mincemeat, you'll love this easy bar cookie. Muffin Mix makes the crust quick to fix.*

> **2 packages (7 ounces each) Martha White Apple Cinnamon Muffin Mix**
> **½ cup (1 stick) butter or margarine, melted**
> **2 tablespoons sugar**
> **1½ cups mincemeat**

Preheat oven to 400°F. Combine muffin mix, butter and sugar in mixing bowl; blend until crumbly. Reserve 1 cup mixture, loosely packed. Press remaining crust mixture into bottom of an ungreased 9-inch square baking pan. Bake for 10 minutes. Remove from oven; cool for 5 minutes. Carefully spread bottom crust with mincemeat; sprinkle reserved crumb mixture over mincemeat. Bake for 20 to 25 minutes or until golden brown. Cool on wire rack. Cut into 2x1-inch bars. Makes 32 bars.

## *Chocolate Chip Cookies

*You can never go wrong with a batch of these all-time favorites.*

> **½ cup (1 stick) butter or margarine, softened**
> **½ cup granulated sugar**
> **⅓ cup firmly packed light brown sugar**
> **1 egg**
> **½ teaspoon vanilla**
> **1¼ cups sifted Martha White All-Purpose Flour**
> **½ teaspoon salt**
> **½ teaspoon baking soda**
> **1 package (6 ounces) semi-sweet chocolate morsels**
> **½ cup chopped pecans**

Preheat oven to 375°F. Grease a large baking sheet. Cream butter and sugars together in mixing bowl until light and fluffy. Add egg and vanilla; beat well. Sift flour, salt and soda together; blend into creamed mixture. Stir in chocolate morsels and pecans. Drop by level tablespoonfuls two inches apart onto prepared baking sheet. Bake for 10 to 12 minutes or until golden brown. Cool on wire racks. Makes about 36 cookies.

*One of Martha White Test Kitchen's ten all-time favorite recipes.

## Peanut Butter Cookies

*An all-time classic favorite. Use a floured fork to make the traditional criss-cross design.*

½ cup (1 stick) butter or margarine, softened
½ cup creamy peanut butter
½ cup granulated sugar
½ cup firmly packed brown sugar
1 egg
½ teaspoon vanilla
1¼ cups sifted Martha White All-Purpose Flour
¾ teaspoon baking soda
¼ teaspoon salt

Preheat oven to 375°F. Cream butter, peanut butter and sugars together in mixing bowl until light and fluffy. Add egg and vanilla; beat well. Sift flour, soda and salt together; blend into creamed mixture. Shape dough into 1-inch balls. Arrange 2 inches apart on ungreased baking sheet. Press balls of dough with floured fork to flatten and make criss-cross design. Bake for 10 to 12 minutes or until golden brown. Cool on wire racks. Makes about 48 cookies.

## Chewy Chocolate Chip Cookies

*A little chewier version of the classic will hold up well for mailing to college students.*

¾ cup (1½ sticks) butter or margarine, softened
¾ cup firmly packed light brown sugar
½ cup granulated sugar
2 eggs
2 teaspoons vanilla
2 cups sifted Martha White All-Purpose Flour
1½ teaspoons salt
1 teaspoon baking soda
1 package (12 ounces) semisweet chocolate morsels
1 cup chopped pecans

Preheat oven to 375°F. Grease a large baking sheet. Cream butter and sugars together in mixing bowl until light and fluffy. Add eggs and vanilla; beat well. Sift flour, salt and soda together; blend into creamed mixture. Stir in chocolate morsels and pecans. Drop by level tablespoonfuls two inches apart onto prepared baking sheet. Bake for 10 to 12 minutes or until golden brown. Cool on wire racks. Makes about 60 cookies.

## Snickerdoodles

*A favorite childhood treat—the cream of tartar adds an unusual flair.*

¾ cup (1½ sticks) butter or margarine, softened
1½ cups sugar
2 eggs
1 teaspoon vanilla
2¾ cups sifted Martha White All-Purpose Flour
2 teaspoons cream of tartar
1 teaspoon baking soda
½ teaspoon salt
2 teaspoons cinnamon
2 tablespoons sugar

Preheat oven to 400°F. Grease a large baking sheet. Cream butter and 1½ cups sugar together in mixing bowl until light and fluffy. Add eggs and vanilla; beat well. Sift flour, cream of tartar, soda and salt together; blend into creamed mixture. Combine cinnamon and 2 tablespoons sugar in small bowl. Shape dough into 1-inch balls; roll in cinnamon-sugar mixture. Place balls of dough 2 inches apart on prepared baking sheet. Bake 8 to 10 minutes or until light golden brown. Cool on wire racks. Makes about 48 cookies.

# ★ Riders in the Sky ★

Seats in the saddle, boots in the stirrups and tongues in the cheek. That's Riders In The Sky. This trail-tenderized trio includes Woody Paul, King of the Cowboy Fiddlers; Too Slim, the Man with a Dozen Friends; and Ranger Doug, Idol of American Youth. Together, this Grand Ole Opry act dishes out the tastiest western harmonies since the Sons of the Pioneers.

## COWBOY COOKIES

2 cups sifted Martha White All-Purpose Flour
1½ teaspoons salt
1 teaspoon baking soda
½ teaspoon baking powder
1 cup (2 sticks) butter or margarine, softened
1 cup granulated sugar
1 cup firmly packed light brown sugar
2 eggs
1 teaspoon vanilla

2 cups quick-cooking or old-fashioned oats
1 package (6 ounces) semisweet chocolate morsels

Preheat oven to 350°F. Lightly grease a large baking sheet. Stir together flour, salt, soda and baking powder in medium bowl. In large mixing bowl, cream butter and sugars together until light and fluffy. Add eggs and vanilla; beat well. Gradually add flour mixture to creamed mixture; blend thoroughly. Stir in oats and chocolate morsels. Drop dough by teaspoonfuls two inches apart on prepared baking sheet. Bake for 10 to 12 minutes or until golden brown. Cool on wire racks. Makes about 60 cookies.

Oatmeal Chocolate Chip Cookies

## Candy Cookies

*Tastes like a buttery version of a chocolate-coated toffee candy bar.*

**Crust Layer:**

> 2 cups sifted Martha White
> All-Purpose Flour
> 1 cup firmly packed light brown
> sugar
> ½ cup (1 stick) butter or margarine,
> softened
> 1 cup coarsely chopped pecans

**Filling:**

> ⅔ cup (10⅔ tablespoons) butter or
> margarine
> ½ cup firmly packed light brown
> sugar
> 1 cup semisweet chocolate morsels

Preheat oven to 350°F. For crust, stir together flour and brown sugar in mixing bowl. Cut in butter using pastry blender or two knives until mixture re-

sembles coarse crumbs. Pat crust mixture firmly into bottom of ungreased 13x9x2-inch baking pan. Sprinkle pecans over unbaked crust. To prepare filling, combine butter and brown sugar in medium saucepan. Cook over medium heat, stirring constantly, until entire surface of mixture begins to boil. Boil for 30 seconds to 1 minute, stirring constantly. Pour hot mixture evenly over pecans and crust. Bake for 18 to 20 minutes or until caramel is bubbly and crust is golden brown. Remove pan from oven and sprinkle evenly with chocolate morsels. Set aside for about 3 minutes. Swirl melted chocolate slightly to create a marbled effect. Cool in pan completely on wire rack before cutting. Makes about 40 small squares.

## Oatmeal Chocolate Chip Cookies

*Fill a cookie jar with these crisp old-fashioned cookies and watch them disappear.*

> 1 cup shortening
> 1 cup granulated sugar
> 1 cup firmly packed brown sugar
> 2 eggs
> 1 teaspoon vanilla
> 2 cups sifted Martha White
> All-Purpose Flour
> 1 teaspoon baking soda
> 1 teaspoon cinnamon
> ¼ teaspoon salt
> 2 cups quick-cooking oats
> 1 package (6 ounces) semisweet
> chocolate morsels
> 1 cup chopped pecans

Preheat oven to 375°F. Grease a large baking sheet. Cream shortening and sugars together in mixing bowl until light and fluffy. Add eggs and vanilla; beat well. Sift flour, soda, cinnamon and salt together; blend into creamed mixture. Stir in oats, chocolate morsels and pecans. Drop dough by level tablespoonfuls two inches apart onto prepared baking sheet. Bake for 10 to 12 minutes or until golden brown. Cool on wire racks. Makes about 70 cookies.

## Dona Hatfield's Orange Cookies

*A favorite of Mrs. Hatfield and her baking class, called The Brunswick Bake Shop, in Brunswick, Georgia.*

1 cup shortening
2 cups sugar
2 eggs
¼ cup grated orange peel
2 tablespoons orange juice
2 cups sifted Martha White Self-Rising Flour
1 teaspoon nutmeg
3 cups quick-cooking oats

Preheat oven to 375°F. Grease a large baking sheet. Cream shortening and sugar together in mixing bowl until light and fluffy. Add eggs, orange peel and juice; beat well. Sift flour and nutmeg together; blend into creamed mixture. Stir in oats. Drop dough by level tablespoonfuls two inches apart onto prepared baking sheet. Bake for 12 to 14 minutes or until golden brown. Cool on wire racks. Makes about 48 cookies.

**Note:** If using Martha White All-Purpose Flour, sift 4 teaspoons baking powder and 1 teaspoon salt with flour.

## Chocolate Peanut Butter Cups

*Rich peanut butter cookie dough formed in little muffin pans and stuffed with miniature peanut butter cups. (These can be habit-forming.)*

½ recipe Peanut Butter Cookies (page 192)
48 miniature peanut butter cups

Prepare Peanut Butter Cookie dough as directed; except—press ½-inch balls of dough into bottom and halfway up sides of greased miniature 1⅞x⅞-inch muffin cups. Place unwrapped peanut butter cup in center of formed dough in each muffin cup. Bake for 12 to 15 minutes or until golden brown, being careful not to burn chocolate. Cool in pans for 10 minutes. Carefully remove from pans and cool completely on wire racks. Makes 48 peanut butter cups.

**Note:** Prepare remaining half of Peanut Butter Cookie dough as cookies, or make additional Chocolate Peanut Butter Cups, if desired.

## KEEPING COOKIES

Cookies are easy to make and can be kept for long periods of time if stored properly. Here are a few storage tips to help keep the cookies you bake fresher longer:

- Store soft cookies and crisp cookies separately.
- A plastic container with a tight-fitting lid is ideal for storing fragile cookies.
- Plastic zipper-lock bags are space-saving containers for sturdier cookies.
- Bar cookies may be stored tightly covered in the pan in which they were baked.
- Soft cookies can be kept soft by adding a piece of apple or bread to the container, changing it every other day.
- Crisp cookies that soften can be recrisped in a 300° oven for 3 to 5 minutes.

Cookies freeze well. Here are a few tips to help guarantee success.

- Cool thoroughly, pack in sturdy containers with a cushioning of crumpled waxed paper, if necessary.
- If cookies have been decorated, freeze until hard in a single layer, then pack for storage.
- To thaw, unwrap cookies and let them stand at room temperature for about 10 minutes.

## Thumbprints

*Holidays wouldn't be complete without these little jam-filled cookies.*

**1 recipe Butter Cookies (page 199)**
**⅓ cup jam or preserves, such as strawberry, raspberry or apricot**

Prepare Butter Cookie dough as directed; except—preheat oven to 375°F. Shape chilled dough into 1-inch balls. Arrange balls 2 inches apart on ungreased baking sheet. Using finger or tip of wooden spoon, make a deep depression in center of each ball. (Center will open as cookies bake.) Bake for 10 minutes. Remove from oven and fill center of each cookie with ¼ teaspoon jam. Return cookies to oven and bake for 5 minutes or until light golden brown, being careful not to burn jam. Cool on wire racks. Makes about 60 cookies.

## Peanut Butter Chocolate Kisses

*These chewy cookies topped with a chocolate kiss are a special treat for the holidays or any day of the year.*

**⅓ cup (5⅓ tablespoons) butter or margarine, softened**
**¾ cup firmly packed brown sugar**
**1 egg**
**1 teaspoon vanilla**
**½ cup chunky peanut butter**
**1⅓ cups sifted Martha White Self-Rising Flour**
**40 large milk chocolate kisses**

Cream butter and brown sugar together in mixing bowl until light and fluffy. Add egg, vanilla and peanut butter; beat well. Stir in flour. Cover and refrigerate for 1 hour. Preheat oven to 375°F. Shape chilled dough into 1-inch balls; arrange one inch apart on ungreased baking sheet. Bake for 5 minutes. Remove from oven and press a chocolate kiss in center of each cookie. Return to oven and bake for 3 to 4 minutes, being careful not to burn chocolate. Cool on wire racks. Makes about 40 cookies.

**Note:** If using Martha White All-Purpose Flour, sift 2 teaspoons baking powder and ¾ teaspoon salt with flour.

## Old-Fashioned Sugar Cookies

*Just honest and simple—take a plateful and a glass of lemonade to the porch and relax with a good book.*

> ½ cup (1 stick) butter or margarine, softened
> 1 cup sugar
> 1 egg
> 1 tablespoon milk
> 1 teaspoon vanilla
> 2 cups sifted Martha White Self-Rising Flour
> Sugar

Cream butter and sugar together in mixing bowl until light and fluffy. Add egg, milk and vanilla; beat well. Stir in flour. Cover and refrigerate 1 hour. Preheat oven to 400°F. Roll out a small amount of dough to ⅛-inch thickness on lightly floured board or pastry cloth. Keep remaining dough refrigerated until ready to use. Cut out cookies with a 2½-inch round cutter; arrange one inch apart on baking sheet. Sprinkle cookies with sugar. Bake for 8 to 10 minutes or until light golden brown. Cool on wire racks. Makes about 48 cookies.

**Note:** If using Martha White All-Purpose Flour, sift 1¼ teaspoons baking powder and ¼ teaspoon salt with flour.

## Chewies

*A thin, chewy little round cookie.*

> ¼ cup (½ stick) butter or margarine, softened
> 1½ cups firmly packed light brown sugar
> 1 egg
> 1 teaspoon vanilla
> 1⅔ cups sifted Martha White Self-Rising Flour

Preheat oven to 350°F. Cream butter and sugar together in mixing bowl until light and fluffy. Add egg and vanilla; beat well. Stir in flour until well blended. Drop dough by teaspoonfuls onto ungreased baking sheet. Bake for 12 to 14 minutes or until golden brown. Cool on wire racks. Makes about 36 cookies.

**Note:** If using Martha White All-Purpose Flour, sift 2¾ teaspoons baking powder and ¾ teaspoon salt with flour.

# Coco Not Cookies

*Potato flakes and coconut extract make these cookies taste just like they were made with coconut—fun and easy.*

- ⅓ cup (5⅓ tablespoons) butter or margarine, softened
- 1 cup sugar
- 1 egg
- 1 teaspoon coconut extract
- 1 package (2 ounces) Martha White SpudFlakes
- 1 package (5½ ounces) Martha White BixMix

Preheat oven to 375°F. Cream butter and sugar together in mixing bowl until light and fluffy. Add egg and coconut extract; beat well. Stir in potato flakes and biscuit mix. Shape dough into ¾-inch balls; arrange two inches apart on ungreased baking sheet. Bake for 12 to 14 minutes or until golden brown. Cool on wire racks. Makes about 48 cookies.

# Party Pecan Balls

*A decorative cookie jar filled with these little cookies will make an appreciated gift for a friend.*

- ½ cup (1 stick) butter or margarine, softened
- 1¼ cups confectioners' sugar, sifted, divided
- 1 teaspoon vanilla
- 1 cup sifted Martha White All-Purpose Flour
- ⅛ teaspoon salt
- 1 cup finely chopped pecans

Cream butter and ¼ cup sugar together in mixing bowl until light and fluffy. Blend in vanilla. Add flour and salt; blend well. Stir in pecans. Cover and refrigerate for about 1 hour. Preheat oven to 350°F. Grease a large baking sheet. Shape dough into ½-inch balls and arrange one inch apart on prepared baking sheet. Bake for 12 to 15 minutes or until light golden brown. Carefully roll warm cookies in remaining 1 cup sugar to coat. Cool on wire racks. Roll again in sugar. Store in airtight container. Makes about 60 cookies.

# Almond Slice and Bake Cookies

*Prepare dough, shape into rolls and refrigerate, then it's easy to slice and bake as needed.*

- 1 cup (2 sticks) butter or margarine, softened
- 1 cup sugar
- 2 eggs
- 2 teaspoons almond extract
- ½ teaspoon vanilla
- 3 cups sifted Martha White Self-Rising Flour
- ½ cup finely chopped blanched almonds (optional)

Cream butter and sugar together in mixing bowl until light and fluffy. Add eggs and extracts; beat well. Stir in flour and almonds. Cover and refrigerate for about 1 hour and 30 minutes. Divide dough into three equal parts. Shape each third into a 6½x1½-inch roll. Wrap each roll in waxed paper, sealing ends. Chill for 3 hours or overnight. Preheat oven to 400°F. Grease a large baking sheet. Cut rolls into ⅛-inch thick slices and arrange one inch apart on prepared baking sheet. Bake for 8 to 10 minutes or until light golden brown. Cool on wire racks. Makes about 75 cookies.

**Note:** If using Martha White All-Purpose Flour, add 1 teaspoon salt with flour.

## Butter Cookies

*Rich and buttery—wonderful with fresh fruit.*

    1 cup (2 sticks) butter or margarine, softened
    ½ cup sugar
    1 egg
    1 tablespoon vanilla
    3 cups sifted Martha White All-Purpose Flour
    ½ teaspoon baking powder

Cream butter and sugar together in mixing bowl until light and fluffy. Add egg and vanilla; beat well. Sift flour and baking powder together; blend into creamed mixture. Cover and refrigerate for 1 hour. Preheat oven to 425°F. Roll out a small amount of dough to ⅛-inch thickness on lightly floured board or pastry cloth. Keep remaining dough refrigerated until ready to use. Cut into rounds with a 2½-inch cutter; arrange one inch apart on ungreased baking sheet. Bake for 5 to 7 minutes or until light golden brown. Cool on wire racks. Makes about 70 cookies.

## Buttery Sugar Cookies

*Create lasting memories by making cut-out cookies for the kids to decorate.*

    1 cup (2 sticks) butter or margarine, softened
    1 cup sugar
    2 eggs
    1 teaspoon vanilla
    3 cups sifted Martha White All-Purpose Flour

Cream butter and sugar together in mixing bowl until light and fluffy. Add eggs and vanilla; beat well. Stir in flour. Cover and refrigerate 1 hour. Preheat oven to 350°F. Roll out a small amount of dough to ⅛-inch thickness on lightly floured board or pastry cloth. Keep remaining dough refrigerated until ready to use. Cut out cookies with a 2½-inch round cutter or shaped cutter; arrange one inch apart on ungreased baking sheet. Bake for 10 to 12 minutes or until light golden brown. Cool on wire racks. Decorate if desired. Makes about 70 cookies.

## Stuffed Monkeys (Cinnamon-Sugar Pinwheels)

*A family favorite of a former member of the Martha White Kitchen staff, the origin of the name is a mystery, but the cookies are delectable.*

- ½ cup (1 stick) butter or margarine, softened
- 1 package (3 ounces) cream cheese, softened
- 1 egg yolk
- 1 cup sifted Martha White All-Purpose Flour
- ¼ cup (½ stick) butter or margarine, melted
- ½ cup finely chopped pecans
- ⅓ cup sugar
- 2 teaspoons cinnamon Confectioners' sugar (optional)

Beat butter and cream cheese together in mixing bowl; blend in egg yolk. Stir in flour. Cover and refrigerate for 30 minutes. Preheat oven to 350°F. Divide dough in half. On lightly floured board or pastry cloth, roll out first half into a 12x10-inch rectangle. Brush with 2 tablespoons melted butter. Stir together pecans, sugar and cinnamon. Sprinkle half of this mixture over dough. Roll up jelly-roll style, beginning with a long side. Cut into ½-inch slices and arrange one inch apart on ungreased baking sheet. Repeat this procedure with second half of dough. Bake for 12 to 15 minutes or until golden brown. Cool on wire racks. Dust with confectioners' sugar, if desired. Makes about 36 cookies.

## Coconut Drop Cookies

*Old-fashioned drop cookies loaded with coconut—perfect with homemade ice cream.*

- ⅔ cup (10⅔ tablespoons) butter or margarine, softened
- 1 cup sugar
- 2 eggs
- 1 teaspoon vanilla
- 2 cups sifted Martha White All-Purpose Flour
- 1 teaspoon salt
- ½ teaspoon baking powder
- ¼ teaspoon baking soda
- ½ cup dairy sour cream
- 2 cups flaked coconut
- ¾ cup chopped pecans

Preheat oven to 350°F. Grease a large baking sheet. Cream butter and sugar together in mixing bowl until light and fluffy. Add eggs and vanilla; beat well. Sift flour, salt, baking powder and soda together; add to creamed mixture alternately with sour cream, beginning and ending with flour mixture. Stir in coconut and pecans. Drop dough by level tablespoonfuls two inches apart onto prepared baking sheet. Bake for 15 to 18 minutes or until golden brown. Makes about 50 cookies.

## Fruitcake Cookies

*Festive and colorful, a nice alternative to the traditional holiday cake.*

- ½ cup (1 stick) butter or margarine, softened

½ cup firmly packed light brown
  sugar
2 eggs
¼ cup milk
1½ cups sifted Martha White
  Self-Rising Flour
½ teaspoon baking soda
½ teaspoon allspice
1 cup chopped candied cherries
1 cup (3 slices) chopped candied
  pineapple
1 cup chopped dates
⅓ cup raisins
3 cups chopped pecans

Known as "The World's Greatest Flour Peddlers," Lester Flatt and Earl Scruggs with the Foggy Mountain Boys stand beside the first "Martha White Express" in 1955.

Preheat oven to 350°F. Grease a large baking sheet. Cream butter and sugar together in mixing bowl until light and fluffy. Add eggs and milk; beat well. Sift flour, soda and allspice together; blend into creamed mixture. Stir in cherries, pineapple, dates, raisins and pecans. Drop dough by level tablespoonfuls two inches apart onto prepared baking sheet. Bake 10 to 12 minutes or until golden brown. Cool on wire racks. Makes about 48 cookies.

**Note:** If using Martha White All-Purpose Flour, sift 2¼ teaspoons baking powder and ¾ teaspoon salt with flour.

## Old-Fashioned Oatmeal Raisin Cookies

*The standard by which other oatmeal cookies are measured.*

1¼ cups (2½ sticks) butter or
  margarine, softened
¾ cup firmly packed brown sugar
½ cup granulated sugar
1 egg
1 teaspoon vanilla
1½ cups sifted Martha White
  All-Purpose Flour
1 teaspoon baking soda
1 teaspoon salt
1 teaspoon cinnamon
¼ teaspoon nutmeg
3 cups quick-cooking or
  old-fashioned oats
1 cup raisins

Preheat oven to 375°F. Grease a large baking sheet. Cream butter and sugars together in mixing bowl until light and fluffy. Add egg and vanilla; beat well. Sift flour, soda, salt, cinnamon and nutmeg together; blend into creamed mixture. Stir in oats and raisins. Drop dough by level tablespoonfuls two inches apart onto prepared baking sheet. Bake for 8 to 10 minutes or until golden brown. Cool on wire racks. Makes about 50 cookies.

Paintbrush Cookies

## Pepparkakor

*Crisp and spicy—the aroma of these Swedish gingersnaps will bring everyone to the kitchen before the cookies are out of the oven.*

½ cup (1 stick) butter or margarine, softened
½ cup shortening
1 cup sugar
2 eggs
½ cup molasses
3½ cups sifted Martha White All-Purpose Flour
2 teaspoons baking soda
1½ teaspoons ginger
½ teaspoon cinnamon
½ teaspoon cloves
½ teaspoon nutmeg
¼ teaspoon salt

Cream butter, shortening and sugar together in mixing bowl until light and fluffy. Add eggs and molasses; beat well.

Sift flour and remaining ingredients together; blend into creamed mixture. Cover and refrigerate for 1 hour and 30 minutes. Divide dough into three equal parts. Shape each third into a 6½x1½-inch roll. Wrap each roll in waxed paper, sealing ends. Chill 3 hours or overnight. Preheat oven to 375°F. Cut rolls into ⅛-inch thick slices and arrange one inch apart on ungreased baking sheet. Bake for 6 to 8 minutes or until deep golden brown. Cool on wire racks. Makes about 80 cookies.

## Paintbrush Cookies

*A simple egg yolk paint makes it fun and easy to decorate cut-out cookies.*

1 recipe Buttery Sugar Cookies (page 199)
2 egg yolks
½ teaspoon water
Food colorings

Prepare Buttery Sugar Cookies as directed, arranging cut shapes on cookie sheet. Mix egg yolks and water in small bowl. Divide mixture among several small cups. Tint each cup of egg mixture with a different food coloring. Paint cookies with small paint brushes. If paint thickens, stir in a few drops of water. Bake as directed in recipe. Makes about 70 cookies.

## Buttery Tea Cakes

*Old-fashioned goodness—plain and simple.*

>     1 cup (2 sticks) butter or margarine,
        softened
>  1½ cups sugar
>     3 eggs
>     3 tablespoons whipping cream
>     1 teaspoon vanilla
>     4 cups sifted Martha White
        All-Purpose Flour
>     1 tablespoon baking powder

Cream butter and sugar together in mixing bowl until light and fluffy. Add eggs, whipping cream and vanilla; beat well. Sift flour and baking powder together; blend into creamed mixture. Shape dough into a ball; place in tightly covered container. Chill several hours or overnight. Preheat oven to 350°F. Grease a large baking sheet. Divide dough into four pieces. On lightly floured board or pastry cloth, roll out each piece to ¼-inch thickness. Cut into rounds with 3-inch cutter. Place 2 inches apart on prepared baking sheet. Repeat procedure with remaining pieces of dough. Bake for 10 to 12 minutes or until edges are lightly browned. Cool on wire racks. Makes 36 cookies.

## Chocolate Pinwheels

*Spiral of chocolate and vanilla that will add a beautiful dimension to an assortment of holiday cookies.*

>  ½ cup (1 stick) butter or margarine,
        softened
>  ⅔ cup sugar
>     1 egg
>     1 tablespoon milk
>     1 teaspoon vanilla
>     2 cups sifted Martha White
        Self-Rising Flour
>     1 square (1 ounce) unsweetened
        chocolate, melted

Cream butter and sugar together in mixing bowl until light and fluffy. Add egg, milk and vanilla; beat well. Stir in flour. Divide dough in half. Add chocolate to one half; blend well. Cover and refrigerate for 1 hour. Roll out each half of dough to a 12x10-inch rectangle on floured waxed paper. Invert plain dough over chocolate dough and peel off waxed paper. Roll up jelly-roll style, beginning with a long side. Wrap tightly in plastic wrap. Refrigerate 3 hours or overnight. Preheat oven to 375°F. Remove plastic wrap. Cut rolls into ⅛-inch thick slices and arrange one inch apart on ungreased baking sheet. Bake for 8 to 10 minutes or until light golden brown. Cool on wire racks. Makes about 60 cookies.

## Candy Canes and Christmas Wreaths

*It's fun to shape colored dough into Christmas cookies—keep dough not being used in the refrigerator.*

1 recipe Buttery Sugar Cookies (page 199)
1 teaspoon green food coloring
1 teaspoon red food coloring

Prepare Buttery Sugar Cookies dough as directed; except—before chilling, divide dough into three equal parts. Tint ⅓ of dough with green food coloring and ⅓ of dough with red food coloring. Leave remaining third as is. Wrap each third of dough individually and refrigerate for 1 hour. Preheat oven to 350°F. Grease a large baking sheet. Shape level tablespoonfuls of dough into 6-inch ropes by rolling back and forth on lightly floured board or pastry cloth. Place two different colored ropes side by side; press together lightly at one end and twist ropes together. Shape into canes or wreaths. Arrange one inch apart on prepared baking sheet. Bake for 12 to 15 minutes or until lightly browned on bottom. Carefully remove from baking sheet and cool on wire racks. Makes about 18 canes and/or wreaths.

## Gingerbread

*Decorating gingerbread cookies or making gingerbread houses will be the highlight of a family Christmas celebration.*

½ cup shortening
½ cup sugar
½ cup molasses
1 egg, lightly beaten
3 cups Martha White All-Purpose Flour
1¼ teaspoons allspice
1 teaspoon cinnamon
½ teaspoon baking soda
¼ teaspoon salt

Preheat oven to 325°F. Combine shortening, sugar and molasses in large saucepan. Bring to a boil over medium heat, stirring occasionally. Remove pan from heat; cool mixture to room temperature. Stir in egg, flour and remaining ingredients until well blended.

*For Houses:* Grease and flour an 17x11-inch jelly roll pan. Turn dough out onto lightly floured board or pastry cloth and knead until smooth and pliable. Roll out dough in prepared pan as evenly as possible, forcing dough into corners of pan with fingers if necessary. Bake for 15 minutes or until deep brown and firm to the touch. Cool in pan for 5 minutes. Cut out pieces using patterns and small sharp knife. It is important to cut pieces while cake is very warm because gingerbread hardens as it cools. Cool pieces on wire racks.

*For Cookies:* Roll out a small amount of dough to ⅛-inch thickness on lightly floured board or pastry cloth. Keep remaining dough refrigerated until ready to use. Cut out cookies with shaped cutters; arrange one inch apart on ungreased baking sheet. Bake for 10 to 12 minutes or until deep golden brown. Cool on wire racks. Decorate with Decorator Icing and trims as desired.

### Decorator Icing

> 2 egg whites
> 2½ cups sifted confectioners' sugar

Beat egg whites with electric mixer on high speed until frothy and slightly thickened. Beat in sugar, ½ cup at a time. Continue beating for 5 minutes or until stiff.

**STEP 1:**
Place each carton on brown paper sack and trace sides A, B and bottom C. Cut out pattern pieces.

**STEP 2:**
Prepare Gingerbread for Houses.

**Note:** House pieces must be cut out while cake is very warm. For each house, cut 2 each of pieces A, B and C. You may want to cut a window and door for each house. Cool pieces on wire rack.

**STEP 3:**
Prepare Decorator Icing. Glue gingerbread pieces to cartons using icing. Frost outside of each house with remaining icing. Use your imagination and creativity to decorate houses with candies.

## Easy Gingerbread Houses

*You will need:*

> 3 small empty cartons: 2 empty cartons (½ pint each) such as whipping cream or orange juice and 1 empty carton (1 pint) such as half-and-half
> Paper sacks
> 1 recipe Gingerbread for Houses
> 1 recipe Decorator Icing
> Assorted candies for decoration (peppermint sticks, caramels, red hots, gumdrops)

(side wall)    (bottom to be used for roof)

(end wall)

# SNACKS
# AND PARTY FOODS

It's 8 p.m. Do you know where the Average American Family is?

The youngest kids are huddled around the glow of the television set. The typical teenage daughter is on the phone while the typical teenage son is in his room hiding from the lawn mower. Dad is practicing his chip shot in the back yard. And Mom is wishing the family spent more time together.

Time at home is not necessarily time together or what those on the talk-show circuit call "Quality Time."

How can you bring the whole family together, subtly and without argument or ultimatum? The secret ingredient is *snack food*. Let the aroma of piping hot pepperoni bread or sizzling sausage bites float through your home, and watch your family magically appear.

Informal and honest, homemade snack foods fit the intimate flavor of family together. Often fondly referred to as "finger foods," snacks free folks from the inhibiting use of silverware, proper place settings and table manners.

Yes, most snack foods are best eaten with your hands. For most of us, eating with our hands is a forgotten pleasure lost from childhood. The satisfying feel of a warm chicken nugget in your palm and the stray cheese crisp crumb on a fingertip are part of the secret flavor fingers impart to food.

In addition to its naturally homey character, snack food dresses up pretty well for social occasions and is the true life of most parties, wedding receptions and debutante balls. In the South, a wedding wouldn't be official without gardenias and crispy cheese straws at the reception table.

As party foods, snacks often serve as the centerpiece of social occasions. They occupy the table of honor around which guests gather. They are a tasteful icebreaker and a welcome alternative to talking about the weather. They offer a solution to the age-old social question, "What should I do with my hands?" And their service and preparation are the perfect responsibility for that aunt or inlaw who just *has* to be involved in the wedding.

But whether served for family or as a social centerpiece, snacks are an enduring American entertainment. Yes, "Quality Time" might just be a new way of saying something that families have enjoyed for generations as snack time.

Left: Party Pizzas (page 210); Right: Italian Parmesan Twists with Dipping Sauce (page 209)

## Cheesy Bread Sticks

*Easy to make because sticks are cut after baking—serve with soup or salad.*

- 1 package (5½ ounces) Martha White BixMix
- ⅓ cup milk
- ¼ cup (½ stick) butter or margarine, melted
- 1 egg, lightly beaten
- 1 teaspoon dry mustard
- ¼ teaspoon crushed red pepper (optional)
- 1 cup (4 ounces) grated sharp Cheddar cheese

Preheat oven to 375°F. Grease a 13x9x2-inch baking pan. Combine biscuit mix and milk in large mixing bowl; stir until smooth. Add remaining ingredients; blend well. Spread dough evenly in prepared pan. Bake for 15 to 20 minutes or until golden brown. Cool in pan for 10 minutes. To serve, cut into 3x¾-inch strips. Makes about 36 bread sticks.

## Cheese Crisps

*Crisp rice cereal adds extra crunch to these sharp cheese wafers*

- 2 cups (8 ounces) grated sharp Cheddar cheese, at room temperature
- 1 cup (2 sticks) butter or margarine, softened
- 2 cups Martha White Self-Rising Flour
- 2 cups crisp rice cereal
- ¼ teaspoon cayenne pepper

Preheat oven to 325°F. Lightly grease a large baking sheet. Combine cheese and butter in large mixing bowl; blend well. Stir in remaining ingredients. Shape dough into ½-inch balls and arrange one inch apart on prepared baking sheet. Press each ball with floured fork to flatten and make criss-cross design. Bake for 18 to 20 minutes or until light golden brown. Cool on wire rack. Makes about 85 crisps.

**Note:** If using Martha White All-Purpose Flour, sift ½ teaspoon salt with flour.

## Cheese Sticks

*Crisp and flaky, delicious with a summer salad or for a holiday party.*

- 2 cups (8 ounces) grated extra sharp Cheddar cheese
- ½ cup (1 stick) butter or margarine, softened
- 1½ cups Martha White All-Purpose Flour
- ½ teaspoon salt
- ⅛ teaspoon cayenne pepper

Beat cheese and butter together in mixing bowl until blended. Stir together flour, salt and pepper in separate bowl. Add flour mixture to cheese mixture; stir to blend or use hands to work in flour. Cover dough and refrigerate for 1 hour. Preheat oven to 375°F. Grease a large baking sheet. Turn dough out onto lightly floured board or pastry cloth; knead gently just until smooth. Roll out very thin, ⅛-inch thick. Cut into 4x½-

inch sticks using sharp knife or pastry wheel. Place sticks on prepared baking sheet. Bake for 10 to 12 minutes or until golden brown. Cool on wire rack. Makes about 72 sticks.

---

## RAISINS ARE A NATURAL

**R**aisins are a natural—the ideal snack for active people, no matter what age. Raisins also combine with other ingredients to make great snacks, breads, cakes, salads and puddings.

*Raisin Hints and Tips*

♦ For easy chopping, toss 1 cup raisins with 1 teaspoon oil and chop with a sharp knife or a food processor.

♦ If a recipe calls for ground raisins, use an oil-coated blender or meat grinder.

♦ To plump raisins, cover the amount needed with very hot tap water and soak for 2 to 5 minutes; drain.

♦ To distribute raisins better in cake batter, stir ¼ of amount needed into batter. Pour batter into pan(s) and sprinkle remaining raisins on top.

♦ Stir ½ cup raisins into bran muffin mix for added nutrition.

♦ Combine raisins with any of the following to make a great tasting snack: nuts, diced dates, chopped dried apricots, pretzels, coconut and granola.

---

# Italian Parmesan Twists

*Fun to make and fun to eat with a zesty dipping sauce.*

1 package (8 ounces) Martha White Deep Pan Pizza Crust Mix
1 cup grated Parmesan cheese
1½ teaspoons Italian seasoning
⅓ cup (5⅓ tablespoons) butter or margarine, melted
Dipping Sauce, below

Preheat oven to 450°F. Grease a large baking sheet. Prepare pizza crust mix according to package directions. Combine Parmesan cheese and seasoning in shallow plate or pie pan. Divide dough into 6 equal pieces; divide each piece into 4 more pieces. (There should be 24 pieces of dough.) Roll each piece between hands into a 4-inch rope. Dip each rope in butter; roll in cheese mixture. Twist rope three times; place on prepared baking sheet. Bake for 7 to 9 minutes or until golden brown. Serve with warm Dipping Sauce, if desired. Makes 24 appetizers.

## Dipping Sauce

1 can (8 ounces) tomato sauce
½ teaspoon Worcestershire sauce
½ teaspoon oregano leaves
¼ teaspoon thyme leaves
¼ teaspoon garlic powder

Combine all ingredients in small saucepan. Heat until warm, stirring occasionally.

## Crusty Sausage Bites

*Little smoked sausages wrapped in crisp pizza crust will be a welcome treat for a casual gathering.*

> 1 package (16 ounces) small smoked sausages (about 50)
> 1 package (6½ ounces) Martha White Pizza Crust Mix
> Mustard Sauce, below

Preheat oven to 425°F. Grease a large baking sheet. Lightly brown sausages in large skillet over medium heat, piercing skin to release juices. Prepare pizza crust mix according to package directions, except—after dough rests for 5 minutes, turn out onto lightly floured board or pastry cloth and knead just until smooth. Divide dough into five equal pieces. Roll out each piece to a 7-inch circle. Cut each circle into ten wedges. Wrap each sausage in a wedge, beginning at wide end and pinching pointed end to seal. Repeat procedure with remaining dough and sausages. Place on prepared baking sheet. Bake for 12 to 15 minutes or until golden brown. Serve with Mustard Sauce, if desired. Makes about 50 appetizers.

### Mustard Sauce

> 1 cup (8 ounces) dairy sour cream
> 2 tablespoons Dijon mustard
> ¼ teaspoon seasoned salt

Combine all ingredients in mixing bowl; stir to blend.

## Party Pizzas

*Little pizzas with a flaky biscuit dough crust will delight young children.*

> 3 cups sifted Martha White Self-Rising Flour
> ⅓ cup shortening
> 1 cup plus 2 tablespoons milk Pizza Sauce, following
> ¾ pound (12 ounces) ground beef, browned and drained
> 1 green pepper, thinly sliced
> 2 cups (8 ounces) grated mozzarella cheese
> Chopped fresh parsley (optional)

Preheat oven to 400°F. Cut shortening into flour with pastry blender or two knives until mixture resembles coarse crumbs. Add milk and stir with a fork only until dough leaves sides of bowl. Turn dough out onto lightly floured

Old-Fashioned Corn Dogs

board or pastry cloth; knead gently just until smooth. Divide dough into 16 pieces. Roll out each piece of dough into a thin 3-inch circle. Place circles on ungreased baking sheet. Spread each circle with thin layers of Pizza Sauce, ground beef, green pepper and cheese. Sprinkle each with parsley, if desired. Bake for 12 to 15 minutes or until cheese is melted and crust is golden brown. Makes 16 pizzas.

### Pizza Sauce

     1 can (6 ounces) tomato paste
     1 can (8 ounces) tomato sauce
     ½ teaspoon salt
     1 teaspoon Worcestershire sauce
     1 teaspoon garlic salt
     2 to 3 drops hot pepper sauce
     1 teaspoon oregano leaves
     ½ teaspoon thyme leaves

Combine all ingredients; blend well.

## Old-Fashioned Corn Dogs

*Nothing else can compare to a homemade corn dog—the coating is light, crisp and golden brown.*

       Vegetable oil or shortening for
       deep frying
     1 cup Martha White Self-Rising
       Flour
     ⅔ cup Martha White Self-Rising
       Corn Meal Mix
     ¾ cup milk
     1 egg, lightly beaten
     2 tablespoons vegetable oil
       Wooden skewers (optional)

     1 pound (16 ounces) weiners, at
       room temperature
       Mustard and ketchup (optional)

In large saucepan or electric fryer, heat 2 to 3 inches of oil over medium-high heat to 375°F. Stir together flour and corn meal in mixing bowl. Add milk, egg and 2 tablespoons oil; stir until smooth. Set batter aside for 10 minutes. Insert skewers into weiners. Dip weiners into batter. Carefully drop corn dogs into hot oil. Fry until golden brown and floating on top. Drain on paper towels. Serve hot with mustard and ketchup, if desired. Makes 8 to 10 corn dogs.

## Party Sausage Balls

*This all-time favorite may be made ahead and frozen for convenient holiday entertaining.*

     ½ pound (8 ounces) sausage, at room
       temperature
     1 cup (4 ounces) grated sharp
       Cheddar cheese
     1 package (5½ ounces) Martha
       White BixMix

Preheat oven to 325°F. Combine sausage and cheese in large mixing bowl, using hands to blend ingredients together. Add biscuit mix and continue to blend with hands. Roll mixture into marble-sized balls. Place on ungreased baking sheet. Bake for 20 to 25 minutes or until sausage is no longer pink. Serve hot or at room temperature. Makes about 60 appetizers.

## Pepperoni Bread

*Pepperoni and Swiss cheese lend a unique flavor to this snack made easy with a pizza crust mix.*

**1 package (8 ounces) Martha White Deep Pan Pizza Crust Mix**
**1 package (3½ to 4 ounces) sliced pepperoni**
**2 cups (8 ounces) grated Swiss cheese**
**2 tablespoons grated Parmesan cheese**
**1 egg, lightly beaten**
**1 teaspoon Italian seasoning**

Preheat oven to 375°F. Grease a large baking sheet. Prepare pizza crust mix according to package directions. Turn dough out onto lightly floured board or pastry cloth; knead gently just until smooth. Roll out into an oval shape (see illustration 1). Cover one half of dough with pepperoni, covering almost to edge (see illustration 2). Sprinkle cheeses over pepperoni; drizzle with entire beaten egg (this keeps the crust chewy and moist). Sprinkle with Italian seasoning. Fold plain half of dough over covered half (see illustration 3). Moisten edges with water; press to seal. Carefully slide bread onto prepared baking sheet. (Bread can be lifted if handled carefully.) Bake for 20 to 25 minutes or until golden brown. Cool on wire rack for 10 minutes before cutting. Slice into 1-inch strips cross-wise with pizza cutter. This is best served warm, but is also good cold. Makes about 12 servings.

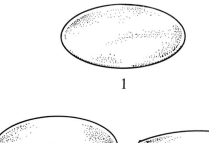

1

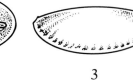

2                           3

## Chicken Nuggets

*Serve with sweet and sour, mustard or barbecue sauce.*

**Vegetable oil or shortening for deep frying**
**3 whole chicken breasts, skinned and boned**
**1 package (5½ ounces) Martha White FlapStax**
**1 cup water**
**¾ teaspoon salt**
**¼ teaspoon pepper**

In large saucepan or electric fryer, heat 2 to 3 inches of oil over medium-high heat to 375°F. Cut chicken into 1-inch cubes. Combine pancake mix, water, salt and pepper in mixing bowl; stir until smooth. Dip chicken cubes into batter. Carefully drop nuggets into hot oil. Fry until golden brown and floating on top. Drain on paper towels. Serve warm with desired sauce. Makes 4 to 6 servings.

## Lemon Cake Pudding

*Delightful—the cake forms on top during baking and leaves a lovely lemon sauce on the bottom —serve warm or chilled.*

1 cup sugar
¼ cup Martha White All-Purpose Flour
¼ teaspoon salt
1 cup milk
2 egg yolks, lightly beaten
¼ cup lemon juice
1½ teaspoons grated lemon peel
2 egg whites, stiffly beaten

Preheat oven to 350°F. Grease a 1½-quart baking dish. Stir together sugar, flour and salt in mixing bowl. Add milk, egg yolks, lemon juice and lemon peel; blend well. Fold in beaten egg whites. Pour mixture into prepared dish. Place dish into a square baking pan filled with one inch of water. Bake for 45 to 50 minutes or until golden brown. Remove baking dish from water and cool 10 minutes on wire rack before serving. Makes 4 to 6 servings.

**Note:** Lemon Cake Pudding may be baked in six 6-ounce greased custard cups. Place cups into a 13x9x2-inch baking pan filled with one inch of water and bake as directed above.

## Old South Strawberry Shortcake

*This flaky butter pastry rolled out and cut in rounds makes a delectable shortcake.*

2¼ cups sifted Martha White All-Purpose Flour
¾ teaspoon salt
¾ cup (1½ sticks) butter, cold and cut into pieces
About ⅓ cup ice water
Sugar
1½ quarts strawberries, hulled, sliced and sweetened to taste
1 cup (8 ounces) whipping cream, whipped with 1 tablespoon sugar

Stir together flour and salt in mixing bowl. Cut butter into flour with pastry blender or two knives until mixture resembles coarse crumbs. Sprinkle water a little at a time over flour mixture, stirring with a fork until dough forms a ball. Roll out dough on lightly floured board or pastry cloth to about ¼-inch thickness. Cut into sixteen 3½-inch circles. Place on ungreased baking sheet. Sprinkle circles with sugar and prick with a fork. Chill thoroughly. Preheat oven to 375°F. Bake for 22 to 24 minutes or until pastry begins to brown. Serve within a few hours or freeze. To serve, place a pastry round on eight individual serving plates; top rounds with half the strawberries. Place another pastry round on top of strawberries. Top with remaining strawberries and whipped cream. Makes 8 shortcakes.

Party Sausage Balls (page 211) and Cheese Sticks (page 208)

## Blueberry Fruit Squares

*Serve as a delightfully different brunch dessert or as a treat for Saturday morning breakfast.*

    **4 cups sifted Martha White
        All-Purpose Flour**
½ **cup sugar**
½ **teaspoon baking powder**
½ **teaspoon salt**
  **1 cup (2 sticks) butter or margarine,
     softened**
½ **cup shortening**
  **1 cup (8 ounces) dairy sour cream**
  **4 egg yolks, lightly beaten**
½ **teaspoon vanilla**
  **2 cans (21 ounces each) blueberry
     pie filling
    Confectioners' Glaze, following**

Sift flour, sugar, baking powder and salt together in large bowl. Cut butter and shortening into flour mixture with pastry blender or two knives until mixture resembles fine crumbs. Add sour cream, egg yolks and vanilla; blend well. Cover dough tightly and refrigerate several hours or overnight. Preheat oven to 350°F. Grease a 15x10x1-inch jelly-roll pan. Divide chilled dough in half. Turn first half of dough out onto lightly floured board or pastry cloth; knead gently just until smooth. Roll out to 15x10x¼-inch rectangle. Roll dough around rolling pin and unroll into prepared pan, pressing corners to fit if necessary. Spread bottom crust with pie filling to within ½ inch of edge. Roll out second half of dough slightly larger than first half. Lightly moisten edges of bottom crust. Unroll top crust over filling, being as exact as possible with placement of crust. Press edges of top crust down onto edges of bottom crust to seal. Bake for 50 to 60 minutes or until golden brown. Cool on wire rack for 10 minutes. Drizzle with Confectioners' Glaze. Cool completely before cutting for neater squares. Cut into 3-inch squares. Makes about 15 squares.

**Note:** Cherry pie filling may be substituted for blueberry pie filling.

### Confectioners' Glaze

  **1 cup sifted confectioners' sugar**
  **2 tablespoons milk**

Combine ingredients in small bowl; stir until smooth.

# INDEX

# ORDER ADDITIONAL COPIES

You may buy additional copies of *Martha White's Southern Sampler* for yourself and your friends from your local book store or gift shop. If you are not near a store, you may order copies from Rutledge Hill Press for $19.95 each plus $1.55 tax for each book shipped in Tennessee plus $1.75 postage and handling for each shipment (even if more than one book is mailed). If you want to send copies as gifts, Rutledge Hill Press will enclose a gift card signed with your name at no additional charge.

To: Rutledge Hill Press
    513 Third Avenue, South
    Nashville, TN 37210

Please send me _____ copies of *Martha White's Southern Sampler* at $19.95 each plus $1.55 tax per book and $1.75 postage and handling per order. Enclosed is my check or money order for $_____. (Make check payable to Rutledge Hill Press and mail to the above address.)

Name _____

Address _____

City _____ State _____ Zip _____

- - - - - - - - - - - - - - - - - - - - - - - - - - - - - - - - - - - -

Please send me _____ copies of *Martha White's Southern Sampler* at $19.95 each plus $1.55 tax per book shipped inside Tennessee and $1.75 postage and handling per address to friends whose names and addresses are listed below. Enclosed is my check or money order for $_____. (Make check payable to Rutledge Hill Press and mail to the above address.) Sign my name on the cards as follows (Please print):

_____

My name _____

Address _____

City _____ State _____ Zip _____

Send copies of the Cookbook to:

Name _____ | Name _____

Address _____ | Address _____

City _____ State _____ Zip _____ | City _____ State _____ Zip _____

Name _____ | Name _____

Address _____ | Address _____

City _____ State _____ Zip _____ | City _____ State _____ Zip _____